The Lonely Days Were Sundays:

Reflections of a Jewish Southerner

To Julie,

all the best.

Eli Evans

REFLECTIONS

OF A

JEWISH

SOUTHERNER

ELI N.

The Lonely Days
Were Sundays

E V A N S

University Press of Mississippi

Jackson

97 96 95   4 3 2
First paperback edition 1994
The paper in this book meets the guidelines for
permanence and durability of the Committee on
Production Guidelines for Book Longevity of the
Council on Library Resources.

Designed by John A. Langston

Library of Congress Cataloging-in-Publication Data

Evans, Eli N.
    The lonely days were Sundays : reflections of a
Jewish southerner / by Eli N. Evans.
        p.   cm.
    ISBN 0-87805-627-0 (alk. paper)—0-87805-752-8
(pbk.: alk. paper)
        1. Jews—Southern States.   2. Southern States—
Ethnic relations.   3. Southern States—Politics and
government.   4. Jews—United States—History.
5. United States—Ethnic relations.   6. Israel—
Politics and government.   7. United States—
Politics and government.   8. Evans, Eli N.
I. Title.
F220.J5E8   1993
975'.00924—dc20   92-42313
                                              CIP

British Library Cataloging-in-Publication data available

To Joshua

Born in the North while his father clutched
southern soil in his pocket,
later used
to plant
a tree in
Israel . . .
with faith that the dirt works

Also by Eli N. Evans

The Provincials:
A Personal History of Jews in the Soutl

Judah P. Benjamin:
The Jewish Confederate

"The lonely days were Sundays—Sundays when I watched the town people going to church, while we stayed upstairs in our apartment. Then I would feel like an outsider in this little community. I would have hunger in my heart for my own people. I would visualize a Utopia—a village like this of all Jews—going to temple on the Sabbath."

Jennie B. Nachamson,
the author's grandmother,
recalling her life
in the early 1900s.

Contents

Foreword by Terry Sanford*

I have known Eli Evans for more than thirty years and have watched his growth as a colleague in public service and as a writer-historian. He has accomplished what is rare in the world of ideas: he has defined and articulated a unique perspective—that of the Jewish South—and has become its most eloquent voice. As this collection testifies, he is at home in many worlds, including those of presidential politics, civil rights, Israeli history, and North Carolina life. He writes as well about films, fashion, sports, and culture, often seeing a lighter side but always with serious purpose. This volume of essays, which explores the meaning of southern, American, and Jewish history, is anchored in the pivotal themes of the last century, ranging from the abolition of slavery to the tragedy of the Holocaust, from the agony of the Civil War to the creation of the state of Israel. By tracing these roots to the present day, Evans adds a new dimension to our understanding of history and its meaning for the future.

*Terry Sanford was a U.S. Senator from North Carolina from 1986 to 1992, Governor from 1960 to 1964, and President of Duke University from 1969 to 1985.

Since the early 1960s, the South has projected itself force-fully into the national consciousness, reshaping the soul of the nation as the South reshaped itself. The forces of social change were stirred by the impatience and stubborn courage of those in the civil rights movement. The sit-ins, demonstrations, and marches stimulated unparalleled national media coverage, as television, especially, came of age and profoundly affected the conscience of the nation.

It has also been an extraordinary period in Jewish history, and television has made us witness to the maturation of the state of Israel, through its four wars and many conflicts, its breakthroughs and setbacks, and with its growing permanence as a nation. As a haven for the oppressed—whether from war-torn Europe, Ethiopia, or the Soviet Union—its history calls on the conscience of the world.

Eli Evans has been deeply involved in these changes as an observer and a participant. He is a native North Carolinian, the son of a prominent Jewish family in Durham, North Carolina, where his father, E. J. "Mutt" Evans, served as mayor for six terms in the 1950s and early 1960s. In North Carolina his father is a near-legendary figure who pioneered in human relations in his community, inspired other cities in the state in his capacity as president of the North Carolina League of Munici-palities, and represented smaller towns on the board of the National Conference of Mayors. Believing in politics as a noble pursuit crucial to the life of his city, he led the campaigns that won a majority in Durham County for Adlai Stevenson in 1956 and for John F. Kennedy in 1960. He was a complete person, finding time to be president of his synagogue and to head up the Bonds for Israel campaign for ten consecutive years in the state. For more than four decades, he and his wife, Sara, a wise and remarkable woman who spoke throughout the South in behalf of Israel, were known across the country as leading Jewish figures in the state, the region, and the nation.

Growing up, Eli Evans was immersed in the atmosphere of

southern politics and the aspirations of Jewish life. He became a writer and historian who turned from time to time to work in government and politics on the local, state, and national levels. In addition, he is a leader in national philanthropy, having served for twenty-five years as a grantmaker for two national foundations—from 1967 to 1977 as a program executive with the Carnegie Corporation of New York and since 1977 as president of the Charles H. Revson Foundation. He has administered philanthropic programs in the South and in the nation aimed at increasing civil rights and opportunities for racial minorities, addressing urban problems, supporting creative projects in public television and Jewish education, and helping to stimulate biomedical research and public policy studies in the United States and in Israel.

Chronicling Jewish life and culture in the South, Evans's writing has fascinated reviewers and southern scholars because it represents the perspective of a particular sort of outsider, both a part of the South and yet distant from it. Evans views the South through the prism of a minority with an ancient history of suffering from prejudice and oppression. As an analyst of Jewish history and culture, he brings to his writing the unique perspective of one who has grown up Jewish in the Bible Belt. It has given him special insights into both worlds.

His first book, *The Provincials: A Personal History of Jews in the South*, has remained in print since it was published in 1973 and, beyond its favorable reviews at that time, has received over the years a continuing positive reaction from younger writers and scholars. On November 12, 1986, more than thirteen years after the book's publication, the *New York Times* reported on a resurgence of interest in southern Jewish history, stating in an article: "Earlier works had addressed the issues of Southern Jewry, but it was Eli Evans who, hugging the topic close to personal experience, laid out the emotional terrain . . . and the compass points. He addressed topics at the quick of every Jew born in Dixie: the impulse toward and anxiety over assimilation; the Old Testament links to southern Blacks; the curious relationship with white fundamentalists, many of whom hold a fascination, even reverence, for Jews."

The research and writing of his second book, *Judah P. Benjamin: The Jewish Confederate*, published in 1988, took nine years and required the tracking down of letters and other documents in Europe and in the South. Benjamin, the first self-acknowledged Jew in the U.S. Senate (from Louisiana) who served as attorney general, secretary of war, and secretary of state to the Confederacy, burned all of his papers, and the idea of looking for his letters to other people as well as the demands of writing a fresh analysis of such a secretive life so frustrated other historians that before this biography no major book had been written on Benjamin in over fifty years. Eli Evans successfully explored the man and his times, and the book has already become a classic in Civil War literature. Yale professor C. Vann Woodward, the dean of Civil War historians, wrote in *The New York Review of Books* that the book was "romantic, improbable, and spell-weaving. . . . Some of the best history is written by historians with roots deeply planted in the past of which they write. The main part of the past Evans relates here lies at an anguished juncture in the history of Jews and Southerners. But the past he taps to illuminate that scene, and especially the Jewish role in it, is much older and deeper. It is a past and a theme rarely available to the understanding of non-Jewish historians. For that reason, we are all the more indebted to him for this very fine and moving book."

After he graduated from the University of North Carolina in 1958 and served in the Far East in the U.S. Navy, Evans received a law degree in 1963 from Yale Law School. He was drawn back to southern politics to work as a speech writer in the 1964 North Carolina gubernatorial campaign of L. Richardson Preyer and in 1964–1965 served on the White House staff of President Lyndon B. Johnson. I asked him to return to North Carolina to work with me at Duke University from 1965 to 1967 on a nationwide *Study of American States*, a report on the future of state government funded by the Ford Foundation and the Carnegie Corporation.

Eli Evans combines knowledge of his region and of his Jewish heritage into a complex and subtle mixture of insights that often intertwines autobiography with observation and informs as it inspires. This collection of his articles and essays will take its place beside his other books as a unique contribution to our understanding of the ways in which southern and American history interact with Jewish history, enriching the American past and its future.

Preface

I have for years been intrigued with the ways in which Jews and southerners are alike—stepchildren of an anguished history. From the period before the Civil War, southerners have used Old Testament analogies to portray themselves as "the chosen people," surrounded and outnumbered but destined to survive and triumph against overwhelming odds. This analogy has endured deep in the southern psyche, influencing subconsciously its reactions to events. For example, in 1967, during the Arab-Israeli Six-Day War, polls showed that the South was caught up in military fervor and admiration for the lightning victory of the Israelis. It was almost as if Moshe Dayan had become the Israeli Stonewall Jackson, outthinking and outfighting his Arab foes, just as the boys in gray had done in the Shenandoah Valley against vastly superior numbers in the 1860s. Israel transformed the image of the modern Jew in the mind of the South.

Southerners have also tended to see the Middle East in religious terms, through the lens of biblical prophecy, which foreordained that there would be a great ingathering of the Jewish people before the Second Coming and Judgment Day.

Innumerable trips to Israel since the early 1950s, when I lived on a kibbutz as a student and worked the land alongside Israeli young people, have made me understand more deeply the southern idea of place, so rooted in the Bible, and the Jewish attachment to homeland, as old as civilization itself. Christian fundamentalist passion has linked the South and the Holy Land psychologically in the soul of the South, which explains the extraordinary sympathy and support for Israel in the Bible Belt since 1948, even though there were so few Jews in the region. Israel was acting out the prophecies in the Book and was the symbol of the beginning and the end of the world. For me, therefore, it is natural that there should be articles about Israel and Jewish history in a collection largely about the South. It was so in my family growing up, and I have inherited that twin legacy as a Jewish southerner.

Essentially, I am a book writer who loves history. I remember the first time I read a nineteenth-century newspaper, imagining that I was a Civil War soldier who had just picked it up that morning. I remember the attraction of old documents—from Maimonides' journals at Hebrew University to Robert E. Lee's letters in the Library of Congress—with their musty smells and time-worn colors and the absolute authenticity of signatures and texts. I remember the thrill of finding a new fact after a week of playing hunches and cross-referencing and chasing clues. I liked the feeling of mission, of pursuing a new theory or a fresh point of view. Writing a book takes me years, because I like to turn a subject inside out, to examine its subtleties and nuances until the ideas crystallize, mature, and ripen.

While I prefer the lasting character of books, over the past twenty years I have also done some heart-and-soul writing in shorter forms—op-ed pieces stirred by events; magazine articles, occasionally assigned but usually written on speculation with the hope of publication; essays for serious audiences; book reviews and reports; speeches that were later published.

When I began to organize the more than forty articles for this collection, a number of themes emerged that flow from my personal history.

My father, Emanuel J. "Mutt" Evans, was a Jewish mayor of a southern town—Durham, North Carolina—for six terms from 1951 to 1963. He served in office as a southern liberal through the turbulent years of the civil rights movement and social change in the South that shaped my adolescence. I campaigned with him, visited precincts, and sat with him on election nights. He shepherded his city through the difficult years of desegregation, successfully integrating the schools, public accommodations, the fire and police departments, and city agencies. And my father did not neglect his Jewish obligations: he was president of the local synagogue and raised funds from both Jews and non-Jews as statewide chairman of the Israel Bonds campaign. He believed that to survive in a non-Jewish world, one had to be openly, actively, and proudly Jewish. When I once asked him why he listed the presidency of the Beth-El Congregation on his campaign poster when his advisors recommended he not do so, he simply said, "People down here respect church work."

My mother, Sara Nachamson Evans, was active in all levels of Hadassah, the women's Zionist organization, most of her life. In fact, my grandmother, Jennie Nachamson, founded the first Hadassah chapter in the South in 1919, and she took my mother on a trip from North Carolina to Jerusalem in 1933, in the midst of the Great Depression, because she wanted to see the Holy Land with the eldest of her eight daughters before she died. My mother, handed the torch of Jennie's idealism, traveled and spoke as "Hadassah's Southern Accent," organizing chapters and continually inspiring its members for more than fifty years.

The pieces in this collection are somewhat eclectic in style and range of subject. I have written for the *New York Times* op-ed page, as well as for its book review, arts, and magazine sections, for *The Village Voice*, *Newsweek*, and *New York* magazine, and for numerous scholarly and professional journals. A

third of this collection represents previously unpublished articles, some written especially for this book. I have added observations to bring the material up to date, merged articles with
similar subjects, and edited out redundancies.

In my travels to interview and do research for *The Provincials*, I discovered that Jews were not aliens in the promised
land, but blood-and-bones part of southern history, passing for
white in that mysterious underland of America. I wrote about
this southern life force with wellsprings far deeper than the
Confederate ancestry that the old families in my hometown
loved to brag about. What I wrote is as relevant for this volume
as it was for my first: "I am not certain what it means to be both
a Jew and a Southerner—to have inherited the Jewish longing
for a homeland while being raised with the Southerner's sense
of home. The conflict is deep in me—the Jew's involvement in
history, his deep roots in the drama of man's struggle to understand deity and creation. But I respond to the Southerner's
commitment to place, his loyalty to land, to his own tortured
history, to the strange bond beyond color that Southern blacks
and whites discover when they come to know one another."

I have called the book *The Lonely Days Were Sundays*, taking a quote from my grandmother's life story, which she dictated at the end of her life. More than that, I felt that phrase
was epigrammatic of the emotional terrain of the immigrant
generation of Jews who arrived in the small towns of the South
in the eighteenth and nineteenth centuries. And that loneliness of soul is at the core of every Jew who lives in the Bible
Belt, and certainly is one of the central influences of my own
writing and point of view. The phrase also serves as a psychological backdrop for the ongoing and unfolding American drama I describe in this book, including the history of Jews in the
South and the impact of Israel and the Holocaust on Jewish and
human history, as well as my own family story.

The subtitle, *Reflections of a Jewish Southerner*, is linked to
identity, and the ties I still feel to the South in spite of the more
than two decades of living in New York. Moving to New York
opened me to the kaleidoscope of ethnic America, as well as

the rich varieties of Jewish life. But I was also fortunate to have found a mission in philanthropy that enabled me to explore and serve these dual interests, to make frequent trips to Israel, and especially to travel in the South. My work allowed me to concern myself with the South's problems and its future, and to stay in touch with the enormous changes that have reshaped its destiny. Beyond that, I kept my attachment refreshed by spending summers back in North Carolina writing—more than ten years researching and writing about the story of Jews during the Civil War—and happily accepted speaking dates across the region, and other obligations that kept me attached and involved. But deeper than that, I believe that no one born and raised in the South, even if one moves away physically, can escape its hold on the imagination. I was touched in childhood by its passions and myths, by its language and literature, by the rhythm of its seasons, by the menacing fear of violence and the love of land, by the complexities of race and religion, by the heartbeat of its music, the intensity of its history and the turbulence of its politics, by its sunlight and its shadows, illusions and mysteries. With such entanglements, a native son remains irredeemably and endurably southern. So it has been with me, immersed in the endless fascinations and dense matrix of southern history entwined with Jewish roots, resonating in my soul forever. The very word "home" still conjures up the South for me, and I struggle to give my seven-year-old son that same feeling of affection, ambivalence, and intimacy with the region that I experienced growing up there.

In selecting the articles for this collection, I have been struck by the way in which almost every one reflects the commitment to social justice that was forged in my early years. While history may cast a different shadow on these pieces of writing in retrospect, they were for me my best thoughts at the time they were written. I hope they hold up, now and in the years to come.

Eli N. Evans
November 1992

Part I

Jews in the South

Southern Jewish History: Alive and Unfolding

When I first went back home to the South in the late 1960s to interview southern Jews and their neighbors for *Harper's* magazine, I didn't know what to expect.

I only knew that Jews lived in the shadow of southern history; that the Civil War and slavery had been powerful legacies, even for those Jews like my grandparents who immigrated from Lithuania in the 1880s. One could hear echoes of this dark past in the conversations with Jews whose origins were part of the earlier waves of immigration. The pressure to assimilate was enormous in a region of so much homogeneity.

One of my early encounters was with a man from Anniston, Alabama, a Mr. Sterne from an old German-Jewish family. "What was Friday night like in Anniston, Alabama?" I asked.

He answered, "Oh, it was memorable. First"—and he lifted his hands up—"Mama blessed the lights, and then we settled down to our favorite Friday night meal—crawfish soup, fried chicken, baked ham, hoppin' John (black-eyed peas and rice), and sweet potato pie." I knew then that I had fallen down the rabbit hole into the complex world of the southern Jewish mind and experience.

I have some wonderful memories from my travels in the South. One of the first persons a number of friends advised me to see was Tom Tobias down in Charleston. His entire name was Thomas Jefferson Tobias, so named because of his great-great-grandfather's admiration for Thomas Jefferson, which was so ardent that he rode by horseback all the way from Charleston to Monticello to shake Jefferson's hand. In each succeeding generation, there was a child named Thomas Jefferson Tobias. I asked Tom, whom I was fortunate to see a short time before he died, "Why is it that of all the families from the Sephardic wave, your family is one of the few that has survived?"

He answered, "We were lazy. We lacked adventure and we were comfortable here; so everyone else went off to the Delta where the cotton was growing strong and high and we stayed."

In North Carolina I met Gertrude Weil, a remarkable woman then in her nineties, one of the original suffragettes and a founder of the League of Women Voters. Entering her house was like going through velvet curtains into another world of old photographs and brocaded furniture. I interviewed her in the very room in which she had been born! I asked her, "Miss Gertrude, who was the first president you ever remember hearing about?"

She replied, "Well, I do remember talking to a man whose father remembered as a boy hearing about Thomas Jefferson's inauguration." It's an extraordinary fact that this country is only two long lives old; what we think of as history in America would be smiled at tolerantly in Israel, as if it were a coin so recent it should be thrown back into the sand.

Differences Between Jews North and South

Whenever I have traveled, I have been asked, "What are the differences between Jews in the North and Jews in the South?" That is one of the central questions that any southern Jewish historian must confront.

After living in New York for some years I can offer one

answer. I think being Jewish in the South is like being Gentile in New York. What I mean by that is that Jews in the South live as a minority in a majority culture. The schools close on Jewish holidays in New York; they don't in the South. When my generation of friends in New York was playing stickball in the streets of the Lower East Side, I was picking blackberries in the backyard. They were upwardly mobile; we wanted roots.

In the North the seamstresses and tailors worked to get their children up and out of the ghettos and out to Long Island; in the South the fathers wanted to build businesses that would keep their sons at home. One of the dramas of Jews in the South revolves around the fathers who built businesses for the sons who didn't want them. The memory of that painful day when I told my father that I wasn't going into the family business echoed time and again in my mind as I interviewed people of my generation. It is a fundamental drama of Jews in the South.

A few years ago, I heard Dr. Jacob Rader Marcus assert that "no Jew was ever the first person to go anywhere. There was always a cousin or an uncle ahead of him." I took Dr. Marcus's statement as a challenge. I vowed to myself that I would find someone who was the first Jew in his community, and so I searched. I found almost no one. Finally I stumbled onto a man in Scotland Neck, North Carolina, a little crossroads of a town, not the kind of place one would just happen to settle in. I asked him, "Mr. Goldstein, I have been looking everywhere for you. Why is it that you settled here in Scotland Neck, North Carolina?"

"You really want to know?" he asked.

"Yes," I replied with growing excitement.

"The horse died," he confessed.

What I found was that, whereas historians and scholars of southern history like W. J. Cash saw Jews as aliens in the promised land, we were indeed not aliens, but rooted deep in the soul of southern history.

I came to this subject for personal reasons, not as a historian. Beginning my research, I explored for the first time the literature of Jews in the South. One question began to gnaw at me. Since the history of Jews in the South is such a rich one— and everyone who has studied it or knows about it agrees that it is a story full of humanity and irony—why hasn't there been more written about it? Where are the poets and playwrights, the essayists and novelists?

Only a handful of novels have been written on the southern Jewish experience in the last decade. Perhaps fifty, fewer than a hundred general books through the years. Compared to the tremendous outpouring from the centers of Jewish life in America, it's almost negligible. Why has this aspect of the American Jewish experience received so little attention?

I think there are several reasons. One is the great concern with the subject of conflict between blacks and whites in the South, the result being that the varieties of the white experience have just been overwhelmed and overlooked. It's not only the Jews that have been neglected; so have Catholics and other minority groups.

Moreover, Jews in the South have acquired the habit of maintaining a low profile, an instinctive shyness. It's something that we grow up with, a deep-seated reticence internalized from one's early years. When I went to New York, my feeling was that southern Jews were unimportant. I had been conditioned throughout my life to believe that we were the Jews on the periphery, that it was New York, the world of our fathers, that was the center of Jewish life in America. Jews in the South were out on the rim where they didn't matter. The Jewish community in New York is self-occupied; we were the country cousins and they were the city slickers. I knew little about them, and I came to realize that they didn't know anything about us either.

Why did the Jews come to the South? Many came as peddlers looking for a better life, since the South was the place of opening opportunity after the Civil War. Many of them had been failures in the North, and even if they were successful later, northern Jews continued to see Jews who came south as those who couldn't make it elsewhere. My grandfather was one of those peddlers. In the North, he had had a dairy route, had run a bakery, and finally, as a last resort, had opened a 3 and 9 cents store, which didn't work either, because Woolworth's was too strong.

But time is changing in the South's loser image. Now that the South is emerging as a major regional force in America, Jews in the South may be experiencing an end of the sense of inferiority and inadequacy, the ingrained lack of confidence that has been a part of Jewish life in the South all these years.

Gaps in Southern Jewish History

Now, at last, with growing interest in the southern Jewish experience, scholars can look more energetically at the gaps in our knowledge. What do we know really about the lives of those peddlers in the South? Because it was such an unhappy part of the Jewish experience, literature is sparse, but the subject deserves to be researched and recorded and preserved. There are many ex-peddlers around the South who are still alive. Historians ought to talk to them soon.

What do we really know about the relationship between blacks and Jews? The interviewing I did in the black community (and I would suggest that sort of broad approach to Jewish scholars—interviews with all kinds of people, not just Jews) revealed that Jewish attitudes and psychology are shaped by the ethos we grow up in.

Look at race and religion through the eyes of the participants. When black people saw the peddler, they said to themselves, "Here is a man with an accent (not southern), who doesn't own slaves, who will smile at me, serve me." (The poet and novelist Alice Walker once told me that her grandmother called the Jewish peddler who came in his wagon "the rolling store man"—a wonderful poetic phrase—as she described how the peddler opened up his packs, and remembered that the smells of spices would go through the little cabin where her grandmother lived.)

From the Jewish point of view, the peddlers had been conditioned to be afraid of the muzhiks, the Russian peasants, who would come storming into the shtetl to rape and pillage during the pogroms. They had no previous experience with blacks, no reason to fear them. Since the ex-slaves were customers, they were both linked economically.

Blacks and Jews were linked in other ways as well. Listen to the spirituals—"Go Down, Moses, Let my people go," "Joshua Fit the Battle of Jericho," "Didn't My Lord Deliver Daniel"— blacks in the South were moved by the story of the Israelites struggling out of the land of bondage into the land of freedom. Moses and the children of Israel were very much a part of the black psyche, and the Old Testament connected blacks and Jews to each other.

What do we know about the history of Zionism in the South? It's a fascinating story, because the longing for Zion and a Jewish homeland is wrapped up with Jewish identity everywhere, a part of the sense of peoplehood felt by Jews all over the world. Yet, the South demands its own loyalty, and generates a powerful sense of place. We need to trace the changing attitudes toward Israel in the twentieth century, contrasting attitudes before World War II to the period after the state was declared in 1948 and in the years since, through its five wars and many perils.

What do we know about growing up Jewish in the Bible Belt, of relationships with Southern Baptists and with Catholics? How do we assess a place where both anti-Semitism and philo-Semitism are in the air? How do children deal with the love-hate syndromes of many southern fundamentalists?

What do we know about Jews in politics? This is a special interest of mine, because my father served as mayor of our town for twelve years. The subject stretches back to the Confederate

Secretary of State Judah P. Benjamin and forward to today. My own informal poll as I went through the South revealed that there have been at least 150 Jews elected to public office in the South since World War II. That's a remarkable statistic, given the relatively small number of Jews in the South. One explanation may be that for the emerging black vote, Jews offered a moderate choice; not all, but most, were moderate southern politicians.

And finally, what do we know of the special experience of southern Jewish women? How different were their relationships with Jewish and non-Jewish men, Yankees and southerners? What can we discover about their attitudes toward home, job, family, and education?

The Search for Roots

We are seeing in America an end to the melting pot theory as the central philosophy governing so much of American life.

People are searching for roots. An Italian writer has said, "We learned to be Americans by learning to be ashamed of our grandparents." No more. The de-shaming of the immigrant experience is a necessary step to understanding and, ultimately, to emerge with a profound sense of pride. There's an explosion of ethnicity, a curiosity about where we came from, as well as about where we are and where we are headed. Today, we celebrate the validity of the southern Jewish experience—for academic research and literature—and take pride in its history and its struggle, in the unique Jewish perspective on southern history. We celebrate the southern Jewish experience as a body of knowledge that needs deeper probing, that can benefit from our perspective as southerners and as Jews. There is much to be discovered about the conflict between southerners' commitment to their own place as a homeland and to the Jewish search for a home.

A Renewed Southern Jewish Historical Society

I suggest that scholars and lay people reactivate and reinvigorate the Southern Jewish Historical Society, not just for aca-
demics and amateur historians and rabbis who have an interest, but for everyone who lives in the South. Such a group
could start a publication that is somewhat loose in format and
not too academic, that could draw articles from young sociologists, both Jewish and non-Jewish, and from southern and
Jewish historians who are interested in this subject as an avo-
cation or as part of their other work. The publication could
include poems and essays and thoughts and oral histories;
prizes and awards could be given for the best books and best
research papers. We know a great deal about the external
histories of the major Jewish communities in the South—New
Orleans, Charleston, Richmond—but what about their internal histories? What about the psychological and emotional
experiences of being Jewish in the South? What would anthro-
pologists say, or psychologists, or sociologists? We must ask
not only what Jews in the South did—whom they married, how
much property they had, what kind of wills they left, whether
they owned slaves—but also *how did they feel*? Out in the
small towns away from the major centers, who is telling the next
generation that their history is important, that they, too, are a
part of American Jewish history and what happened to them
matters because it is part of the tapestry of American Jewish
life? As one man told me, "When the Jewish stores were here,
all these towns were different, and then the chain stores came
and now every little town looks alike." We need to learn the
stories behind all those families before it's too late.

When I was growing up, southern Jewish history was the
province of the aristocratic southern Jewish families who
wanted to show how deep their roots were. The rest of us were
newcomers, and we were treated that way by the old Jewish
families as well as by the old Gentile families. There was a
preoccupation with the Civil War among people who wanted to

show that they had a good claim to membership in the United Daughters of the Confederacy. Yet, most of the Jewish immigration to the South occurred *after* the Civil War. As Mrs. Goldberg of Richmond said to me, "The immigrant generation had to be remade. Your generation is different." I would like to know more about the fascinating story of what it meant to be the immigrant generation in the South and to be remade.

Recently, I spent several days with Alex Haley, the author of *Roots*, along with historian Shelby Foote as lecturers on a university-sponsored trip down the Mississippi River. He listened to my family story and took me aside to talk about the Jewish store owners in Hennings, Tennessee, who treated his parents with respect. He recalled the shared history of the slaves and Jews and spoke, the next day, about the importance of written history, such as the Bible, and of oral history. He told about a visit to the village of his forefathers in Gambia where he visited with the *Griot*, who was the living oral archivist of his tribe. He sat for hours listening to this old man trace the fragment of the name of Haley's great-great-grandfather, Kunta Kinte, recounting the entire history of the tribe for many, many hours, all from his memory. The old man was an oral historian. It was the tradition of the tribe which had no written history. From him, Haley learned the story of his ancestor who was dragged to the slave ship and grabbed two handfuls of earth from the beach at Gambia to take to that ship.

I would like to recount my own experience with oral history, how it was linked with my discovery of self and what I believe all southern Jewish historians, indeed every family, must do.

Interview Your Grandparents; Write for Your Grandchild

The increasing mobility of Americans has left most families scattered across the country, with the old people at "home" floating in memories and their offspring in various places phoning in on anniversaries and holidays. Distance deprives the young of roots, of any feeling for family or attachment to place. It robs the old of a close relationship with grandchildren, and of the roundness of life that should come from easy talk about the past in the natural warmth that connects the old to the very young.

Some years ago, I worked with the Kin and Communities program of the Smithsonian Institution, which was trying to do something about encouraging families to record their histories. Under the direction of Margaret Mead, the program produced booklets to encourage families to hold reunions, read family diaries, look at scrapbooks, letters, and wills, and record conversations with each other. Dr. Mead advised, "Interview your grandfather or write for your grandchild."

Historians are now calling this approach the "New New Social History," the aim of which is to leave records not of the men and women who stand out in history, nor of great moments, but of ordinary people in everyday life. While it is true that such family histories will provide a legacy that will be useful for future historians searching for the texture in the lives of everyday people, they can also have a profound impact on future members of every family.

Some time back I chanced upon a yellowing typed manuscript, fewer than a hundred pages, that my grandmother Jennie Nachamson had dictated to one of her eight daughters during the last year of her life in 1939. The story told of her life in Lithuania, the family debate about coming to America, the family's first years in a Baltimore slum, and my grandparents' decision to gamble on the South. She described raising a large Jewish family in the eastern North Carolina tobacco belt in the early 1900s, where they ran a small store and tried to cope with the loneliness that plagued small-town Jews throughout the South. Jennie's story offered me a connection to the life force in my family's past and personalized the pain of the immigrant struggle. And she stirred the southerner in me by revealing those Jewish wellsprings, a genesis far deeper than the Confederate ancestry the old families in my hometown of Durham, North Carolina, used to brag about.

It was a large family—Jennie and Eli produced eight consecutive daughters and finally a son, who begat twenty-two first cousins. I interviewed my aunts about their childhoods and asked my artist aunt (there's one in every family) to do sketches depicting their years of growing up. My mother, the oldest, had custody of the family photograph albums, and together we picked out the best pictures (her sisters had fought over them for years). We gave everything—Jennie's story, the interviews, the sketches, and photographs—to a local printer who offset it and bound it like a book. Every member of the family, and friends as well, received a copy.

After that, my interest mushroomed into a three-year project. I traveled through the South talking to old and young people; I pored over dozens of family histories; I interviewed my own mother and father. I finally wrote a book that combined Jennie's story with those interviews, entwining our family saga with the history of other Jews in the South.

It was one of the most deeply fulfilling experiences in my life, and I recommend collecting your own family history to everyone. While all of us hear stories about our families from parents and older relatives, I found that gathering information in a systematic way as a reporter freed me to ask questions of my parents that I would never have asked as a son. Here's how to do it:

Talk to the family and make it clear that what you seek is more than dates and events—you want to know about personalities, feelings, memories, and experiences. You are hoping for richly detailed stories to pass on to future generations of your family. Remember that myths are as important in a family as "truths," that mystery nourishes history. It matters not at all whether the story of your family is a noble one, whether it is filled with success or failure. What matters is that it happened.

Prepare yourself by charting a family tree with as many dates and events as you can put down—family moves, marriages, children. The chart will guide you in your questions, enabling you to calculate how old parents and grandparents were in the 1920s, or in the Depression, or where they lived during the wars.

Borrow or buy a tape recorder and about a half-dozen tapes (perhaps you can share the expense with several other families or a church or civic group). Practice operating it; nothing is more disconcerting to someone talking than a listener who keeps fiddling with a tape recorder. Look them in the eye so they are not performing for the tape recorder but talking to you. I recommend a recorder with a non-directional microphone, one that is built into the machine so all you have to do is turn it on and put it on the coffee table in front of the person being interviewed.

Set aside several weeks to do the interviews so that you can let your parents or grandparents (or yourselves) unravel memories at a leisurely pace, not more than an hour or so a day. That way, they will look forward to the sessions and add their own energy to the project.

Let's assume that you're talking to your parents. Ask them about their own parents, the neighborhoods they grew up in, the nicknames of friends, the games they played as children. Ask them to sing childhood songs and recite bedtime stories. Don't forget pets, toys, and jokes.

What were winters like? Who were their favorite teachers? When did they first see an automobile, first hear a radio? Do they remember the first movie they saw, the first television show?

Ask about love—how your mother met your father, when they first kissed, what it was like when he proposed. How did they spend Saturday nights, and what were holidays like— Rosh Hashonah, Yom Kippur, Passover, or the Fourth of July? What holiday dishes do they remember eating? Did they keep kosher? Who built the local synagogue and what were rabbis like?

Don't be afraid of unpleasantness—funerals, illnesses, accidents, anti-Semitism, political fights in the town, the impact of war and depression are all a part of life. What is painful to one generation is insight for the next.

What gossip do they remember in town? Whom did they admire and whom did they despise? Did they vote for candidates for governor or mayor and why? What did people think of Roosevelt and Truman?

Ask your mother or grandmother about growing up—the clothes she wore, how she fixed her hair, her first dance, what dances they did, and whether she wore makeup. Ask your father or grandfather about fishing or hunting, about skinny-dipping, about whether he ever saw Babe Ruth play baseball. Ask what the Great Depression was like for the family, what jobs he got and who his bosses were. What was he doing when Pearl Harbor happened and when Franklin Roosevelt died? If you get stuck, open photograph albums and discuss the pictures.

Interviewing my parents and aunts made me feel less lonely somehow, as if I were no longer a particle of sand on the beach but a part of all our family and the immigrant generation who went before and struggled, wandered, settled, loved, married, and bore children. Talking about our family history provided me not only with a bridge to the past but with an anchor for the future. My grandmother always hoped one of the grandchildren would write her story, for she was aware of the drama of her voyage from the old world to the new. What she didn't realize was that I could never have done it had she not sat down with my aunt in the summer of 1939 and told her own story in her own words. No one can predict the impact of interviewing your family or telling your own story to your children or grandchildren—but do it. It will be a contribution to history, but that's incidental; it will leave a treasure for your family.

Southern Jewish history is alive and unfolding, and the search must continue not only for what events took place, but for what people felt, hoped, and feared. Looking at southern Jews—Jewish southerners—creates a prism to re-examine southern history, to explore these new participants in the southern drama and discover a vital part of the Jewish experience in America.

2

In Search of Judah P. Benjamin

Joseph Cohen, head of the Department of Jewish Studies at Tulane University, interviewed me in New Orleans in February 1988, when I went down for a speech after the publication of my biography of Judah P. Benjamin. It was an emotional trip for me, a return to the city Benjamin lived in and the state he represented in the U.S. Senate. It was also a rare audience that came to hear me speak, a combination of members of the Jewish community and Civil War buffs, and the warmth of their reaction was memorable.

Because Cohen prepared himself so thoroughly for this interview, it was the most searching conversation I have had on the subject.

We sat in a hotel room with a grand view of the Mississippi River, an immense presence sweeping southward toward the gulf through a land that has known slavery and civil war. This raucous port is perhaps the only city in North America which, at the time, could have nurtured the enigmatic man who became the Jewish senator from Louisiana and a Confederate statesman.

JC: How did you first become interested in Judah P. Benjamin?

EE: Judah P. Benjamin in a way was always there for me. When I was growing up I was always proud that Hank Greenberg, the home run slugger of the Detroit Tigers, was a Jew, and Sid Luckman from the Chicago Bears, who was their quarterback, was a Jew. I was proud of the fighters Benny Leonard and Max Baer. And I was always glad that Judah P. Benjamin was a Jew. The origins of my feeling about Benjamin were for me, as a southern boy growing up, grounded in Jewish pride. There were other factors, too. As you know, my father ran for mayor of Durham in 1950 in the middle of my adolescence, was reelected six times and served twelve years. Because of his campaigns, I was drawn into the politics of a southern town. Dad was elected in a liberal reform victory in the city as an openly Jewish figure supported by the black vote. He was a remarkable leader for our city. I wrote about him in *The Provincials.* He helped to integrate the schools and the lunch counters and the public accommodations. We had a downtown store with a lunch counter in it, and when the sheriff came and said he couldn't serve an integrated clientele at his store, Dad asked his lawyer to look at the law, and he found that the law enabled us to serve anybody so long as they were standing at the counter. So he had the stools at the counter removed. That, incidentally, was the origin of writer Harry Golden's famous "vertical integration plan." The secret to solving the South's problems, Harry said, was to take all the seats out of the restaurants and the schools and then everybody could integrate. As long as black and whites were standing up together, integration was easy.

In Dad's political campaigns there were, of course, instances of anti-Semitism in the city. Durham was in the middle of the Bible Belt, and I had always wondered what running for office in the Bible Belt was like for the first Jews who came into the South. My imagination was drawn to Judah P. Benjamin then, but I never really pursued the matter until I was doing research for *The Provincials* because, as you know, American Jewish history jumps straight from Haym Solomon to Louis D. Brandeis in its recording of important figures. Their stories were not complicated by southern history in the way that Benjamin's was. Researching materials for *The Provincials*, I came upon Judah P. Benjamin anew and I read much about him. It occurred to me even then that there was something wrong in the way historians had treated Benjamin. I came to feel that Judah Benjamin was a much more important figure than historians in this country—Jewish or southern—had given him credit for being. There was a psychological dimension to him that had not been explored, because he was the first Jew to break through the barriers of bigotry into the councils of national power. It did not matter what kind of Jew he was. What was important was that he was the first Jew in American history that other Jews and the non-Jewish community had to react to as *a Jew with secular political power*. I knew from my father's experience that non-Jews as well as Jews in the community react in complicated ways to a Jew who has that influence and power. I began to feel that there was a real untold story here, and a story that perhaps I was uniquely equipped by personal history to research and to tell.

JC: What do you consider the most important discoveries about Benjamin that you made in the course of your research and writing the book? What were the surprises?

EE: Well, there are a number of things. I think the first thing I discovered was that Benjamin, while he left no papers, did leave a lot of impressions. In a sense, we are captives of the impressions that other people had of Benjamin, because when they spoke of him he was more of a Rorschach test on how they felt about Jews than how he really was as an individual. Their feelings that he was "exotic" or a "fatalist" or a dark Mephistophelian figure, I think, got transmogrified into fact, hardened from repetition over time in history books, almost like an ancient fossil. It is that impression that history has brought down to us, when indeed we are looking at a symbolic figure, particularly in the eyes and comments of his contemporaries. All of them had various reasons to dislike Benjamin.

So my first realization was that there was something more to this man than what newspapers or political figures or contemporary writers had to say about him. And the one way to get at Benjamin's complexity was to come at it through broad and comprehensive research. That approach, dictated by circumstance, I think makes the book unique. Emory Thomas, a historian from the University of Georgia whom I respect enormously, said in his review in the *Washington Post* that I was deprived of the opportunity to do a conventional biography by the fact that Benjamin had burned his papers. I had to pursue another technique, he wrote, which involved "monumental research" in order to surround the figure in the middle whose papers were missing. Dr. Thomas described that line of approach as a "conversational biography." I had to take the hard evidence that has survived—official papers, his letters to others—and be honest with the reader about what the real meaning of that evidence was. That gives to the book a speculative quality, but at least it's honest speculation, and I try to draw reasonable conclusions.

The truth is, I did not mean to get involved in a task this extensive when I began with Benjamin nine years ago. What initially was a fascination obviously turned into an obsession. Perhaps it was because of my father that the search became a "roots" experience. I've been reading a lot about the art of biography in the last few years, and there's no question that a biographer is attracted to a subject with whom there is a commonality of spirit. There were parallels in our lives: I also was born Jewish in the South, my father was in politics, and I myself worked in politics. I was a speech writer in the White House and an aide to a number of people who ran for office or were in office, in much the same way that Benjamin was an aide to Jefferson Davis. And I felt that I understood the role of the aide to famous political figures in a way that perhaps other writers would not because I had been one. I was on the White House staff of President Lyndon Johnson and worked for former North Carolina Governor, now U.S. Senator, Terry Sanford. I had worked in several campaigns. I thought I understood that role very well.

There were other parallels as well. I had gone to Yale Law School, and while Yale by the time I got there in 1960 was a far cry from the Yale that Benjamin went to as one of its first Jews when he was a fourteen-year-old, there were still remnants of feeling there of the "old blues" and the social exclusion from the eating clubs. So I got something of a feeling for what Yale must have been like in Benjamin's student days. I felt some empathy. In the end I felt that Judah P. Benjamin had found his biographer.

The most important consideration to me, I think, was that I was willing to take an unconventional approach to the research and immerse myself totally in his times. It required hiring researchers in London and Paris, in Richmond, New Orleans, and Charleston. It required retracing Benjamin's steps, as well as months of sitting in the Library of Congress sifting through the manuscript collections to look at the papers of scores of other people. It was certainly a new form of biographical research for me, and there were surprises.

One large surprise early on was my discovery that in order to understand Benjamin and his rise to power one had to understand New Orleans and Catholicism in Louisiana. I think that Benjamin's rise to become the first acknowledged Jew elected to the United States Senate—by that I mean everyone knew he was a Jew—could perhaps only have happened in New Orleans and in Louisiana. There was something unique about the nature of early nineteenth-century New Orleans, especially its incredible growth as a port city that doubled in size between 1830 and 1840 and then more than doubled again in the following decade. That rapid growth allowed an outsider like Benjamin to emerge, because the city was cast loose from the moorings of its traditions and the control of old social structures. It was chaotic, diverse, and Catholic in an otherwise Protestant, fundamentalist South. A brilliant Jewish lawyer could make a fortune and enter politics.

Another surprise was the character of Jefferson Davis, who played a key role in Benjamin's rise to power. You have to give Jefferson Davis his due. He was the first chief executive on the North American continent to appoint a Jew to his cabinet, and he did it not once but confirmed it three times in the face of enormous criticism and pressure to let Benjamin go. Why keep someone in your cabinet who is drawing such controversy, such fire, such criticism? The truth is, the criticism of Benjamin deflected criticism from Davis, but that explanation is not sufficient. Why was Davis different from his contemporaries? On investigation, I found Davis had a history of interaction with Jews that was intriguing. Davis is almost a bigger sphinx in the history of the Confederacy than Judah P. Benjamin. These were two extraordinarily enigmatic men at the center of southern history. That was a surprise. And the discovery of Varina Howell Davis, about whom I knew nothing when I started, was also a surprise to me. I think much of the key to Benjamin's influence and survival has to do with her.

Lastly, I was surprised about the depth of the bitterness and fear and even anti-Semitism following Lincoln's assassination. I had never really read the literature of the post-assassination period before. It was a shockingly terrible time in American history. In some ways it is a wonder that this country survived it. The emergence of radicals taking over the United States government and running roughshod over the Constitution, trying to impeach a president for the most cynical of political reasons, stirring up bitterness and tensions—it's no wonder it has been called an "age of hate." It was a time of accusations and wild rumor and suspicion, when everyone in power seemed to be accused of complicity in the assassination of the president, particularly the Confederate leadership. All of that was fairly shocking to me, but the Kennedy assassination provided a frame of reference that made it easier to project back into that time in a way that might not otherwise have been possible. In some ways, it was more intense because Lincoln was a wartime father figure; it was a horror, as if Franklin Roosevelt had been shot in 1945. The bitter aftermath of the Lincoln assassination was a great surprise to me.

JC: It's gratifying when you are doing research to find things that are so immediately rewarding.

EE: I must say, though, that my initial reasons for being attracted to Benjamin were deeply personal, and all of these other things came afterward—the rewards, the fascination.

JC: Now that the book is published, what is it, in retrospect, that intrigues you the most about Benjamin? What is the most enduring impression you have?

EE: I think the most enduring impression for me is the fact that Benjamin, psychologically, remained a Jew all his life. And that is the key to explaining everything about him. Ordinarily, I wouldn't have accepted that as a thesis except for the fact that his father was one of the twelve dissenters who founded Reform Judaism in America. It began in 1824, and Philip Benjamin was one of its leaders and served on the central committee of Beth Elohim in Charleston. Judah P. Benjamin was a thirteen-year-old boy, perhaps one of the first confirmed in the new congregation, so he was raised not in an indifferent home but in a passionately intellectual one in which the absence of rituals, if they were absent, had a rationale, a reason, and a perspective. But there were boundaries, even in revolt. His father was expelled from the new congregation for keeping the family fruit stand open on the Sabbath, and that may explain some of Benjamin's alienation from Judaism. But he carried a Hebrew prayer book with him to Yale, and even though one doesn't find him talking much about Judaism over the course of his life, there were a few instances in which he did. Knowing about his boyhood changes so much of the way we look at Benjamin, causing us to think of him as a subconscious Jew but a Jew nonetheless. Think of Henry Kissinger, if you will, who also served as secretary of state to an isolated, suspicious president, and you will have something comparable.

Benjamin was attacked almost daily with snide remarks about his Jewishness in the press or on the floor of the Confederate Congress. This was another enormous surprise to me. The bitterness and ugliness of those attacks I couldn't believe at first. I actually read through the daily accounts of the *Richmond Examiner* and the daily accounts of the Confederate Congress. I finished reading the material in a state of shock. The hatred was all there. Benjamin was a foil, the "dark prince," the symbol. Think what that must have done to him day after day. Given who he was, his Jewishness was something he simply could not run from or ignore. And yet this man emerged, in a sense, triumphant. He survived. It is really one of the extraordinary Jewish stories in American history. If I had any sort of mission in writing the book, it was to put him in context and thereby give Judah P. Benjamin back to the Jews as part of our history.

JC: You've produced a superb book in spite of the fact that Benjamin destroyed all of his papers. Do you have an explanation for his need to leave no traces behind him? Usually, accomplished people with strong egos who are active in public life want to leave as voluminous a record as possible. Was it his disastrous marriage or some other sensitivity or secret that led him to silence the record?

EE: He burned papers over the course of his whole life, not just at the end. He said that he didn't want a biography written, and therefore he tried almost to disappear, to remain hidden from history. He never wrote about or spoke about the war. Just think of the book that Judah P. Benjamin could have written about the war. It would have been an extraordinary book. Something happened. And I came to believe that what silenced Benjamin was the assassination of Lincoln and the accusation against the Confederate leadership. Suddenly, he had to realize that the Jewishness he had fled from all his life was going to be a basis for an accusation against him and that the prejudice of the times might destroy him. If Benjamin had been captured, we might well have had a Dreyfus trial in America. Benjamin was not guilty of plotting the assassination and neither was Jefferson Davis. Official investigations and a hundred years of inquiry have exonerated them. After all, the South had everything to gain from Lincoln's survival. Benjamin knew that. Lincoln's postwar policy was the only chance the South had for a generous peace. There would have been no real reason even to participate in such a plan. The whole thing was just an accident of history from Benjamin's perspective. I think it frightened him, and that fear was the major emotion of the last twenty years of his life.

Lincoln was the first president of the age of photography, and his photograph was in every home. As you know, he was killed on Good Friday of what became known as Black Easter. There were 2,500 sermons about him that Easter Sunday. I actually read through scores of those sermons because they're in the Library of Congress. Lincoln was instantly compared to a martyred Christ figure. John Wilkes Booth was called the "American Judas." The southern leadership was accused. Within hours of Abraham Lincoln's death, Union Secretary of War Stanton said that the assassination was a plot "hatched in Richmond." It was in the interest of the radicals like Stanton to blame the Confederate leadership. Jefferson Davis spent two years in jail under a charge of treason and a cloud of suspicion over the charges of complicity in the assassination. Judah P. Benjamin was never charged, but the Canadian spies were. John Surratt, Benjamin's courier to Canada, was sought for four years as the most wanted man in the world because Booth and four other conspirators stayed in Mary Surratt's boardinghouse in Washington. Benjamin didn't know what Surratt was going to say to save his neck or the life of his mother. Then Mary Surratt became the first woman hanged in American history.

So what cruelties would Stanton not have stooped to had Benjamin been captured? Benjamin would have become the

Jewish scapegoat in this Civil War passion play. Only something this shocking, I think, could have caused one of the most formidable orators in American history to remain silent, a man who some experts on the subject have called the equal in oratory and debate to Calhoun and Webster, a man who was a brilliant writer, a man with an extraordinary legal mind and analytical talent. He simply chose never to speak of the war publicly again and to disappear.

JC: Why was it so important to Benjamin to keep his marriage going in view of Natalie's treatment of him and of her known extended infidelities?

EE: First, divorce was not very prevalent in those days and not acceptable for men in politics. Second, Benjamin's parents actually lived apart—his mother in Beaufort and father in nearby Charleston—and therefore he had a model in his boyhood of a marriage which, in a sense, had dissolved, though it appeared intact. Benjamin was really continuing the pattern in his own life that he had experienced as a child. Third, he did end up in Paris with Natalie but only in the last two years of his life. He was constantly humiliated whenever they were together, and the rumors of her adulterous affairs are recorded in diaries and letters of the times. I think that in the end it was just easier to be separated than to do anything else, and there weren't any alternatives in that age for someone in his position.

JC: Is there any likelihood that any of Benjamin's correspondence to Natalie survived in Paris?

EE: It's a question that keeps haunting me. I had two experienced historical researchers in Paris looking for Benjamin material. First, I thought there must be a portrait of Natalie around. She was a vain enough woman. It's hard to believe that it's not somewhere in Paris. Second, she was part of Louis Napoleon's court and social circle and so she must have been mentioned in the newspapers. And third, since the Rothschilds ultimately bought the Benjamins' mansion, the furnishings, one would think, would have survived. There must be records and deeds. But the researchers couldn't find anything. Curiously, quotations of some of Benjamin's letters about Natalie appeared in Pierce Butler's biography, which he received on loan from relatives, so at one time there were some letters in New Orleans. Those letters have since disappeared. I've advertised and looked everywhere, but perhaps they will show up now, and Tulane University can publish a volume of his papers. I would like to help with that.

JC: As remarkable as Varina Howell Davis was, she always had to play second fiddle to Jefferson Davis's first wife, the dead Sarah Knox Taylor. But given Benjamin's marital situation, his charm, his eloquence, his urbanity, and Jefferson Davis's rural background, it seems natural to me that Varina and Benjamin would have been strongly attracted to each other. Just how close was their attachment?

EE: It was a deep friendship. It certainly was a kind of love affair of the mind, if I can put it that way. She wrote at the end of her life that "his greatness was hard to measure . . . [and] I loved him dearly." She's on the record about her feelings. Even after the war, Benjamin was her lawyer and personal advisor for the rest of his life. And she was very dependent on him. Varina Davis was a remarkable woman who was related to a former governor of New Jersey and therefore came from a political background. But Jefferson Davis hated politics and politicians. Benjamin was a man who really understood her and accepted her intellectually. In a way, it was a manipulative relationship on both sides because it was convenient for Benjamin to have someone as close to Jefferson Davis as Varina Davis was, and for Varina it was important to understand events and participate in the affairs of state. Benjamin was a kind of court Jew, like so many of the Sephardic Jews who had served for centuries the royalty of Europe. He wasn't in competition with Jefferson so Varina saw him as a colleague. She was proud of the fact that Benjamin never withheld secrets from her, that he trusted her. She wanted to be more consequential than just another wife and first lady who entertained. Benjamin played to her need to be consequential. And who better than she could he have relied upon? At different times Benjamin was actually the acting president of the Confederacy.

Jefferson Davis suffered from neuralgia and neurasthenia— the nineteenth-century terms for depression and ulcers—and at times he was totally immobilized. But he lived a long life, so these weren't ailments that were totally physical but more psychosomatic. He lived until his eighties and was quite healthy after the war. He simply couldn't deal with the pressure of the situation. That explains Benjamin's writing 2,500 memos over the course of the war. Actually, in some ways he was the president. I think he and Varina formed a partnership to enable Jefferson Davis to perform his duties, to ride horseback through Richmond and leave to go buck up the troops and see people and play a public role while somebody was handling the paperwork at home. In a sense, Varina and Benjamin were the twin parts of Jefferson Davis's soul—his love life and his working life. Varina Davis and Judah P. Benjamin had a unique relationship, there's no doubt about it. It's clear that Varina really cared for Benjamin. She knew that he was not happy. They did have a very close and affectionate relationship, but not an affair really because one didn't do that sort of thing with the first lady of the Confederacy. Certainly, no other historian has written of it. But it was quite an intense and passionate friendship.

JC: Was there any malicious gossip about Varina and Benjamin?

EE: Malicious gossip? Not of that sort, not that I found.

JC: Varina was certainly an attractive person. I suspect most people don't think of Jefferson Davis that way. I've always thought of him as rather forbidding. But your image of him is still a sympathetic one. He comes across in a human way. I still

have lingering doubts about his capability in running the Con-
federacy. How capable was he?

EE: Well, that is an interesting question. I worked very hard
on Jefferson Davis, hoping to get him right because I knew the
book would be judged by Civil War historians on the one hand
and American Jewish historians on the other. That gauntlet of
critics was not going to be an easy thing for me to face because
the book was vulnerable on all counts. But Frank Vandiver, the
distinguished historian and president of Texas A & M who also
serves as editor of the Jefferson Davis papers, said that he had
learned new things about Davis from my book. Historians had
never viewed Davis from a southern Jewish perspective. There
is still a great biography of Davis to be written and it hasn't
been done yet. He was without question a very complicated
man.

As to his capability, my research makes me feel that in some
ways Davis was the wrong man for the Confederacy but in other
ways the right man. His cabinet ministers were an arrogant
crowd. But as I look at the choices, I don't think Senator
Robert Toombs of Georgia would have been a better president,
and I know Alexander H. Stephens wouldn't have been a better
president. They both would have been terrible. Of course,
Jefferson Davis suffers greatly because we have a tendency to
contrast him with Abraham Lincoln. But Lincoln was probably
the greatest president in American history, soulful and profound, and Davis does not come off well in contrast. Lincoln
was able to unify the North, but Davis was not a unifying
figure. He did not command great respect because he seemed
so cold and distant, too rigid and straight-laced. Hindsight
suggests that as bad as the final two years of the war were for
the South, a less proud man and a more pragmatic one might
have ended the fighting earlier in an honorable way. Perhaps
another southerner would have found a way out rather than
proceed, as Davis did, right down to the bitter end, forcing
everybody to suffer with him. He had several opportunities to

stop the war. And Lincoln offered him a way out. But he was so much the proud southern military hero that he could not do it. That's the tragedy of it and the tragedy of Jefferson Davis as president. I've never expressed this view until now, but I think it is the truth about Davis.

JC: Since Benjamin stands out in southern history and southern Jewish history, how do you account for the fact that the Jews in the South have hardly had their presence acknowledged by southern historians? And, indeed, until very recently southern Jews have had only a scant regard for their own history. Or maybe you don't agree with the premises of the question.

EE: Yes, I do agree with the premises of the question. I had to face those questions when I was writing *The Provincials.* It's puzzling, but I would say that the answer is linked to southern fundamentalism with its twin polarities of hatred of the Jews and love of the Jews. It's a situation very little understood by people outside of the South. Because of this fundamentalist ambivalence, I think that Jews in the South have internalized a deep lesson: that the best way to survive was to be quiet about their presence. If trouble came and the blacks were blamed, the Jews felt they would not be far behind. That reticence seemed wise because Jews, Catholics, and blacks were all part of the hierarchy of hate to the Ku Klux Klan. There was fear in the southern Jewish mind. The Leo Frank case in 1915 under- scored it. I never would have believed that the fear was so pervasive had I not interviewed old people in the late sixties and early seventies for *The Provincials.* They still carried scars from the Frank case. And it wasn't just in Georgia, it was all across the South. The fact that this Brahmin, German-Jewish, assimilated, well-to-do man could be the victim of anti- Semitism was an incredible shock to them. Southern Jews just learned to keep a low profile and hope for the best. The Ku Klux Klan was always there. The bigotry was there and it didn't take much to set it off.

When my father ran for mayor of Durham, some members of

the Jewish community feared that if anything bad happened, they would be blamed. They were threatened by my father's decision to run. I'm not saying all were, but some were, enough to know that somewhere deep in them was a fear of what might happen. That fear is certainly one major reason why there's been so little written by southern Jews about themselves. That's part of it. The other part is a deep-seated inferiority complex—the feeling that the only part of American Jewish history that mattered was the story of the immigrants and their rise to greatness in New York and the East. The Jews who went to the South were outside of the mainstream, unimportant even in their own eyes. That's why I called them "the provincials." They were down in Dixie making history where it didn't matter. The significant history of Jewish life was being made by Eddie Cantor, Al Jolson, Irving Berlin, Leonard Bernstein, and the other sons of the immigrants who settled in New York and Boston. Nobody wanted to write about what was happening in the provinces in the largely rural South. But I think the story of the Jews in the South is a dramatic story, a wonderful story. It's a story full of achievement and courage and hard work and triumph. After *The Provincials* was published, people wrote to me and said, "You took our family story, which I was always very ashamed of, and the story of my grandfather who was a peddler, which I've never really liked to talk about, and you made us proud." That mattered. The story of the Jews in the South deserves to be told as part of the story of Jews in America.

JC: Having been born and reared in the South myself, I've always felt that southern Jews were unique. And I think perhaps you may share this feeling as well. What in your view makes southern Jews different from northern Jews?

EE: I think that the most important thing is that they live as a minority in a majority culture. They have to interact with a non-Jewish community every day. That interaction shapes southern Jews. It turns them into testifiers, carriers of Jewish history to their neighbors. When I was growing up as the only Jew in my high school, I discovered that I was representing all the Jewish people in everything I did. I was changed by that experience. I knew they would judge all the Jewish people by the few Jews they knew. In the South, the interactions with the non-Jewish community are daily, constant, on all levels, and one learns about oneself in a much different way than Jews in larger communities do, like New York or the largely Jewish Long Island suburbs. I think that's one of the major differences. Of course, I may be talking about a chapter in Jewish life in the South that you and I know that has now passed. The southern Jews are leaving the small towns and coming to the major cities, where there are growing Jewish communities and institutions.

JC: Do you see Jews and southerners as being alike in any significant ways?

EE: Yes. I've always been struck by the fact that southerners considered themselves the Chosen People. They have a bonding to the Old Testament, and blacks do in particular. I think southerners and Jews each have a tortured history, a history of torment and passion and pain. In essence, there is a lot of similarity between southerners and Jews.

JC: What were your own experiences, growing up Jewish in the South? What was it like? Were there personal attacks, anti-Semitic incidents?

EE: Well, yes and no. I think the overwhelming impression and memory I have is that there was a strong philo-Semitism, a love of the Jews. Every small-town Jew experiences this: being considered the expert on the Old Testament, being a symbol instead of a person. I do remember my best Christian friend being concerned that I was going to go to hell when I died. He told me once how worried he was because I didn't believe in Jesus, and he was sure I was going to go to hell. The idea of soul-saving is very much a part of southern small-town life.

JC: Did you ever have people pray over you?

EE: Oh, yes. When my father was mayor of Durham we suddenly became semi-celebrities. As you know it's very important for fundamentalists to convert celebrities. I became a special target to the "fundies" in school. But I didn't really think of being prayed over as an anti-Semitic experience. There were some anti-Semitic incidents because when my father was mayor it was the time of the Supreme Court decision, the beginning of the Civil Rights era—a passionate time in the South. The conservative, right-wing, white working class was embittered by the black vote, and there was a newspaper that attacked my father in print as the "Jew mayor" of Durham and all the rest of it. I can remember several instances of that kind. But you know, it didn't produce fear. On the contrary, it caused other Christians to go out of their way to act positively with respect and it made for an acceptance and a pride in our being Jewish. Dad put "President, Beth El Synagogue" on his campaign poster because, he said, "People down here respect church work." He would take me to go to greet the preachers who came to hold tent services in the summertime. I'd go with Daddy to listen to him giving the mayor's greeting to these itinerant preachers, and I can remember their saying, "Y'all listen to the mayor because he's the same religion as Jesus," and people would perk up, I mean really perk up, and Dad would deliver his greeting. Of course, there was a Klan element. Our house was threatened. We moved out one night after a bomb threat, and the police watched the house. The KKK is a distorted, twisted Christianity run amok, a cross-burning, psychotic Christianity. It was there, but my feelings were not ones of fear and hatred. They were very different.

JC: Our experiences were very much alike. My closest friends when I was in high school were all farmers' sons. In the summertime I used to go out to the evangelical meetings. I would never have gotten into graduate school at Vanderbilt if I hadn't learned so much Christianity as I did at those tent meetings, listening on those hot summer nights to all that hellfire and damnation theology. But let me broach another subject. Despite the fact that the Jews played important fringe roles in the southern literary renaissance, the southern Jewish community has never produced any great novelists or poets. Do you see any reasons why this is so?

EE: There has been a lack of self-consciousness among Jews in the South, that is, in terms of thinking they have a special history. They have one in the way that they relate to fundamentalists or grow up in the Bible Belt, but they don't really think about themselves that way.

JC: That is a special history well worth writing about. Maybe the next generation will do it. Maybe your book will help them to recognize the possibilities.

EE: I'd like to think that could happen.

3

Miss North Carolina Is Jewish

The night she won the title, the newspaper story about the new Miss North Carolina of 1972 mentioned casually that she was "the daughter of Jewish immigrants persecuted in World War II," and that she had made a brief reference to Auschwitz.

That September, as I drove down the New Jersey Turnpike to the Miss America finals to interview Connie Lerner and her parents, I suddenly felt as if I should turn back and leave the Lerners' memories at peace.

What would her parents be like, having survived the most horror-filled experiences known to any human beings in history? How could I even dare ask them about it, or blame them for a possibly sullen reaction to one more emissary from the prying press, marketing human miseries again for the momentary thrill of the public?

And what kind of child would such a couple raise? Had they encouraged her to enter a beauty contest?

Mostly, it was the irony that attracted me. I was both a Jew and a southerner, and while I had the southerner's instinctive adoration of beauty queens, they had always seemed distant and forbidding to me—untouchable super-Gentile symbols of sweetness and hoop-skirt sexuality, throwbacks to the lazy elegance of plantation days, conjuring up mental ghosts in the southern psyche I neither understood nor felt a part of.

Now I was about to meet my consummate fantasy: the southern Jewish beauty queen. It was that fascinating thought that lured me to Atlantic City.

"When I think of what my mother was going through at my age—do you realize her head was shaved completely? She had nothing to eat, she was running around in the snow without shoes, and here I am, state queen at the Miss America contest—it's really unbelievable."

Miss North Carolina and I were sitting in a corner of the cavernous 25,000-seat convention hall in Atlantic City. We were taking a lunch break during all-day rehearsals for the Miss America finals that night. Bert Parks was sipping a soft drink at one side of the stage, and the state queens were nibbling sandwiches and chattering to each other like fifty tropical birds on a sandbar. Sitting with us was a pudgy Atlantic City matron wearing a flowery pillbox hat. An official hostess, she oozed the artificial helpfulness of the professional censor.

"No embarrassing questions, young man," she warned, her singsong voice and saccharine smile no doubt masking the stilleto tucked in her corset. "No, you cannot talk with a queen without a hostess. It's a long-standing pageant policy."

Her presence didn't inhibit Connie, who continued to talk easily about the death camps. "At first they kept it from me," she said. "Mother didn't teach me Hungarian, for instance, because it reminded her of too many bitter experiences. In the last few years, I began to ask a lot of questions, and then they told me because they thought it was important for me to know. My father lost everybody in the camps—his parents, his brothers and sisters. My mother lost her brother and her parents."

The Atlantic City hostess shifted peevishly in her seat, her face somewhat ashen from the stark turn in the conversation.

I asked Connie how she felt about the criticism that she was frivolous or trite for entering a beauty contest.

The question stung her, and she fired back, "I want to *use* the title, not just win it. If I win the Miss America contest, I'll use it to do something with my life."

In terms of the Miss America pageant, Connie Lerner was something of a kook. The press kits listed the honors, ambitions, and favorite sports of each state queen: "Miss Louisiana—Campus Beauty, Pompom Line"; "Miss Georgia— Campus Crusade for Christ"; "Miss Alabama—Athletic Officer in Social Sorority."

Connie's biography said: "President of Eastern Region of B'nai B'rith Girls" and mentioned her involvement with the "Committee for Responsibility for War-Burned and War-Injured Vietnamese Children."

While most of the state queens sought acceptable degrees in nursing, elementary education, home economics, and physical education, Connie wrote that she intended "to go to law school . . . and become an ambassador in a foreign country." Most girls leaned toward water skiing, swimming, and tennis as their favorite sports; Connie listed "playing chess and running track." A gifted pianist, she chose a non-crowd pleaser— Chopin's "Revolutionary Etude"—for her talent entry because it had been played twenty-four hours a day in defiance of the German invasion of Poland in 1939 and had meant a great deal to her parents.

To protect her from the inevitable childhood hurts, her parents had infused Connie with a fierce pride in her Jewishness. "I was the only Jewish girl in a Catholic school, but it didn't bother me. I just taught the nuns some Hebrew words."

Permitted to make her own choices about dating, she decided to go out only with Jewish boys. "I soon realized that if I started dating a boy who wasn't Jewish, that because I am so open and seek out the good in people and really do love people, I would open myself up to complications I couldn't handle."

Connie is a first-generation American with a profound respect for her parents and admiration for her father, who had to start again in a new country to salvage a life for his family. Remnants of her mother's family had chosen Israel after the war, and the Lerners had visited them two years before. "The first thing I thought when we landed and I got off the plane was 'I'm home!' I have a deep feeling for the land of Israel. Maybe it was because my mother had her 'sweet sixteen' birthday party in a concentration camp. Some 'sweet sixteen.'"

Yet she felt herself a southerner as well. "I eat grits and corn bread. But my mother makes great chicken soup, too."

Her enthusiasm and openness about being Jewish were starting to amaze me. In my day, southern Jewish kids were private and defensive about their religion, often ashamed that they were different. Some would do anything to blend in and belong, pretending they were whatever seemed convenient. Miss North Carolina was comfortably Jewish, even assertively so. Who else but a self-assured but intensely Jewish beauty queen could lead a march of 225 United Synagogue Youth convention delegates in Charlotte from Temple Israel to the courthouse, dance the hora, and make a speech protesting the Soviet treatment of the Jews in Russia? The newspaper printed "Connie Lerner—Extremist?" under her picture. Did she feel any conflict about having the title and leading the protest?

"No. Because the people of North Carolina are liberty-loving people. Besides, the Jaycee creed believes and states that service to humanity is the best work; and besides that, I *am* Jewish, you know."

Connie's beauty isn't flashy, but her olive skin and blue-green eyes were starting to bother me. An unselfconscious queen, she was taking big noisy bites out of an apple, and I found myself wondering if she had ever dressed up as Queen Esther at the Jewish holiday of Purim, pretending that she had saved the Jewish people by admitting her religion to the king who had innocently selected her only for her beauty.

Connie does not question values; she asserts them. In many ways her most firmly held values are the approved ones—love of family, church, and country. But some of her views, resulting from a deep belief in the dignity of man and a reverence for individual freedom, would seem radical to many North Carolinians.

When she pointed out that there had been a black runner-up in the Miss North Carolina contest that summer, I told her that one of my friends had said, "Wouldn't you know that the same year they pick a Jewish queen, they'd put a black girl on the court?" She frowned and said that one of her proudest moments was when that same girl was chosen Miss Congeniality by the sixty other contestants.

She feels that school integration is the only way to break down the barriers of hate between the races. "It's gotta come; it's the only way to get rid of prejudice. It doesn't mean you have to marry people. But there will be more interracial and interreligious marriages because people will learn about each other as people."

She thinks that parents ought to be more forthright in sex education. "What is everybody going crazy about?" she said. "My father said that from ages six to nine, the Jewish boys in Hungary knew everything—who to sleep with and who not, sodomy, adultery, pornography . . . it's all in the Bible and Jewish children knew it from studying the Torah. They learned what's right and wrong, what's clean and unclean. They knew the Bible, and it's a matter of helping children form values."

She likes the idea of coeducational dorms at colleges. "People who want to do anything will do it anyway. Treat 'em like adults and they'll act that way."

I asked about the University of North Carolina at Chapel

Hill and why she refused to join a sorority. Suddenly our
nervous chaperone exploded, "That's an improper question!"

The boardwalk settles down after Labor Day, the absence of
crowds revealing Atlantic City in a state of tawdry, sagging na-
kedness. The beaches, the hotels, the restaurants, are transformed into a vast home for the aged, a gala of wheelchairs and
canes and crowds of doddering women with shawls to protect
themselves from the September chill. The paint is peeling off
everything by now, and the boardwalk crowds are quiet; no
squeals of the young here . . . definitely not a place for
swingers. The smells, the sounds, the sights, are resort-
Americana; greasy luncheonettes, cheap auctions, wig shops,
pizza parlors, offers of handwriting analysis, bingo, ski ball,
wax museums, saltwater taffy, smelly hotdog stands, frozen
custard, a place called "Pretzel City," and in Woolworth's the
biggest display of Dr. Scholl's footpads I have ever seen in my
life—a thirty-foot counter crammed with callus pads, corn
plasters, bunion cushions, metatarsal supports, arch bands,
and foam insoles. This little old ladies' festival of waddling
straw hats with bright ribbons mixes easily with the Kentucky
Jaycees in string bowties and Kentucky colonel hats, all bustling about the Miss America contest, as if the annual rite of
worship, a little girl's dream, will restore this decrepit city's
budding beauty and lost youth.

Harry and Lilly Lerner were staying in the Howard Johnson's
Motor Inn where the lobby was the same as anywhere, USA—
plain and predictable. We sat on a couch in a cheerless corner
to talk.

The Lerners spoke a heavily accented but fluent English,
only rarely searching for words. They were disarmingly direct,
and the conversation was animated with spontaneous and honest replies.

"You are Jewish?" he asked.

"Yes," I answered.

"Just checking," he said.

Mrs. Lerner was frail and small, and, though edgy from the pressures of the day, she greeted me with warmth and friendliness. Her eyes were marked with the pain of memories impossible to wash away, yet she seemed to radiate an inner peace that drew me to her, close and true. It was natural, for example, to address her by her first name.

Mr. Lerner, more crisp in personality, studied me carefully with piercing and suspicious eyes. At last, he seemed satisfied.

"I returned to the village after the war," he began. "It was a small village called Kisvarda near the Russian border in Hungary. I went back because I did not know for certain that everyone had perished in the war, and if anyone had survived, I knew they would come back to the village. I stayed there until 1947. When I found out from an eyewitness that all of my people had perished, I had no more reason to stay, and so I left."

How many had he lost? "My parents, my four brothers and their wives, their five children, and my two sisters, all lost at Auschwitz, Buchenwald, and Dachau."

Had they tried to keep it all from Connie and their other children? Lilly Lerner answered, "I tried to tell them everything. I don't think you should shelter them. It's history; it's actuality. I don't think it helps to hold back. It makes them better persons. Besides, it's our life, you know."

Mr. Lerner picked up: "And you can't hide it. Other families have grandparents who buy dolls and toys for little children. Our children wanted to know why they had no grandparents."

Lilly broke in: "We cannot have family reunions, for example, and that's a tradition in the North Carolina mountains. There are only four or five of us left so we had to explain why we didn't have what other families had."

But how does a parent answer a child who asks questions about an experience like that? Lilly gazed at me and then dropped her eyes. "How does mankind answer it?"

I edged gently into questions of what it had been like, and

Lilly pressed on. "We were in cattle wagons; we were hurried onto a train—hardly any air and no sanitary facilities and taken for miles to what the Germans said was 'a place where you could live.' Even when we got to Auschwitz, we didn't know where we were going or where we were. We stood outside in Auschwitz for maybe three days with nothing to eat but finally a little black coffee. They separated my sister and me from my fourteen-year-old brother and my mother and we never saw them again. They gave us, how do you say, letterheads to write my mother to tell her that we were all right. I remember well that a Polish girl who had been in Auschwitz many months came up to me and said, 'What do you mean, *where* is your mother? *There* she is.' And she pointed to the smokestacks over the ovens."

Then it seemed that Mr. Lerner had to make me understand why it could happen. "It was the big lie," he said. "We didn't know until it was too late." He sat straight in his chair and his grammar became garbled. "If we had known we could have stood and fought at our homes and they never could have taken so many people and killed them. You think that if people had not known where they were going we would not have taken hammers or anything else against the Germans?"

"We didn't know," Lilly interjected. "That's why so many people voluntarily walked to their deaths."

How does any human being survive such an ordeal? Mr. Lerner answered, "Life is always better than death; no matter how bad life gets. Of course some were not convinced of that and they did not hang on."

Suddenly, Lilly changed the mood. "It's a sheer miracle I am alive," she said brightly. "And to be here at Atlantic City at the Miss America contest. It's like our lives are a storybook. It's a living story. She is such a remarkable girl and we wanted her to enter because people in Asheville asked us and we love America and it's part of America to be in this pageant."

I told them that Connie had said she was going to write a book, and Mr. Lerner tried to make a joke. "Maybe she will call it *From Auschwitz to Atlantic City*." Somehow I couldn't laugh.

"I never believed I would get out alive," Lilly went on. "They didn't even waste the ink to tattoo the numbers on us because it was late in the war, and we were to be killed and they were not keeping track of who was killed by then. 'Everybody has to be killed' was Himmler's final order" (she repeated it in German) "and the only reason I survived was that three-thousand girls were taken to Lithuania to dig ditches, and from there the order came for five-hundred girls to work in an airplane plant in Germany. I cannot believe now, when I think back, that we were once working, digging long trenches while Nazis armed with guns stood over us, and there was an electric wire alongside and if you touched the wire, you were dead. We were in Lithuania in a place close enough to the North Pole that it was always light. I looked around at the mountains and the sky and said to myself, 'What a beautiful place to come back to and enjoy someday.'

"So funny to me now that I would think of such a thing. None of the girls in Lithuania survived other than the five-hundred of us who went to Germany. It was rumored that they were put on a ship to Riga and taken out to sea where it was sunk. I am lucky to survive; and then lucky again to survive normally. Maybe it was because we were young and didn't think."

Two North Carolina Jaycees in blue blazers walked by and waved. "Good luck, Miz Lerner. She'll come through." She waved back and nodded a thank-you.

Mr. Lerner continued, "Well, out of that experience came Israel. That is number one. And out of it also came a self-consciousness for all minorities across the world. Perhaps no people will let this happen again."

But could a child like Connie and her three younger siblings be expected to carry the burden of their parents' suffering?

Lilly was firm. "I am telling my children so it will not be forgotten. Parents say today, don't upset children, but they have to know. Life should not be taken for granted and neither should freedom. If people like us do not speak, a hundred years from now what happened will not be remembered."

I wanted her to know that I was listening and caring and I tried to reach out by recalling the afternoon I spent in Dachau, the death camp near Munich, in 1955, when I was nineteen.

I had been the only Jewish boy in my high school class, and I had little understanding of the connection with other Jews as a people linked together by history. That day in Germany, I stood in a gas chamber, my head almost touching the ceiling, and heard a guide tell how the Nazis herded people into "this room" under the pretext of giving them showers. The gas came from "over there," he said, pointing to several small nozzles. He told us that the Germans sometimes found families clinging together. Messages in Hebrew and English were scrawled on the walls: "In memory of my dear mother and father," "God, don't let this happen ever again," "We shall never forget." Prayer shawls were draped over the ovens that burned human flesh and scattered ashes and smoke across the countryside. Outside there were small signs on mounds of earth now covered with grass and flowers. One simply said "Graves of thousands unknown." The red brick barracks where the Jews had stayed and starved and waited were to haunt my dreams.

That afternoon at Dachau had redefined my life, I told Lilly Lerner, and in telling her, the memory of that sickness in my depths came flooding back.

"You can sympathize but you cannot know," Lilly murmured.

We walked out into the lobby and passed two men talking about the contest. "Ah'ed bet a hundred dollars on Connie in the bathing suit competition . . ." one of them was saying.

Lilly didn't hear but she spoke as if for the first time conscious that this was an interview that others might read. "We are very indebted to the people of North Carolina. They have been overwhelming to us and to Connie."

The North Carolina delegation of sponsors, friends, and pageant officials was gathering in the lobby to walk over to the contest, but I wanted to ask a last question of Mr. Lerner. "Do you hate?"

"No," he said, turning his head slowly and looking through me. "It's my way of defeating them."

I walked onto the boardwalk and sat down on a bench. The crumbling carnival that was Atlantic City looked even more surreal through the blur of tears. It was dusk and the parade of people were passing aimlessly, enjoying the breeze and the sea. My mind wandered to a hospital room after the war; I pictured Lilly being told that she had given birth to a normal child she hadn't even been sure she could ever have.

A man in a yellow dinner jacket walked by, name tag on his lapel, movie camera slung over his shoulder, his wife beside him in glittering black gown with swept-up hairdo; they were obviously on their way to Convention Hall. Suddenly, he stopped and turned to her, flinging open his arms, and sang out loudly, "There she is . . . Miss Amer—i—ca . . ."

For the moment, I was certain that America had gone mad.

Connie stood tall on stage in a long-sleeved flowing white gown and gave a deep sigh when Bert Parks didn't call out her name for the finals. I hunted for the Lerners in the darkness, and when I told Mrs. Lerner that Connie was too unique to win, she smiled a wise half-smile and shrugged her shoulders. "There are greater tragedies, you know . . ."

An old friend from Mr. Lerner's village in Hungary was with them, a man who had gone to Israel when the Lerners came to America.

"There is so much sameness in the girls," he observed. "Why must they be so attracted to cookie-cutter beauty?"

Lilly turned to him and sparkled, "Some 'kookies.'"

I stayed in touch with the Lerner family through the years, and interviewed them again in the 1980s at the request of the American Jewish Committee in New York, which had sponsored a national study of the children of survivors, the first comprehensive study of the next generation. A year and a half after the Miss America contest, Connie married a young medical student whose parents had lived in a Hungarian village fifty miles from the Lerners. They, too, had survived the camps. It was not unusual, I discovered from the study, for the children of survivors to marry each other and, because of the loss in Europe, to be determined to have a large family. Like her own family, Connie and her husband are parenting four children.

Lillie Lerner became well known in North Carolina, and because of her status as the mother of a former state beauty queen, was welcomed as a visitor to many North Carolina public schools to testify about her experiences during the Holocaust. She had once spoken to Outward Bound participants about the challenges of survival, and so impressed them that she was invited to serve on the state board of directors of the organization. She even wrote a book about her memories and about her life before the war, entitled *The Silence*, to give her lost family, as she wrote, "one minute longer in eternity." When she died in 1988, at the relatively young age of 59, the inscription on her tombstone identified her as a "Holocaust survivor" and included the following: "In memory of her mother, Kornell, and her brother, Ernoke, who perished in Auschwitz. Let love preserve their memory." Now, when Connie and her family visit the grave, they remember, just as her mother wished.

4

Zionism in the Bible Belt

Because of our family's visible role in supporting the creation of the state of Israel, Zionism in the fundamentalist South— the reaction of non-Jews and Jews to the idea and then the reality of Israel—has fascinated me for years. It touched my boyhood and my travels, and it relates deeply to Israel's place in the soul of America. The United Nations resolution of 1975 that called Zionism a form of racism so outraged my family that my mother wore a button saying "Proud to be a Zionist." She would have been overjoyed when the UN repealed that infamous resolution in 1992, paving the way for the Arab-Israeli peace talks.

At a luncheon in Jerusalem in the summer of 1975, I happened to be seated across from Shalom Rosenfeld, the editor of *Ma-a-Riv*, the largest Hebrew language daily in Israel. The interim Sinai agreement clearly was going through, with levels of aid signaling a new dependence by Israel on the United States. Someone asked him about the future.

"If we are asking America to make sacrifices for us," he

said, "we can't expect Jewish interests alone to carry the day. We will need to develop new friends in America."

The UN resolution equating Zionism with racism and the Security Council recognition of the PLO in January 1975 may have given Israel new friends out in middle America. The resolution struck at the very premise of a Jewish state; it was an attack from the Arabs so blatant that no one could mistake its intent. For fundamentalists in the South, the resolution and the Security Council debate over sovereignty came close to being antireligious.

I spent three years traveling across the South from 1970 to 1973, interviewing Jews and Gentiles about Israel and exploring other southern attitudes toward the Jewish people and Judaism.

One never had to argue with the typical southerner about Israel's right to exist, nor about the moral justification for the establishment of a Jewish state. With the exception of Senator William Fulbright of Arkansas (the Rhodes scholar intellectual whom Truman called "that over-educated s.o.b."), virtually every southern senator and congressman since 1948 has represented this support. If anything, it grew stronger as the Soviet Union began to pour arms first into Egypt and then into Syria.

The support for Israel in the South has been rooted in the acceptance of biblical prophecy that there would be a great ingathering of the Jewish people in the land of Zion. The creation of Israel was the acting out of this drama, the link between the beginning and the end of things. If Zionism were racism, then the Jewish longing for a homeland described in the Old Testament would be racist too, and that is an unacceptable idea to southern Christians. As a local minister wrote in a letter to my hometown paper in North Carolina, "Zion is mentioned 157 times in the Old Testament."

There is a Bible-based attachment to Israel in the minds of black southerners as well. Blacks feel a strong identification with the Moses story, the leading of the children of Israel out of the land of slavery into the land of freedom. "Go Down, Moses" and other spirituals reflect the longing for deliverance that provided fertile ground for the emergence of the civil rights movement and was part of the secret of Martin Luther King, Jr.'s hold on black people's imaginations.

In addition, Israel's daring military exploits in 1967 and at Entebbe appealed to southerners' notions of their own mythology. As the boys in gray had been underdogs, so were the Israelis, who were surrounded by an overwhelming force of arms. The stereotypical Jews—scholars and victims—were transformed into a tough and scrappy military power. No longer were Jews just rabbis and fiddlers on the roof; they were tank commanders, too.

Southerners see Israel in racial terms, as well—whites surrounded by dark, Arab masses representing Islamic danger. To southerners, if anything is racist, it is the Arab attack on Jews in Israel and Christians in Lebanon, a view in some ways strangely parallel to the PLO view of Israelis as white Europeans on Arab lands (especially ironic since 50 percent of the Israeli population is now Sephardic in origin). Racism is in the eye of the beholder.

The southern philo-Semitism, as writer Harry Golden called it, exists as counterpoint to the classic southern xenophobia regarding any outsiders or foreign influences and includes an anti-Semitism that reflects the dark side of southern authoritarianism and orthodoxy. Like so many attitudes in the South, fundamentalist feelings about Jews are ambivalent and unpredictable, fed by the traditional view of Jews as being responsible for the death of Christ. The ambivalence can manifest itself in peculiar ways: for example, the anti-Israel tension in the South during the Arab oil boycott just after the Yom Kippur War quickly gave way to resentment against the sheiks with the Cadillacs living in the desert while the rest of us shivered at the gas pumps at home.

Most indicators internationally show a growing U.S. and

European dependence on foreign supplies of oil. In August 1975 in Israel, I was asked over and over again by Israeli students how long America could hold out against Arab oil pressure. One answer, I think, is out in the heartland of the country. Moshe Dayan, before he died, asserted that Israelis have only themselves, Jews all over the world, and America standing between the country's survival and annihilation. The reasons for the support from the Bible Belt may be unusual, but America's capacity to sustain a commitment to Israel may ultimately depend on tapping that goodwill.

5

Harry Golden (1902–1981)

Harry Golden was an editor, publisher, and a best-selling author who fought bigotry with humor and became a famous literary figure in the South writing about his memories of New York and civil rights.

Born Harry J. Goldhirsch, he was raised on the Lower East Side of New York. He moved to Charlotte, North Carolina, to work as a salesman and a reporter during the Depression, and in 1941 founded *The Carolina Israelite*, a one-man newspaper with a national circulation (at its peak, forty-thousand), which he published until 1968.

"I got away with my ideas in the South," he said, "because no southerner takes me—a Jew, a Yankee, and a radical— seriously. They mostly think of a Jew as a substitute Negro, anyway."

A collection of his pieces, *Only in America*, was published in 1958. It became a national bestseller and was followed by nineteen other books, including *For Two Cents Plain* and *Enjoy, Enjoy*. His anecdotal biography of Carl Sandburg, who once called him "a force for good," was the fruit of a long-standing friendship between the two men that developed from

Golden's many visits to the Sandburg goat farm in Flat Rock, North Carolina.

The newspaper was published out of his two-story frame house and, as the *Washington Post* once editorialized, the paper "became a bigger part of American folklore each time it came off the press."

A roly-poly American original, he sat in his Kennedy rocker with his feet barely touching the floor, looking like a twinkling Jewish Buddha with a cigar. The walls were crowded with books and with dozens of autographed pictures of famous acquaintances who subscribed to the paper, including Carl Sandburg, Harry Truman, William Faulkner, John F. Kennedy, Bertram Russell, Ernest Hemingway, and Adlai Stevenson. In the corner stood his celebrated cracker barrel, where he threw finished articles for the paper, which would go to press when the barrel was full. He interspersed recollections of his New York boyhood with essays on politics and folkways.

His numerous "Golden plans" infuriated segregationists and delighted southern intellectuals, not because they were absurd but because they were rooted sufficiently in southern myth to work perfectly well if anyone was astute enough to try them. When the South became embroiled in school desegregation and "massive resistance," he proposed the "vertical integration plan," which stated that:

> The white and Negro stand at the same grocery and super-market counters; deposit money at the same bank teller's window; pay phone and light bills to the same clerk; walk through the same dime and department stores and stand at the same drugstore counters. It is only when the Negro "sets" that the fur begins to fly.
>
> Instead of all those complicated proposals, all the next session needs to do is pass one small amendment which would provide *only* desks in all the public schools of our state—*no seats*. The desks should be those stand-up jobs, like the old-fashioned bookkeeping desk. Since no one in the South pays the slightest attention to a vertical

Negro, this will completely solve our problem . . . in fact
this may be a blessing in disguise. They are not learning
to read sitting down anyway; maybe standing up will help.

His "white baby plan" sprung from his mind when he read of
two black schoolteachers who wanted to see a revival of Oliv-
ier's *Hamlet* in a segregated movie theater and borrowed the
white children of two friends to take in with them. They were
sold tickets without hesitation.

People can pool their children at a central point in each
neighborhood, and every time a Negro wants to go to the
movies all she need do is pick up a white child—and go.
  Eventually the Negro community can set up a factory
and manufacture white babies made of plastic, and when
they want to go to the opera or to a concert, all they need
do is carry that plastic doll in their arms. The dolls, of
course, should all have blond curls and blue eyes.

Golden punched the paunches of a lot of southern politicians
who took themselves too seriously. He had no peer when it
came to poking holes in southern segregation and pointing up
the South's hypocrisy by manipulating its mores. Here is his
solution to the problems of busing and prayer in the schools in
one grand step:

Why not amend the Constitution to permit prayers on the
bus instead of the classroom?
  We could have praying buses and nonpraying buses.
The constitutional lawyers will be happy because religion
will not be invading the classroom; it will be invading the
highways (where it can do the most good). The ministers
will be happy, and the intransigent parents will of course
commit their kiddies to the buses because the kiddies will
get a longer time to pray.
  For the life of me, I cannot see what is wrong with this
plan. It is not only gradual enough to satisfy Southerners,
but it will reinvigorate the parishes.

With his national fame came the revelation that, in 1929, Golden had been sentenced to four years in prison for mail fraud resulting from the misdeeds of a brokerage firm he had run. He pleaded guilty and served eighteen months, after which he was paroled and returned to his Irish-Catholic wife, the former Genevieve Gallagher, and his four sons.

Adlai Stevenson wrote, "I suspect that this experience deepened Harry Golden's understanding, lengthened his vision and enlarged his heart." Golden changed his name and moved to North Carolina to start a new life. In December 1973, President Richard M. Nixon gave him a full pardon.

He was often the target of threats of violence, yet his humor seemed to be his armor, and he was eventually accepted by the southern establishment, which honored him with degrees and awards. When his home was burned down in 1958, the Charlotte police and the FBI helped him decipher the charred list of *Carolina Israelite* subscribers.

Two years before he died, he summed up his life by saying he was "a newspaper man, an American, a Jew, a Democrat and a Zionist, in that order." At the time of his death, the *Raleigh News and Observer* added that "he was also a highly literate prophet and satirist whose views and commentary made a beneficial difference in the affairs of the South and the nation."

6

Strangers in a Strange Land: The Jewish Communities of Savannah, Mississippi, and Atlanta

Five books about Jews in the South that appeared during the 1980s give added dimension and depth to the southern chapter of the American Jewish story. Each is different and yet, together, they represent the kind of literary output previously lacking and therefore perhaps signal some new turning in the mysteriously small number of books written in the last century about the Jewish experience in the region.

Third to None: The Saga of Savannah Jewry 1773–1983 by Rabbi Saul Jacob Rubin fills an important void in southern history by giving us at last the story of the first Jewish community in the South and the third in North America.

B. H. Levy's *Savannah's Old Jewish Community Cemeteries* is a valuable document of source material from the gravestones and community records of the 1733 burial plot granted the Jews of Savannah by General James Oglethorpe. There are short biographies—all that is known—of each person buried there. Historians, novelists, and scholars from all disciplines will be able to draw on this book for years.

A book mainly of photographs, *Jews in Early Mississippi*, by Evelyn and Leo Turitz, gives us portraits of people and pictures of places of business, families, and houses of worship taken in towns throughout Mississippi. The faces and scenes tell stories of struggle and happiness, of sorrow and triumph. Photographs of Confederate soldiers, children in Purim costumes, wedding lockets, country stores, and horse-drawn wagons invite the viewer into a world of small towns and rural settings. It is a book that one can linger over for hours, putting oneself in the photographs and trying to experience another time and place.

One Voice: Rabbi Jacob M. Rothschild and The Troubled South is Janice Rothschild Blumberg's personal reminiscence about her husband, Rabbi Jacob Rothschild, the rabbi of Atlanta's Hebrew Benevolent Congregation, known in a grand shorthand simply as The Temple. Rabbi Rothschild served from 1946 to his death in 1973. He reflected Atlanta's most decent instincts through the stormy years of the civil rights movement, was a close friend of a young minister named Martin Luther King, Jr., and became a spokesman for justice in the city. It is also Janice Rothschild's story, so there are additional insights from an informed native who knows what makes Atlanta tick. It makes one wish for more such books, personal writing about Jews in the South by the people who have lived the stories. Useful not only as a biography, this book is a valuable addition to our understanding of Jewish-black-Christian relations during the stormiest era of recent history.

Stephen Hertzberg has augmented Janice Blumberg's chronicle of modern Atlanta with *Strangers Within the Gate City: The Jews of Atlanta—1865–1915,* which makes use of computer techniques for an analysis of the history of the Atlanta Jewish community.

These five books—an interpretive history of the South's oldest Jewish community, a book of source material about the original settlers of that same community, a collection of photographs from almost every city and town in a southern state, a personal biography of a leading modern figure; and a history of the Jews in the South's largest city—reflect in their variety a renewed confidence that the southern Jewish story is vital and worth telling in all its dimensions. The books will provide fascinating information for ardent researchers and interested readers.

Third to None is a long-overdue history of the third American community—Savannah, Georgia—to have Jewish settlers. The Savannah Jewish colony, in Jacob Marcus's foreword, "A band of Jewish argonauts—financed by London's Sephardic notables—debarked on the site of Georgia's first settlement." This group of forty-two Portuguese and German Jews, the largest Jewish migration during the colonial period, arrived in 1733, a year or two after the first North American synagogue was dedicated in New York and the second in Newport, Rhode Island.

Rabbi Saul Jacob Rubin, of the historic Mickve Israel Congregation, has written a careful book, with forty-five pages of more than eighteen hundred footnotes, twenty pages of photographs, and a thorough index. This effort, sponsored and financed by the Jewish community, could be an important model for other communities.

Covering 250 years of history, the book provides many interesting details. Two of the original settlers, Dr. and Mrs. Samuel Nunes Ribeiro, were the forebears of Uriah Phillips Levy, who saved and then restored Monticello. Jacob Nunez Cardozo was a prolific writer and editor of newspapers in Charleston, Atlanta, and Mobile. His great-grandnephew was Supreme Court Justice Benjamin Cardozo.

Drawing the attention of national leaders, the Savannah Jewish community received letters from three American presidents—Washington, Jefferson, and Madison—on the subject of religious liberty.

Rubin writes about Jewish attitudes in the North toward the Savannah Jews during the Civil War. In 1865, during Pesach, in the midst of the hardships and hatreds of the war, Jews in New York and Philadelphia shipped five thousand pounds of Passover food to the Jewish community in Savannah. These symbolic acts of support reflected a sense of national community.

Third to None, in pulling together research from many sources to tell its story, belongs with Reznikoff and Engelman's *Jews of Charleston*, Ezekiel and Lichtenstein's *History of the Jews of Richmond*, and Bertram Korn's *Jews of Early New Orleans* as an important volume that future scholars must read if they are to write informed southern Jewish history.

B. H. Levy, a lawyer in Savannah who was fascinated with old cemeteries, undertook one of those painstaking four-year efforts that can only be termed a "magnificent obsession." After sifting through records and copying information from the gravestones of the town's early settlers, he wrote *Savannah's Old Jewish Community Cemeteries*, a jewel of a book which serves as a companion to the Rubin history. Graveyards cry out with their own tragedies, such as the deaths of infants and small children and the toll taken by "warm fever" and other forms of pestilence that shortened life expectancy in that era. But Levy also looked at wills and other writings, building brick by brick a house of details populated by a parade of characters and stories behind the worn gravestones and forgotten inscriptions.

Both Rubin and Levy acknowledged their great debts to the superb writers on southern colonial history, Jacob Marcus and Malcolm Stern.

In researching *Jews in Early Mississippi*, Rabbi Leo Turitz and his wife, Evelyn, called on community leaders, public librarians, and curators and archivists in the Mississippi Department of Archives and History, but they mostly collected the scrapbooks of families they knew or had heard of in thirty-eight cities and towns across Mississippi. The result is a charming volume of photographs and an almost innocent text of local legends. The book is organized by city so that a reader can turn, for example, to Yazoo City or Meridian and read short histories of the Jews there as well as view photographs of the leading families, in both formal and informal pictures. As the authors point out, the collection concentrates on the years since the advent of photography in 1840, and many of the Jewish communities exist no more, having been uprooted by the coming of the railroads, a disastrous flood, epidemics, or just new opportunities.

The writing style is similar to that found in a family album—a straightforward and uncritical listing of the facts of marriage, economic achievement, local officeholding. There is little analysis of the material. There is no point made, for example, of the number of wives who managed local stores and businesses, once their peddler husbands earned enough to buy a horse and wagon and then to settle down.

But there are wonderful nuggets in the local anecdotes recounted in the book. Woodville, Mississippi, had such an active Jewish community that it was called "Little Jerusalem." The earliest rabbi was a circuit rider for the region, and the town was also served by a young rabbi, Henry Cohen, who would later shepherd thousands of Jews arriving in Galveston, Texas, to the small towns of the South and the Midwest. When Rabbi Cohen reached an accommodation with the Jewish store owners at least to close their stores during Sabbath morning services, local farmers each Saturday morning joined not only the Jewish store owners but also the Gentile store owners, who also closed so they could hear the skillful preaching of the engaging young rabbi. Assimilation came in many forms: Natchez called the rabbi's house "the parsonage"; because there was no temple in Starkville, Carrie Fried got married in the local Methodist Church in a Jewish ceremony; the Dreyfus family of Meridian changed its name to Threefoot and the Blums changed to Flower; Bishop Brunini of the Vicksburg diocese had a mother named Blanche Stein of Canton and gave a mezuzah to the new temple in Vicksburg at its dedication.

Surprising stories of quiet courage also appear: Joe Weinberg of Greenville saved Hodding Carter's newspaper from unscrupulous stockholders when the pressure built in reaction to Carter's liberal editorials; the Wechsler School in Meridian, the first brick school building in Mississippi for black children, was named, according to a plaque, "for Rabbi Wechsler on request of the Negroes of Meridian because he led the movement to provide public school facilities for their children."

The book reflects another southern Jewish phenomenon: Mississippi boys scoured the state looking for wives and often married local girls. Thus the families across Mississippi were entwined like wisteria vines, with every family having "kinfolk" in almost every city in the state.

But the photographs leave the most profound impressions: Julius Yaretsky, the mayor of Shuqualak for several terms, in full regalia as an officer in the Grand Lodge of Masons; the storefront of a struggling Jew in McComb with the locals lounging on the porch under the sign "A. Heidenreich Cheap Store"; little children in Confederate sailor suits; a family of beautiful daughters, in giant picture hats with plumes and ribbons hanging down, southern belles indeed. The Turitzes have mined a boxcarful of treasures in collecting the visual images that historians often overlook and have pioneered a technique other states could well emulate. They have captured the spirit of a period in southern Jewish history lost in time.

In *One Voice*, Janice Rothschild Blumberg records the role played by her husband, Rabbi Jacob M. Rothschild, during the events in Atlanta over a twenty-seven-year period when he was head of the Reform congregation and an outspoken leader in the civil rights movement.

Jacob Rothschild was the right man at the right time to succeed David Marx as the rabbi in The Temple when Marx retired after fifty years in the rabbinate. Marx had seen Atlanta through the lynching of Leo Frank in 1915 and had become an ardent advocate of the most extreme forms of Reform Judaism as well as one of the leading anti-Zionist critics of the creation of the state of Israel. The Temple's congregation changed after

World War II, and Captain Jack Rothschild came from Gua-
dalcanal to sweep away the cobwebs. His name, they at first
thought, connected him to Europe's most aristocratic Jewish
family. At his twenty-year anniversary, one of the congregants
wrote a song about him:

"Rothschild! What a lovely name,
And what a lovely family tree.
He probably is a nephew of that charming Baron Guy.
But this Rochschild hit Atlanta like a Jewish General Sher-
man;
He wasn't related to Baron Guy
He wasn't even German!"

His friendship with Martin Luther King, Jr., was authentic
and deep. Janice Blumberg tells a poignant story about the
Kings' coming to dinner one night, unable to find the Rothschild house because of poor streetlights. The Kings finally
had to drive up to another house to inquire, but "as Martin told
us this, he quickly added, 'But we were careful not to embar-
rass you with your neighbors. I let Coretta go to the door so
they'd think we were just going to serve a party'." The author
adds, "I still get a lump in my throat when I think of it."
Coretta King wrote the introduction to the book, saying that
Rothschild "was in great measure responsible for the Atlanta
dinner honoring Martin as a recipient of the 1964 Nobel Peace
Prize, an occasion that heralded a new era in race relations in
our country."

Another highlight of the book is the story of the bombing of
The Temple in 1958. Blumberg tells of the crowd that was
packed into the bombed-out sanctuary the following Friday
night, "gathering as a family might in time of trouble," to listen
to Rabbi Rothschild's greatest sermon. She confesses to the
sad realization that "after so many years of saying the same
things, the same things had to be said." She describes the
revolutionary impact of his statement on Rosh Hashonah in
1970 that Israel "has kept us faithful to our heritage and been

our salvation as Jews as surely as we Jews have played a part in ensuring its survival as a Jewish state." She adds: "That statement alone probably represented the greatest change that had taken place in the congregation during the quarter of a century of his leadership."

It is a tribute to the book that a reader wants to know more of what is intimated between the lines. For example, the tensions between Rothschild and Marx, who lived until 1962 and saw his congregation change, are only alluded to, as are the disagreements, which must have been tumultuous, between Rothschild and the establishment leadership of his congregation. The author has a tendency to be too modest about her own role in opening the way for Rothschild's support of Israel and in easing his task of making changes in rituals and religious customs. Janice Rothschild was admired for her beauty, independence, and the self-confidence that came from her deep roots in Atlanta, and a reader longs to know more of her inner life as the renowned rebbitzin of a remarkable man.

Jacob Rothschild once considered putting his sermons into book form under the title *Sermons from a Southern Pulpit.* Fortunately, his wife has provided us with them, as well as speeches and letters, and enriched the collection with her own story. Coretta King wrote, "Her memoir is an eloquent reaffirmation of the bonds of solidarity that unite Jewish and black Americans as well as an inspiring story of commitment and brotherhood during an exciting, creative period in American history."

The preceding four books were written by passionate amateurs who have done commendable jobs. In addition, however, while the Jewish South has long been one of the last bastions of such writing, more scholars at southern universities and colleges are also beginning to grasp the rich opportunities to be found in research on the Jewish South and to delve more deeply into the heart of its history and the soul of its people.

In *Strangers Within the Gate City: The Jews of Atlanta—*

1865–1915, Stephen Hertzberg, a professional historian, has synthesized the dry data of census tracts and synagogue lists, using computer techniques of the modern scholar to write a careful, definitive, and meticulous history of the Jewish community of Atlanta. It takes its place with the half dozen other important histories of Jewish communities in the South and sets a standard for future scholars regarding thoroughness of analysis and organization.

Through careful examination of ledgers, minute books, and membership lists of the Hebrew Benevolent Congregation and the B'nai B'rith Gate City Lodge, Hertzberg tried to identify every Jew who lived in Atlanta from 1870 to 1900. These records also identified renters of seats for the High Holy Days and unsuccessful petitioners for membership. The names were checked against the census schedules, naturalization and cemetery records, and the other membership lists of the East European Congregation Ahavath Achim formed in the 1890s. Hertzberg probably missed a few unaffiliated Jews but, as he points out, the small size of the Jewish community and the southern tradition of religious affiliation meant that he wouldn't miss many.

The author fed into a computer data on 284 persons from the 1870 census, 570 from 1880, and 1,501 persons from 1896. By correlating this information with tax records and property assessments, he could draw precise conclusions about age, occupation, country of origin, geographic and economic mobility, wealth, and marital status. Tracing the influx of new immigrants, he was able to determine how many of them were professionals, managers, peddlers, or shoemakers and to follow how they changed neighborhoods or economic status over time. His material is presented in more than sixty graphs, tables, and maps.

What emerges is a Jewish community that grew along with a booming post–Civil War Atlanta—from fewer than fifty Jewish souls to over four thousand in a city that expanded from 21,789 people in 1870 to 154,837 in 1910.

While the history of the Jews in the South has been carefully documented in the colonial period, there has been little research on the five decades covered by Hertzberg. Atlanta is probably the best locale for such a study, because it is a relatively new city, incorporated in 1843, destroyed by Sherman's army in 1865, and resurrected as the jewel of the "New South" in the decades between Appomattox and World War I.

Hertzberg found that by 1890, most of the East Europeans who had settled in Atlanta were not "greenhorns" but immigrant Americans who had come to Atlanta after living a few years in another city; they were already acclimated to America, with the language proficiency and business skills necessary for success. A large percentage came without wives or families (creating a five-to-one ratio of men to women at one point), seeking to establish an economic base before marrying or bringing relatives. They liked the climate and wanted to escape the sweatshops of the northern ghettoes, but what they left behind were flourishing Yiddish newspapers and theaters and hundreds of synagogues and friends. One man summed it up: "In New York, I would have found my soul but without my body, and in Atlanta, a body without a soul."

They largely were not professionals—doctors, lawyers, accountants—nor were they laborers. Many had been peddlers, and statistics show that 75 percent were retail merchants in 1870. These store owners immediately faced a southern Jewish dilemma—whether to keep the stores open on Saturdays, when the farmers came to town and the blacks who worked in factories were paid, or to face economic ruin. Yiddish poet I. J. Schwartz, who settled in the South in 1918, wrote:

> The joke was:
> That one worked on the Sabbath
> Even harder than on the week day,
> Because on Saturday people got their wages;
> They fitted shoes and pants on Negroes,
> And talked their hearts out—

But as soon as the stars appeared,
The merchant immediately stopped his business,
Withdrew quickly behind the partition
And said the *Havdoleh* (prayer at the end of the
    Sabbath) out loud.

Because the German Jews had migrated to Atlanta a generation earlier, they were already successful entrepreneurs by the
time the East Europeans arrived. Residential patterns and exclusive social clubs began to divide the rich Jews from the poor
ones, the Germans from the Russians and the 150 new Sephardim who arrived between 1906 and the outbreak of World War
I, mostly from the Isle of Rhodes. Between 1896 and 1911,
there was a five-fold increase in the number of Russian Jews,
but they had had almost no social interaction with the German-
Jewish community. Rabbi David Marx, who headed the Reform
congregation for fifty years, was pleased that so few of the new
immigrants were attracted to The Temple. "We have sacrificed
no principles to secure numerical strength," he said.

But Atlanta was growing, and the new immigrants would
prosper with the rest of the city. They, too, could form social
clubs, build attractive synagogues (bringing the total to six
different congregations by 1915), and emerge as leaders in the
community. Finally, though divided philosophically over politics, philanthropy, and Zionism in ways that would last another
generation, the leadership of the two communities came together in 1910 to form the Jewish Educational Alliance, to
which the Russians flocked because it housed a gymnasium,
Hebrew school, meeting rooms, kindergarten, and night
school. It was the center of concerts, dances, plays, and activities for some members of the German community as well.

The statistics indicate that by 1896, more than half the adult
Jewish males were professionals or proprietors, and 30 percent
were white-collar workers. Atlanta's economy was based on
distribution, not manufacturing, and the character of the Jewish community, the author believes, was influenced by "selective immigration." He says that "few Jews or other foreigners

who lacked capital or marketable skills settled in the community. Those who came tended to be uniquely equipped to make the most of the opportunities available in the expanding regional center, and their acceptance by native white Gentiles was facilitated by their small numbers and assimilative bent."

Jews in Atlanta's early history played a major role in civic affairs, but as the city matured, the ambivalence of the Gentile community became more apparent. The author traces the steady erosion of the Jewish position—the growing social exclusion and the suspicion. Fewer than two dozen families of the Jewish elite, he states, had much contact with the Gentile community, and in the twenty-five-year period between 1890 and 1915, only eleven Jews sought public office, out of which two were elected.

A curtain of fear dropped over the Jewish community in 1913, when fourteen-year-old Mary Phagan was found murdered in the basement of a factory managed by a leading member of the German community, Leo Frank. The painful aftermath—the trial, the mobs, the anti-Semitic slurs and public degradation, and finally, the pardon and the 1915 lynching—left a scar on the Atlanta community, "confirming that economic success was no protection against bigotry."

The result of Hertzberg's scholarly approach contrasts with much of the recent community histories written in the South. The author quite rightly points out that many of those local histories were by "well-intentioned amateurs . . . [who] regarded history not as an end in itself, but as a weapon for self-respect and social advancement." He complains, with some overstatement, that the resulting works, written by "enthusiasts with deep local commitments, who are intent on building a good case for their communities, continue to be poorly researched" and are often "filiopietistic, biographical, impressionistic, antiquarian, and anecdotal, with a tendency to include as many names as possible and ignore the unseemly aspects of communal life and the shady side of individuals."

Herzberg's strength is that he brings to his project the cold professional eye of an outsider who must rely on the painstaking accumulation of data for his conclusions. I would like to see every Jewish community in the South assemble the data of its past in just this way. But there is room with this sort of impartial fact-gathering for the non-professional, also, to fill in the demographics and the tax records with the warmth of oral histories.

A city like Atlanta is not that old, and the Jewish community contains many people living there today who remember hearing stories about its earliest days in their childhoods. This book gives any local interviewer an intelligent start and a common set of new insights about how to collect stories and word pictures. Interviewing grandparents will encourage the younger generation to search for its roots in the memories of the old of each family. To the people of Atlanta and elsewhere, I say, "Do an oral history of your community." Let each family collect its own history, display collections of family photograph albums in the community center, and bring in a professional historian, perhaps a young Ph.D. candidate like Steven Hertzberg, to build the precise basis for a complete and total historical project, balancing the graphs, maps, and printouts with the poetry of recollection and memory. Such records would be an invaluable legacy, not only for historians, but for each family as well.

7

The Jewish South in Novels

A Lynching in Georgia

Richard Kluger's *Members of the Tribe*, published in 1977, is one of the best novels about the Jews who settled in the South. The story's critical event is a fictionalized version of the Leo Frank lynching in 1913.

Kluger traces the history of the Jews of Savannah through the eyes of a new arrival in 1878 named Seth Adler, a German Jew who wears around his neck the Congressional Medal of Honor awarded his father, who died for the Union in the Civil War. Adler apprentices as a lawyer and eventually becomes one of the defense counsel in the trial of Noah Berg, who is accused of murdering Jean Dugan, a fourteen-year-old girl found strangled in the basement of the factory that Berg manages.

In a disconcerting way, the novel is almost two separate books. The first half, which takes place up until the time of the murder, is told through Seth's eyes, and the second half is told through the memoirs of Seth's daughter, Judith, who observes the entire trial.

Seth Adler's confrontation with the South introduces him to

hog meat, slave beatings, a delicious belle named Amanda, rednecks who teach him to shoot doves and eat whole bob-olinks in a gulp, and a fiery populist named Tom Watson. The novel traces Watson's transformation from populist in 1907 to bitter racism and anti-Semitism. After the trial, he whips the Georgia mob into such a blood frenzy that when Noah Berg is pardoned, twenty-five men break into the state prison at Milledgeville and take Berg 125 miles to hang him from the big oak tree in front of the house where the young girl, Jean Dugan, had been born.

With humor and insight, Kluger traces Seth's personality change from northern immigrant to southern Jew through de-scriptions of southern smells, Jesus-loving friends, and his slow adoption of speech patterns, accent, and cadences. It is courageous terrain for a Yankee writer, and Kluger comes off surprisingly well, though he has a tendency to catalogue every flower in Savannah and to use every southernism in existence, from "diddly-squat" to "ain't worth a pitcher of warm spit." It is no criticism to say that Seth Adler, like Richard Kluger, has a Yankee view of the South, and that the book, though set in a southern context, is not really of the South; it is ultimately more a Jewish novel than a southern one.

In the second half of the book, Kluger develops the skill in depicting legal drama that was evident in his earlier book, *Simple Justice*, capturing the flavor of the trial: the crowds lining the streets screaming "Hang the Jew"; the judge walking into the courtroom and showing the jury a red newspaper head-line that says "State Adds Links to Chain"; a photograph of the victim dumped into a coal bin clutching a phony note describ-ing her assailant; the women packing the sweaty courtroom for three weeks in July to hear 250 witnesses, fans fluttering at the salacious testimony from such witnesses as the county coroner who says, "There are no signs of the hymen," and suggests a "sexual assault" from the blood that was found on her under-garments.

While the book is true to the original atmosphere and much

of the testimony of the Frank trial, its departures from actual events are disturbing, not because the novelist has any obligation to relate exactly what happened, but because the 1913 date and the characters Tom Watson and Governor Slaton (who pardons Berg) suggest that trial, and it may be that more people will experience Kluger's version of the trial than the real one.

Kluger paints Noah Berg as something of a lecher who confesses to the defense team the truth in a story told by a disgruntled paymaster that there was once "a stenographer on her knees in his office" while Berg had "his drawers dropped." In the novel, there is testimony from an "office boy who once said that Mr. Berg made improper advances toward him . . . and touched his body." This is unsettling, because the Georgia prosecutors in the original trial tried to establish that Leo Frank was a "pervert" (or, as Tom Watson actually wrote, "this filthy, perverted Jew from New York") with trumped-up stories from girls he had fired that "he barely touched my breast"; with a statement by a well-known Atlanta madam that Frank was a "frequent customer" and had called that very afternoon to reserve a room at her house "for him and the girl"; and with charges from a well-rehearsed black janitor who changed his story three times that Frank often had girls up to his office for immoral acts. The janitor testified that he had once caught a glimpse of Frank with a lady "sitting down in a chair and she with her clothes up to here . . . and he was down on his knees and she had her hands on Mr. Frank." Kluger includes that testimony in the fictional trial but leaves out the preposterous statement by the janitor that Frank said, "Why should I hang? I have wealthy people in Brooklyn."

The author adds an additional sexual dimension to the story by painting the innocent "little Mary Phagan" of the original trial as the more worldly Jean Dugan, with a "precociously developing body . . . one girl speculated she may have been molested by her stepfather . . . Jean went out with older men."

In the real trial, Frank said under oath that "the story as to women coming into the factory with me for immoral purposes is a base lie and the occasion that he claims to have seen me in indecent positions with women is a lie so vile that I have no language with which to fitly denounce it."

The character Noah Berg is not the upstanding earnest German Jew and community leader that Frank was. "Noah Berkowitz . . . came from Polish-Russian Jewry whom the defenders of Nordic purity found so deformed and loathsome . . . who changed his name to something less provocative." He was "a limp spirit . . . no tallow in him, only wick and flame"; he marries Naomi Klein, "whose family sold sheets throughout the state to the Ku Klux Klan." Leo Frank married Lucille Selig of a highly cultured and well-to-do Atlanta family, manufacturers of chemical products. In fact, it was Frank's Brahmin Jewish roots that struck such terror in the minds of the East Europeans across the South—if the most elite and most assimilated Jews could be framed and lynched, what chance would the rest of them have? And it gave Tom Watson the yeast to tie Leo Frank to "Wall Street bankers" and an international conspiracy.

"Frank belongs to the Jewish aristocracy," Watson bellowed, "and it was determined by rich Jews that no aristocrat of their race should die for the death of a working girl."

Still, the trial in the book makes exciting reading, and Kluger even adds a twist with the confession of a plausible and previously unsuspected murderer who actually played a role in the original Frank trial.

Only a few novels have been written about Jews in the South in the last sixty years, and the Frank case is one of the reasons—southern Jews learned to keep a low profile, are conditioned by an instinctive wariness in a land where cross-burnings were frequent reminders that they were hated, too. And northern Jews have been too preoccupied with recording and reading about the world of their fathers to worry much about the Jews in the Bible Belt. Perhaps Richard Kluger's provocative fictionalization of the Frank trial and lynching will help to dispel the phantoms that have held back novels about southern Jewish life in America.

The Jews of New Orleans

In *Crescent City*, a romance novel set in the Jewish New Orleans of the Civil War period, Scarlett O'Hara is a haunting presence. It may be difficult to believe that at this point in American literary history anyone would even try a rewrite of *Gone With the Wind* using Jewish characters, but Belva Plain, the popular novelist who started writing at the age of fifty-nine, was undaunted by the creative risks of such an undertaking. She uses almost every Southern cliché, but with seven and a half million copies of her three previous bestsellers in print, she seems to have found a formula for placing the elements of the romance novel in period settings and using historical information as background for heartaches and secret liaisons.

Her Scarlett is Miriam Raphael, who arrives in America from Germany as a little girl and comes of age in New Orleans, where she lives with her wise slave girl, Fanny, and assorted unpleasant family members. She is trapped in an unhappy arranged marriage with the wealthy planter Eugene Mendes, a lout and plantation owner who counts among his slaves his own illegitimate son, has a quadroon mistress with a heart of gold, and tries to protect his Tara from both the rampaging Yankees and scalawag southerners. On her wedding night, sixteen-year-old Miriam thinks, "Surely one was not supposed to loathe one's husband."

Will she remain faithful to him, or will she be seduced by the handsome, Rhett Butler–like blockade runner who whisks her into an all-white room and unpins her chignon while "wire hoops and twenty yards of yellow cloth fell to the floor"? Or will she come to her senses and embrace her brother's childhood friend, the young lawyer Gabriel Carvalho, who is warm and considerate like Ashley Wilkes and has loved her from afar all her confused life?

Her stormy romances make Miriam an emotional Oke-fenokee, churned up as well by responsibilities to her children, a high-living father who goes bankrupt and moves into her house, and an abolitionist brother who is up to his neck in nighttime adventures with former slaves and finally flees north but returns from medical school just in time to save her life. Miriam herself is, at least from time to time, a northern sympathizer opposed to the war, slavery, the role of southern women, and almost everything else about the Old South she lives in.

The southern Jewish experience is fascinating terrain waiting for its William Faulkner or Thomas Wolfe. The rich fictional possibilities invite a great novelist to capture the world of the insider-outsiders in a Bible-dominated land of slavery and mystery. Thousands of Jews fought for the Confederacy during the Civil War; Charleston and New Orleans had thriving Jewish communities that in the early nineteenth century were the largest in the United States. Reform Judaism had its beginnings in Charleston in 1824 and flourished in the South.

Belva Plain uses this history but does not explore it. Her own sensibilities are clearly close to the characters in *Evergreen*, her first successful saga, about members of the first generation of Jewish immigrants to come to the North (her own father came to New York from Germany). She writes about the southern Jews as if they merely transferred ghetto values to plantation life en masse.

Historic figures pass through the story as dinner guests or sources of gossip and conversation. Judah P. Benjamin, the New Orleans lawyer, United States senator, and ultimately attorney general, secretary of war, and secretary of state in the Confederacy, is denounced by anti-Semitic Gentiles and denied by the Jews. Judah Touro, the first great American Jewish philanthropist, is first disparaged, then admired. Rabbis in the North and South are commented on.

But in the end, Plain, like the Jews she writes about, is a

stranger in a strange land who has not mastered the intricate emotional life or the psychological dilemma of Jewish southerners. That, however, probably will not bother her fans, who will surely be as enthralled by this book as they have by her previous bestsellers. Her research shows like the stitching in a hoop skirt, but all the elements of romance are here, and as a romance, *Crescent City* can't miss. Southern literature, however, still must wait for the masterpiece novel about Jews in the South that the subject deserves.

Part II

Southern Politics
and History

8

Southern Liberals and the Court

In 1954, the South faced in September the first reopening of schools after the historic United States Supreme Court desegregation decision of the previous May. The 1954 decision in *Brown v. the Board of Education of Topeka* shattered sixty years of "separate but equal" precedent, and southern moderates like my father, E. J. Evans, who was mayor of Durham, North Carolina, were thrust back into their classic role of trying to pull their communities through the turmoil. The South had staggered through a summer of the jitters, a crumbling social order punctured by shock and defiance. Governor Herman E. Talmadge in Georgia vowed to use troops, saying, "There will never be mixed schools while I am Governor," and Senator James O. Eastland of Mississippi had announced that "the South will not abide by nor obey this legislative decision by a political court."

In my hometown, local officials predicted that the decision would cause "no race warfare" while my father and other leaders urged calm and "a sincere effort" to comply with what the most fearless local leaders were already calling by that lofty phrase "the law of the land." The harshest anger seemed directed at the southerners on the Court—Hugo L. Black of Alabama, Tom C. Clark of Texas, and Stanley F. Reed of Kentucky.

The local paper, The *Durham Morning Herald*, expressed some surprise at the unanimity of the Court and that "not a single member felt that the separate but equal doctrine was constitutional." President Eisenhower's tepid reaction ("The Supreme Court has spoken and I will obey," without any effort to commend its fairness or lead public opinion) undercut southern liberals further. Despite the intensity of southern feelings, the reaction to the decision had to compete for front-page attention with the Army-McCarthy hearings and the "amazing success" of young Billy Graham's crusade in England.

When a thousand blacks attended a mass meeting called by the Durham Committee on Negro Affairs, the paper reported that "restraint prevailed, but joy was obvious in scattered references to the Supreme Court decision . . . and in the fervor with which the group sang 'My Country Tis of Thee.'" That issue of the paper also carried photographs of members of my high school graduating class, for the decision had come down like a cannon exploding in the midst of spring exams. Most of us had been in the same class together for twelve years, grown up with each other through bicycle tag and Halloween mischief. We would scatter now to college or to the army or to jobs in Durham or just off to somewhere, most of us never to see each other again.

The hallway had come alive with whispering and alarm that afternoon.

"Did y'all hear the news about the Supreme Court?" The words raced each other to get out, full of uncertainty and shock. "They say we're going to have to integrate. Go to school with *them*. Right here!" The story came out in harsh snatches, rushing over me in waves: "The niggers," "next year probably," "they'll mess up everything."

Still none of us realized the implications; by the end of the day the talk was all about putting in extra water fountains and "colored" restrooms.

It had never occurred to any of us so starkly that there were no Negroes in our class, but at the graduation dance I worried about next year and what the sons of the millhands would do if a black student came to a prom. I felt so distant from my classmates. Every high school scene began to take on a black dimension: the lunchroom, the classes, the football practice, the games.

My father served as mayor for twelve years, from 1951 to 1963, when the Court jolted the South into responsibility and changed all the rules of living. He played the role of peacemaker, presiding over transition years until blacks would demand concessions as a human right and whites would yield as an economic, political, and ultimately moral necessity. He always tried to guide his town, pleading for respect of the law and the courts, seizing the openings, and bringing his slice of the South through the difficult times when whole corners of his universe were turning to demagogues and false prophets for comfort and obstruction.

9

The Transformation of Southern Politics

In the early 1950s, political scientist V. O. Key wrote in his classic *Southern Politics: In State and Nation* that "whatever phase of the Southern political process one seeks to understand, sooner or later the trail of inquiry leads to the Negro." The South in the years since Key's book has virtually dominated the American political landscape; the rest of the country has watched a lusty and violent upheaval in a region where the dust never settles but just waits for the next mule team to come rambling through.

Technological changes on the farms drove millions of blacks to major cities in the North and South while the industries flooding into the South attracted hundreds of thousands of non-native southerners to the voting booth. Court-ordered reapportionment broke up the old rural courthouse gangs gathered around Harry Byrd in Virginia, Eugene Talmadge in Georgia, and Huey Long in Louisiana and laid the groundwork for suburban Republican gains and black political participation. The system of rigid segregation finally crumbled under the weight of the Voting Rights Act of 1965, as millions of new black voters entered the political process.

This stormy era was captured in all its variety and complexity in *The Transformation of Southern Politics: Social Change and Political Consequences since* 1945, an ambitious book published in 1979 that reveals the broad panorama of change through surveys of each of the eleven southern states, using the methodology and style of Key's original work. The authors, Jack Bass and Walter DeVries, worked from Duke University for two years with grants from the Rockefeller and Ford foundations. They drew their material, as Key did, from 360 interviews with retired and active politicians (fifty of them black) and added graphs, charts, and maps illustrating population shifts and voting trends. They created a rich tapestry of colorful detail written in a journalistic style that is as fascinating for lay readers as for scholars.

By 1979, the nation had gotten the message (though not the one George Wallace wanted to send in 1972) that the Democratic party in the South had changed politically and had entered the national mainstream. The ebb-and-flow history of southern Republicans had been less publicized.

According to the authors, "Dwight D. Eisenhower made inroads in 1952 with victories in Virginia, Tennessee, Florida, and Texas. . . . The Eisenhower Republicans in the South often included leadership from the professional and business elite and a reform element that perceived the need to develop a two-party system and to challenge entrenched Democratic statehouses and courthouse organizations that generally were unresponsive to the needs of a changing society."

But Republicans couldn't resist the temptation to stir the pot. In 1961, Barry Goldwater declared in a speech in Atlanta that "we're not going to get the Negro vote as a bloc in 1964 and 1968 so we ought to go hunting where the ducks are." Goldwater voted against the 1964 Civil Rights Act and became the first Republican ever to sweep the Deep South. He got the ducks all right, but he lost the rest of the country.

"Goldwater's strategy killed the chance for the Republican Party to assume the role of reform in the one-party South," the authors asserted, "and the GOP increasingly attracted the most reactionary elements of the region to the party." Ironically, moderate Democrats owe a measure of their success to the Republicans, who drained money, energy, and people from the conservative Democrats.

Even after the Goldwater debacle, there was a chance. "Blacks tended to form political coalitions with white Democrats, who were adjusting to changed circumstances," wrote Bass and DeVries, "but a handful of successful Republican candidates—such as Governor Linwood Holton in Virginia, Senator Howard Baker in Tennessee, and Governor Winthrop Rockefeller in Arkansas—have demonstrated that moderate Republicans who address themselves to issues meaningful to blacks can receive significant black support at the polls."

But Nixon's "southern strategy" treated the South as a monolith, ignoring the differences in tone, the range of personalities and history of each state. Republican leaders under the spell of Sunbelt conservatism should read profiles describing individual states in the late seventies to understand the subtlety of southern politics. The rectitude of a self-righteous Virginia ruling class breaking out of the "Byrd cage" contrasted with Louisiana, where the Longs left a legacy of graft and corruption. (T. Harry Williams, Huey Long's biographer, told the authors, "I always suspected the carpetbaggers were learners down here. They didn't bring it with them; they were taking lessons.") The "politics of resistance and confrontation" in Mississippi at the time appeared even more futile alongside the "politics of accommodation" in South Carolina. The "conservative blandness" of North Carolina in 1979 was completely unlike the "pitched battles" between conservatives and liberals in Texas. The political situation in Florida was totally different from the one in Arkansas, which was still in the Faubus shadow, but both states had moderate Democratic leadership in Governor Reuben Askew and Senator Dale Bumpers. While Tennessee stood alone as the only genuine two-party state in the South, Georgia had returned to one-party Democratic control based on "a new political consensus" shaped by the so-phisticated influences of Atlanta. Even in Alabama, where George Wallace had "frozen political development," the forces of change were just below the surface, waiting for liberation.

The new voices in the South of 1979—the 1,652 black elected officials who learned politics in the civil rights move-ment (there were only 75 in 1965 when the Voting Rights Act passed)—animate the book with down-home truths. Listen to Congressman Andrew Young of Atlanta describe the process of change to the Association of Southern Black Mayors in 1974: "It used to be that southern politics was just 'nigger' politics, who could 'outnigger' the other—then you registered 10 to 15 percent in the community and folk would start saying 'Nigra' and then you get 35 to 40 percent registered and it's amazing how quick they learned how to say "Neegrow' and now that we've got 50, 60, 70 percent of the black votes registered in the South, everybody's proud to be associated with their black brothers and sisters."

Though there were by the late seventies black mayors and over one hundred black state legislators, "blacks still comprise barely two percent of all elected officials in the region" and none had been elected to statewide office. Almost none are Republicans and, according to the authors, "maturing Repub-lican conservatives" in the South, who saw their party in 1974 lose eighty-two state legislative seats and nine congressional incumbents in the Watergate aftermath, have begun to question rebuilding the party on the "Southern strategy that not only has driven away the mass of black voters . . . but also turns off many whites who perceive the arousal of racial emotions as a threat to stability."

The authors have an ear for the expressive quotation and an eye for the telling vignette: Virginia's Governor Linwood Holton escorting his daughter into a 95-percent-black high school during a busing controversy in Richmond; once-governor Earl Long of Louisiana pleading with his state legisla-ture that "you got to recognize that niggers is human beings";

George Wallace answering Winthrop Rockefeller, who had called him a "demagogue," with "I just don't understand it. Our folks always bought plenty of kerosene from his folks"; Senator Albert Gore, who played the fiddle in his early Tennessee campaigns but did not "after he became a senator and many of his admirers felt he had become too aloof."

The authors acknowledged gaps in the study for others to fill. For example, the book deliberately bypasses the courageous federal judges and the drama around crucial decisions, though the role of the courts is mentioned in a 1973 interview with the governor, Jimmy Carter. "Once we had to confront the fact that we were right or wrong in the eyes of God," Carter stated, "we said we were wrong, and if we can find a way to make this change without losing face, we'll do it. And the Supreme Court and other court orders were the things that permitted us to do it without losing face. And in many instances, we did it with a sense of relief."

Little attention is given to campaign finances or to nongovernmental institutions such as the church, the press, and the broadcast media. There are intriguing hints about the impact of television from Georgia's Senator Herman Talmadge. "I use a calm, deliberate, rational, reasonable approach on TV," he confessed. "The viewer sitting in the quiet comfort of his home is not subject to the emotional hysteria of the stump."

The vigorous prose of Key's book raised political science to the level of literature and will last beyond the South he wrote about. In 1949 he said, "The South is changing rapidly. . . . He who writes about it runs the risk that change will occur before the presses stop."

The South is now at the brink of yet another era, and *The Transformation of Southern Politics* is a useful document of the one just past.

During the Reagan-Bush era historic trends were reversed in the South, as the white South largely deserted the Democratic party in national elections, and the Republicans began to be defined more dramatically in the South, as elsewhere, by their conservative base. The Carter years, in retrospect, seem like an aberration resulting from Watergate. Republicans won five out of six presidential elections, having made inroads in the South using the old issue of race while introducing new ones such as prayer in the schools, gun control, fear of homosexuals, and abortion, and enlisting televangelists to be messengers of "family values." Running up a federal deficit on a scale beyond anything previously imagined in American history, Ronald Reagan and George Bush rode an overheated economy and a Wall Street boom that enabled Republicans to defeat Walter Mondale and Michael Dukakis and sent the Democratic party back to its 1976 formula of nominating a son of the South to try to recapture the White House. Arkansas governor Bill Clinton would be the moderate southern governor to lead his party in 1992, and he would select Senator Al Gore, Jr., of Tennessee, another southern moderate, as his running mate.

The Republican convention of 1992 seemed like a time warp, harking back to the 1964 Goldwater convention, when the right wing of the party captured the nomination from the eastern leadership of New York Governor Nelson Rockefeller and rammed through a platform of conservative dogma on both economic issues and race. In Houston in 1992, President Bush turned over the platform and the planning for the convention to the far right of the GOP and, in prime time on the opening night, Pat Buchanan, Bush's conservative challenger in the primaries, declared a "religious war" in America. As a symbol of the battle for the souls of original sinners, the platform urged a constitutional amendment banning abortions, with no exceptions even for rape and incest. Women, already alienated from the Republican party by the Clarence Thomas–Anita Hill hearings the previous spring, abandoned the Republican ticket in droves, even in the South. Extreme rhetoric, from fundamentalist televangelists Pat Robertson and Jerry Falwell, echoed in the platform and caused Jewish voters, north and south, to react as well.

Clinton's campaign strategist, James Carville, a Louisiana Cajun nicknamed the "mad dog," kept a sign in his office that said "It's the economy, stupid." Taking that advice, the Democratic ticket ran an impressively disciplined campaign that refused to be sidetracked into any peripheral issues. George Bush's 1988 pledge of "Read my lips—no new taxes" came back to haunt his campaign based on trust, as the deficit doubled in four years and a sluggish economy became the incumbent president's undoing. If Lyndon Johnson's domestic triumphs of the Great Society could be unraveled and tarnished beyond recovery by the Vietnam War, the opposite would be true of George Bush. His domestic economic failures completely overwhelmed his international triumph in the Gulf War.

The New South candidacy of two southerners, born just after World War II, have led the Democrats back to the White House, assisted powerfully by a weak economy and rising unemployment, issues that lured back home the working-class Reagan Democrats who had become the bedrock of Republican strategy in the 1980s.

A new transformation of Southern politics is now inevitable, led by the potential of a Clinton-Gore Administration, perhaps into the twenty-first century. Though the Democrats carried only Tennessee, Arkansas, Georgia, and Louisiana, they were close in Florida, Texas, North Carolina, and Virginia. This was a solid showing against a sitting president representing a party appealing to "the real America" and a sea of white faces at the Republican convention.

Yet this was a campaign in which the discussion of race was strangely muted. President Clinton can open the doors to national reconciliation only if he can rally the country over the next four years with a call to ideals. Writing in *The Nation*, novelist E. L. Doctorow observed that "with each new president, the nation is conformed spiritually. He is the artificer of our malleable national soul . . . the face of our sky, the conditions that prevail . . . . I would want a presidential temperament keen with a love of justice and with the capacity to recognize the honor of humbled and troubled people." He condemned George Bush as one "who speaks for civil rights, but blocks legislation that would relieve racial inequities."

President Bill Clinton is uniquely positioned to free the South of the chains of its history, to turn it away from its angry past. He knows the region is pivotal; that a progressive South means a more reasonable nation. If he could speak its language and touch its soul, there could indeed be a new community in America.

10

In the Shadow of Southern History

Some years ago, during my first few days in New York, I was driving up Third Avenue when a car forced me over to the curb. I prickled with that rush of fear of random violence that new arrivals instinctively feel in the big city. The car's window rolled down so that I could see a black couple with kids piled in the back seat. The man hollered in an unmistakable accent, "Hey, man, where in North Carolina y'all from?" "Durham," I answered, relieved to know that it was only my license plate that had attracted his attention. "We're from Rocky Mount," he said. "Sure is good to see some home folks." We laughed and the kids waved goodbye.

I haven't thought much about that incident since then, but it came back to me recently during a trip to Nashville, where a white bus driver reacted to the mention of New York City problems. "Let 'em squirm," he said. "If they can't pay their bills, to hell with 'em. Let 'em just go into bankruptcy like they deserve."

Most southerners and many members of Congress, too, see New York City as a seething center of ethnic conflicts, brimming with corruption, narcotics, garbage, and crime. But the folks down home are laboring under a massive misconception. The truth is, New York City and the South are bound by history in a permanent relationship that makes ironic any one-sided discussion of urban problems.

It is an ongoing struggle, however, to persuade nonurban representatives and senators to help break the downward spiral of the major American cities. Sweeping welfare reform, changes in housing policy, and other issues on the urban agenda will always have difficulty attracting southern and midwestern votes in Congress unless funds for cities are coupled with programs for rural areas. However, urban and rural ills are rarely related in congressional debates, even though migration connects them together, as two sides of the same problem. A new presidency with a unique coalition of southern and northern voters might be activated to support a comprehensive package of urban and rural programs based on a frank discussion of the southern roots of the northern urban crisis.

In the mid-1970s a Southern Regional Council Task Force on Southern Rural Development (which included then-Governor Jimmy Carter and two future cabinet officers—Secretary of Commerce Juanita Kreps and Secretary of Labor Ray Marshall) urged that the federal government formulate a national rural development policy, consolidate current rural programs into a new agency or department, and support a National Rural Development Bank aimed at small farmers and businesses in growing small towns. The report, entitled "Increasing the Options," pointed out that 4.5 million blacks live below the poverty line in the South, more than half in nonmetropolitan areas. They are being lured to southern and northern cities, the report said, in a migration stream that connects rural nondevelopment to continuing urban problems. "To ignore one at the expense of the other," said Vanderbilt University president Alexander Heard, the task force chairman, "is virtually to guarantee that neither will be solved."

The nation's cities cannot escape the shadow of southern history; statistics prove the connection. Since the Depression, the migration of blacks to the North has represented one of the most massive population shifts in American history. During the 1940s, approximately 1.6 million blacks left the South; during the 1950s, about 1.5 million left; during the 1960s, about 1.4 million headed north. Most of the blacks came north in a state of despair. Depression farm prices plummeted at the same time that mechanization in the cotton fields made human hands superfluous. The descendants of the freed slaves found themselves trapped in a twentieth-century dilemma of unwanted labor and foreclosures.

They looked north for the same reason that European immigrants had flocked to New York City throughout the nineteenth century—blacks saw in its bustling streets and economic vitality the golden door of hope, the possibility of jobs, escape from the chains of hunger and poverty. To the ethnic immigrants from a generation earlier, the needs of the black newcomers struck a deep response. The welfare add-on of 25 percent that constitutes a major depletion of New York City's finances was a result of those citizens' most generous impulses. The second generation of Jewish and Catholic immigrants did not want new immigrants to New York to suffer the indignities of the world of their fathers.

Farm-to-city migration continues, but growing Dixie ghettos are the new destination. Even though welfare payments in New York City still exceed those in some southern states by a four-to-one ratio, 60 percent of all rural black migration now goes to southern cities such as Atlanta, New Orleans, and Birmingham. The big cities in the North are not alone, even if it is New York City's troubles that dominate the headlines.

Nor do the statistics always reflect realities. For the first time, in the period 1970–1975, for example, the Census Bureau reported a sharp drop-off in migration to the North, with the number of blacks leaving the South about equal to the numbers returning. Experts believe, however, that middle-class and skilled blacks are going back to jobs in the booming southern and southwestern cities while the poor are still leaving rural areas and small towns.

The migration is not all black, of course. There was a time in the struggling South when many whites as well as blacks tried to eke out a living with a plow and a lot of luck. Millions of whites have also fled to the urban centers from Appalachia and other rural southern areas—more than 3 million since 1940.

The welfare problem, then, is a national crisis that requires a two-hundred-year perspective to understand; it is, in part, a living legacy of slavery, the dark side of America's past. But it is not only New York City's problem nor is migration of the poor just a black phenomenon. Indeed, the American urban problems created by migration from Puerto Rico and Mexico can also be viewed as a rural development issue.

If the only solutions to New York City's problems continue to be program cutbacks, rising taxes, and fleeing industries (the Northeast lost 781,000 manufacturing jobs from 1960 to 1975), the time will come when the northern cities will resemble the modern version of the rural wasteland of the Depression-wrecked old South—oppressive, cold, uncaring, and brutal places where millions of people have flocked to a jobless chasm almost as barren of opportunity as the land they left.

Urban problems are one end of a pipeline linked to rural poverty, and neither set of problems can be solved piecemeal. Programs and policies that combine rural development with urban initiatives would find a responsive audience among southern congressmen who are growing more sensitive to the rising numbers of black voters. An effective rural-urban coalition in Congress could influence the decisions in millions of families—people now in the rural South who are considering moves to cities and people in New York, Detroit, Chicago—black and white—who might even choose the option of going home if given half a chance.

The deep concern generated by rising welfare costs in the late 1970s has come full circle in the 1990s. In August of 1992, the number of New Yorkers on welfare rose past the one million mark for the first time since the fiscal crisis in the late 1970s. New problems fueled the numbers: rising waves of immigrants, the AIDS epidemic, growing numbers of drug addicts, and teenage pregnancies. Looking back, in the aftermath of the 1992 riots that ravaged Los Angeles, one has to wonder: has America learned nothing from the last twenty-five years of its recent history? How long can we neglect the tragedy of urban deterioration and desperate riots and ignore the roots of the urban crisis on the farms and in small towns? It is ironic that once again, in 1992, a southern governor from a small town, who has been elected President with support in both the South and the cities, is struggling to deal with the joint future of urban and rural America. But the challenge is growing more complex—illegal immigration (by some estimates, more than a million illegal immigrants are in New York City) is a sharp reminder that a global economy will generate global problems. Unless there is a new spirit of shared destiny, New York, as a metaphor for the national urban crisis, will become a twenty-first century tale of two cities—of vast wealth and deep poverty, of sunshine and shadows.

In a 1991 book entitled *The Promised Land: The Great Black Migration and How It Changed America*, Nicholas Lemann (whose father I interviewed in New Orleans in 1970) put into perspective the current pessimism about the black slums in the big cities.

"The framers of the Constitution," he wrote, "idealists though they were, couldn't imagine an American nation without slavery—but in the long run slavery was ended. In this century legal segregation looked like an unfortunate given, impossible to eliminate, until well after the end of World War II. That black America could become predominately middle class, non-Southern, and nonagrarian would have seemed inconceivable until a bare two generations ago." He concluded that the solution to deprivation, ignorance, and the ill health of the black ghettoes of the major cities "now . . . is the most significant remaining piece of unfinished business in our country's long struggle to overcome its original sin of slavery."

To restore a sense of community to America, ambitious,

organized national action in behalf of the poor will be one of the greatest challenges of the Clinton presidency. Those who imagined an end to slavery in the nineteenth century and to segregation in the twentieth century believed in a new America true to its ideals. Those who can imagine an end to the black ghettoes of the cities believe in another new America in the twenty-first century, true to its promise of equality, its birthright of inalienable rights, and its destiny as a society of opportunity, open to all.

II

The City, the South,
and the Caribbean

In the early 1950s, down in North Carolina, where I was raised, my father took me to a ribbon-cutting for a new plant. As the mayor, he proudly introduced the main speaker, Governor Luther Hodges, an ebullient ex-textile executive who was once shown in a picture in *Life* magazine taking a shower in an effort to boost nonshrinking North Carolina—made underwear. The governor boasted about the new jobs and about how the state was leading the Southeast in new plant locations because "our schools are good and our people are great." No one mentioned unions or tax breaks for new industry. No wonder the well-dressed Yankee owners smiled when the high school band played "Nothing could be finer than to be in Carolina."

It was a strange sight. The plant had moved its dress and shirt operation from the North into a windowless cinderblock building. Inside, there was nothing but row after row of sewing machines lined up like black insects feeding on discarded bread crusts. The only difference between this scene and a similar one on the Lower East Side of my grandmother's day was the present use of electricity; in an earlier time, the starched young immigrant girls in puffed sleeves and ribbons had worked the machines with their feet.

In New York today, in thousands of ghostly Soho lofts transformed from the cavernous workplaces of that era, one can still almost hear the restless clatter of immigrant history. The first generation of Jewish immigrants was willing to work in the sweatshops but would form unions to protect their sons and daughters. Up and out of the ghetto they struggled, out of sweatshops to suburban Brooklyn and Queens and then to Long Island.

Just as the Irish famine and the pogroms of Eastern Europe had driven ethnic groups to America, the Great Depression triggered the black migration to the northern cities. In the post–World War II job boom, millions of blacks forced off the cotton farms by picking machines began the long trek north.

But, ironically, while black southerners were moving north in record numbers, manufacturing jobs were moving south. The sweep of the exchange was staggering. The Northeast lost 750,000 manufacturing jobs between 1960 and 1975, while more than two million immigrants came to New York City from the South and the Caribbean.

The South and the Caribbean have been linked throughout American history. The Spanish, English, French, and Dutch colonists virtually destroyed the native Indian populations on the islands and imported millions of black slaves from Africa to work the giant plantations. The islands became part of the great trade triangle: slaves, sugarcane, and rum. Because of the presence of slaves, the pastoral islands were turned into vast agrarian factories, producing for the white man the delights of sugar, tobacco, spices, coffee, and cocoa. Later, "King Cotton" plantations in the Mississippi Delta required the same sort of human product from the Indies, and the market in slaves rose to a fever pitch for a hundred years.

The abolition of slavery in the nineteenth century replaced physical bondage with economic chains, creating a peasant class in the Caribbean and a tenant-farmer class in the South. Depressions and world wars stirred aspirations, and New York looked as attractive to poverty-stricken Puerto Ricans as it did to black sharecroppers (and as easily reached).

The South was like an underdeveloped country and so was Puerto Rico, despite its legal status. The city of New York reacted with a foreign aid–like program of its own. The city human resources budget between 1960 and 1970 increased from $1.1 billion to $5 billion; welfare payments rose from $235 million to $1.4 billion; city jobs pushed payroll costs from $1.6 billion in 1964 to $6 billion in 1976. But New York City alone could not correct the history of Alabama's racial neglect or the economic problems of the overpopulated small islands of the Caribbean.

In the 1950s and 1960s, immigration to New York stepped up. Political and economic refugees from Duvalier's Haiti and Trujillo's Dominican Republic joined southern blacks who had suffered under "Bull" Connor in Birmingham and the Ku Klux Klan in the rural South. Most of the publicity, however, focused on the middle class fleeing Cuba for Miami.

To American eyes, the colonial-inherited differences in language, economy, racial mix, political history, and legal status all blurred in the multiracial and cultural diversity of the many Caribbean islands. As always, the news media dramatized personalities and ideologies, and the clamor confused the issues.

But a profound, unrecognized change was occurring. The population ecology of New York City and the future of urban America were merging with the crosscurrents of change in the South and in the Caribbean.

Immigration is now a major source of annual American population growth. But old images mislead us: for example, the immigration of Jews to New York City in the nineteenth century was a permanent relocation of people yearning for assimilation. There would be no return and each family knew it. But the pattern of migration from Puerto Rico is a circulating one, fluid and filled with ambivalence and doubt. The numbers rise when jobs are available in New York and decrease when jobs are scarce.

The United States Civil Rights Commission recently reported that this constant migration "places Puerto Ricans in a uniquely precarious situation. . . . [It] results in cultural and linguistic alienation from fellow citizens, denial of equal opportunities, decreased social and economic stability."

The commission did not address the unofficial issue—the fact that Puerto Rico serves as one of the major gateways for growing numbers of illegal aliens from the repressive politics and economic deprivation of the other islands and countries bordering the Caribbean. Unrest in Kingston, Jamaica, or actions by strong-armed governments in the Dominican Republic and El Salvador mean thousands of new immigrants for New York City. And beyond the islands ticks the population clock undermining the fragile governments of Central and South America. Yet the American public seems constantly surprised by the unrest and instability in Latin America.

The Census Bureau's report in the early 1970s of a net out-migration of blacks from the Northeast back to the South was applauded by the southern press and the "New South" governors. This trend seemed later to be continuing with the return of two hundred thousand Puerto Ricans to the commonwealth during New York City's fiscal crisis in the late 1970s. But new figures were released in the spring of 1978: the black population in New York City and the state was increasing because of an in-migration "of 138,000 blacks between 1971 and 1975, mostly from the Caribbean." Presumably, they represent the legal tip of the illegal iceberg.

These statistics dramatize new movements of families along class lines. The black middle class is joining the whites fleeing the inner city while the poor continue to arrive. The departure of whites is an old story, but demographers are calling the new phenomenon "black flight," not only to the South but to the suburbs. A Brookings Institution report points out that this net outflow of people will have a profound political impact on the city's future when redistricting occurs after the census, and all cities across the country will lose representation in the state legislatures and the Congress.

With traditional Yankee condescension, the city pleads for special federal help based on the Big Apple arguments of cultural elitism and international fame. But Bible Belt senators have to defend their votes to constituents filled with impressions of decaying ghettos and crime in the streets. Both impressions are parochial. Sugarcane fields in Puerto Rico seem as far away from Spanish Harlem as George Wallace does from Bedford-Stuyvesant, but a nation that will not face its past cannot cope with its future.

Until the nation perceives the interrelationships of our problems, regional conflicts and narrow economic interests will checkmate solutions. In such an atmosphere, the Sunbelt versus the Snowbelt battle over federal largesse disintegrates into a spitting match over who has the most poor folks to take care of in the worst weather. Beneath the "New South" publicity is the reality that about two out of three blacks in the inner cities of the South are employed in low-wage jobs and live below the poverty line. And the blue Caribbean waters of the television ads mask a Puerto Rico in which over 60 percent of the population of 3.2 million receive food stamps and a Haiti where the per capita income for over 4.5 million people is $190 a year.

While the migration to the North seems to have abated momentarily, the rural populations in the South and the Caribbean continue to move to their own cities—Dixie ghettos in Atlanta and Nashville, while the Caribbean poor gather in San Juan and Kingston. But what will happen in the next decade as the cut-and-sew operations in New York City, the South, and Puerto Rico move on a massive scale to places where even cheaper labor pools are available in Mexico, Central America, and Taiwan?

We will curse the outcome rather than the years of dereliction. We do not yet realize that the rural-urban divisions in the

Congress are self-defeating, that the long preoccupation with Castro and Cuba has blinded us to the problems in the rest of the Caribbean, and that all of us in this hemisphere are intimately linked by proximity and history to a common future.

In the approaching decades, the banks, universities, governments, and news media will either have to think interdependently about urban, rural, and international problems or face the possibility of police-state solutions on our borders and in our central cities. Accelerating these conflicts will be the whites' tax revolts slashing government budgets, supported after the censuses of 1980 and 1990 by the increasingly suburban state legislatures and the Congress. And we will suffer as much from our own ignorance as from the innocent hopes of the impoverished minorities seeking a new home behind the golden door that now leads into a jobless slum.

12

A Step toward Equal Justice

For almost four years, from 1969 to 1973, while I was on the staff of the Carnegie Corporation, I worked on a major program designed to increase the number of black lawyers in the South. I traveled throughout the South to talk to deans of the seventeen southern state university and private law schools and found, to the surprise of many, that the schools were willing to accept black students if the deans did not have to provide special scholarship funds, which were not plentifully available at that time to white students either. Because of segregationist sentiments in some state legislatures, what the deans wanted, it seemed, was the existence of an independent fund of money at some distance and out of their control, to which the black students who were admitted could apply for scholarship help, independent of the law schools themselves.

The result of the informal survey in 1969 was the creation of the program described here five years later, which ultimately attracted the support of more than seventy corporations and foundations contributing more than $3.75 million for a range of initiatives: law student scholarships, stipends for summer internships in civil rights organizations, and funds for a law library and for civil rights representation if a graduate returned to a town that did not have a black lawyer. The report was published in April 1974 and generated requests for over eighteen thousand copies, an unprecedented figure at that time.

The report summarized an extensive evaluation of a five-year period of grants made by private foundations, corporations, and individuals to increase the number of black lawyers in the South. The money supported programs of the Earl Warren Legal Training Program, Inc., a new educational entity affiliated with the NAACP Legal Defense and Educational Fund (LDF), and the Law Students Civil Rights Research Council (LSCRRC)—organizations involved in every aspect of encouraging black students to enter law school and then practice in the South. These programs provided for recruiting of students, as well as scholarships, tutoring, and counseling and offered summer experience working on civil rights litigation. Postgraduate fellowships were also given to a limited number of graduating black lawyers so they could work for a year in law firms doing civil rights cases or in a civil rights legal organization. Funds were provided over an additional three years for fees for civil rights legal work done by the young lawyers, either in a new law practice of their own or with a larger law firm in the South specializing in civil rights.

This series of grants constituted a broad-system approach to the needs of black communities in cities and counties across eleven states. While the programs were open to students in the four predominantly black law schools in the South—Texas Southern, Southern University in Baton Rouge, Howard University, and North Carolina Central—the report focused on the impact of these programs in seventeen predominantly white southern law schools—thirteen state university law schools and four private schools (Duke, Vanderbilt, Tulane, and Emory). These efforts told the profound human story of black students arming themselves with knowledge of the law and upon graduation openly committing themselves to the rigors of a civil rights law practice.

The evaluation summarized here was commissioned by the Carnegie Corporation and focused primarily on grants to the Earl Warren Legal Training Program and to LSCRRC by that foundation corporation and the Ford Foundation. The detailed administrative analysis and the interviews and observations run to several hundred pages and prompted Jack Greenberg, then director of the NAACP Legal Defense and Educational Fund, to say that in his twenty-five years at LDF, "There has never been a report on any of our activities with the depth and humanity of this report." It was also one of the most ambitious collective foundation and corporate undertakings ever, that still serves as a model for private funds in joint venture to accomplish something that public funds could never do.

The results of the evaluation of these programs indicated that from 1969 to 1973:

■ Larger numbers of black students were staying in the South to go to law school and were intending to stay there to practice. From 1969 to 1973, the number of first-year black law students at these seventeen southern law schools increased from 22 to about 171. The total number of black students enrolled in those same schools in the fall of 1973 was 375. Of 210 students who responded to a questionnaire, 171 intended to practice in the South.

■ Since almost every one of these law schools was recruiting black students, applications from blacks had risen steadily. Under a special recruiting program run by the Law Students Civil Rights Research Council, the students themselves were returning to campuses to persuade other undergraduates to join them. Law school applications from black undergraduates had increased in these schools from 396 in 1970 to 768 in 1972.

■ Increasing numbers of black students made it easier to recruit and appoint the first black law professors at six state university law schools—Virginia, South Carolina, North Carolina, Florida State, Louisiana State, and Alabama.

■ The number of black students graduating from these seventeen law schools increased dramatically since 1969. By June 1972, the program had produced 127 graduates; in June 1973, the Warren program could count 102 additional graduates, for a total of 229 graduates, most of them in the last two years.

■ The summer internship program, which LSCRRC administered, placed more than 481 students of both races (approximately 50 percent of them black) in the South into summer working experiences in civil rights law firms or organizations and government programs. The program, evaluated as "an important skills building experience" increased the desire of students to complete law school by giving them the confidence that they could function as civil rights attorneys. The program also provided a way for black students in northern law schools to evaluate the South for a summer as a place where they might practice after graduation.

■ The attrition rate for Warren scholarship students, which was 30 percent in 1969 when all recipients were first-year students, declined to 10 percent in 1971 and dropped off significantly for second- and third-year students. Actually, the overall rate was one-third less than the unanalyzed figures indicated. (The report sought to reach dropouts and found a significant percentage who were either readmitted in subsequent semesters or had transferred to other law schools.)

■ Larger numbers of young black lawyers were establishing law practices across the South. More than forty-nine were members of the bar in Mississippi in 1974, more than quadruple the 1969 figure (there were three in 1965), and the numbers were up sharply in many other southern states.

■ Young black lawyers inevitably were being drawn into a larger leadership role in their communities. Especially impressive was the performance of the post-graduate Warren fellows. Since 1970, there had been thirty-nine first-year fellows, twelve of these in the first year of the program in

1973–1974. Of the other twenty-seven, all but two were then in practice in the South; all but one had passed the bar examinations. Former fellows were serving, for example, as the mayor of a town in Alabama, in the state legislature in Arkansas, as a municipal judge in Houston, on the board of elections and the Selective Service Board in North Carolina, as a Democratic county chairman in Mississippi, and on the city council in Arkansas.

While the gains pointed out in the report were real, the problems of lack of representation and injustice continued to plague the nine million blacks living across the South. Forty-nine black lawyers in Mississippi is a significant increase from three—but there are approximately 800,000 blacks in Mississippi. The ratio of one lawyer to every 16,000 blacks did not begin to approach the level of legal services available to the white population in the state. By contrast, 1,400,000 whites could call on the services of 3,200 white members of the bar— a ratio of one lawyer to every 450 whites. Black people by and large still viewed the law as a force that acts to deny justice, not to protect their rights. To most of them, the law is still the sheriff and the white jury, not the black lawyer or the impartial judge. Moreover, the bar exam results in some states have called into question the fairness of that process—especially in one state where all forty-one blacks who took the exam failed it, including a few black graduates of Harvard and Columbia law schools. Students filed law suits charging discrimination in bar exams in at least four southern states.

Two powerful forces had been at work in the South, stirring the aspirations of young black people across the region. First was the Voting Rights Act of 1965, which opened up registration to more than two million disenfranchised blacks and resulted in an increase of black elected officials from about 75 in 1965 to more than 1,300 in 1973. As voting opened, so did opportunity. Black students discovered possibilities for themselves in the South as lawyers, government employees, elected officials, and political leaders.

The atmosphere was slowly changing: after years of arduous and painful efforts to break down the barriers of segregation, young black people could see the promise of a future in the South. This was not another "New South" heralded so many times in southern history by writers and poets. This time the change was deep down in the very grit of the political life of the region, rooted in a profound shift of power and influence and participation.

The other force for change was the impact of integration on the law students of both races. I have traveled the South as a journalist and as a foundation official, going over much of the same ground in 1968 as this report covered in 1973. In 1968, the few black students in predominantly white law schools were complaining of racial slurs, an atmosphere of antagonism, the loneliness of learning in an alien environment. In 1973, while the mood at some schools still was tense, on the whole students worried more over academic and financial matters and the uncertainties of the job market.

Black students and white students alike had changed. The presence of larger numbers of blacks meant that each individual student was less of a novelty and also created a supportive black community, and the white students no longer viewed their black classmates as intruders. As one white student said when asked about integration, "So what's the big deal?"

Still, tensions in 1974 had not disappeared in the classrooms, nor was the curriculum relevant, nor did the environment lack suspicion. Law schools from state to state in the South differed enormously—the University of Virginia, under the leadership of Dean Monrad Paulsen, had graduated all but one black student who had been admitted, and thirty-two were currently enrolled; the University of Mississippi, which changed its policies dramatically during Joshua Morse's deanship when it enrolled thirty-nine black students, dropped back a few years after he left to a disappointing six admissions in 1973, with only two of them new first-year students, according to LSCRRC. While the total number of black law students had increased since 1969, they still represented about 3 percent of the total number of students enrolled in these schools. No predominantly white school had a proportion of black students higher than 7 percent of its student body.

The great dangers in the future, according to the report, were that the law schools would cut back both because of increased pressure resulting from rising numbers of overall applications and because the DeFunis case, in which a white law student from Washington State had an appeal pending before the U.S. Supreme Court, had cast a cloud of doubt over the constitutionality of the practice of admitting minority students according to criteria other than grades and test scores. The report warned that "the fact that DeFunis is being litigated could encourage a 'go-slow' attitude on black admissions among state legislators or law school deans." It was important to note, the report pointed out, that many black students whose admission had been based on factors including their motivation, potential as lawyers, or capacity to contribute to the community had graduated, passed bar exams, and were practicing law successfully in the South.

The Earl Warren Legal Training Program included grants of approximately $3.75 million from 1969 to 1973 from twenty-one foundations, including major grants from the Field Foundation, Carnegie Corporation of New York, the Ford Foundation, the Rockefeller Brothers Fund, the Alfred P. Sloan Foundation, and the Fleischman Foundation, and scores of other individuals and corporations contributing through the NAACP Legal Defense and Educational Fund. The LDF estimated that approximately $2.9 million of this amount was spent on its southern program. The national programs of the Law Students Civil Rights Research Council (LSCRRC) had been supported by thirty-eight foundations and more than fifteen thousand individuals who had contributed more than $1.6 million since 1969. LSCRRC estimates that about $650,000 of this amount had been spent on programs in the South.

It is important to note that while the report covered the period from 1969 to 1973, the programs had their roots in an earlier period. The NAACP Legal Defense and Educational Fund, after its successful litigation had opened the way, began in 1964 to recruit and offer scholarships to black law students to enter the then-all-white state law schools of the South. A year earlier, with the help of the Field Foundation, it had begun a four-year postgraduate program for young black lawyers, which provided special training in civil rights law and help during the first years of practice in southern communities with no black lawyers. This pioneering effort came about because of the difficulties in implementation of newly won legal rights for blacks without local lawyers available to help carry the burden of litigation on large public issues.

Some years earlier, a report on the rising number of black lawyers graduating from predominantly white southern law schools might never have been made public. Racial progress had to be achieved quietly; otherwise the law schools ran the risks of legislative investigations, alumni pressures, and threats of budget cuts and dismissals.

Those risks to the institutions were minimal in 1974. The alumni of the law schools, the bar associations, and the bar examiners had an obligation to make the legal system free of discrimination. While it was true that the southern law schools had changed with the rest of the South, it was also clear that these institutions and others in all areas of southern political and economic life would have to step forward with even greater commitment if they were to meet the rising expectations of the minority community for a more representative and open system of justice.

The report pointed out that a large class of black lawyers would graduate in June 1974, and that there were early indications of great difficulties for many of them in the job market. They were looking for jobs at the very moment when the federal government's commitment to the Office of Economic Opportunity (OEO) Legal Services Program was uncertain and when the economy was in a downswing. Where would they go? What would they do? It would be the greatest irony if black students who chose to stay in their home states for law school had to leave the South to find jobs. There were still only a handful of integrated law firms in the South; the offices of district attorneys, local prosecutors, and public defender agencies were still largely segregated; state and local governments had a long way to go as employers of equal opportunity. Southern business and economic life, with help from the rising number of black officials, would have to find ways to use and support these lawyers, with special concern for the young person who decides to go it alone as the only black lawyer in his or her community.

What this report showed was that black lawyers can matter—that on the day they open an office, they are the chief defenders of human rights, major catalysts in putting together ideas for economic development, and important civil rights strategists. They become responsible leaders of their people, working within the legal system to improve local and state governments and to keep the courts unbiased and the juries integrated—they are symbols to other blacks of hope for a future.

The 350-year-old contest for the soul of the South will not end suddenly but with a long process of healing. A strong, vital black community lending its minds and talents to the South of the future remains the key to regional vitality and national reconciliation. White southerners are discovering that truth in Atlanta and Raleigh and dozens of other cities across the South where they are helping to vote black officials into office. The passions of southern history are still present and can explode into violence at any moment. Yet, in many ways, the region is today the most optimistic section of America, for black people are electing new faces in the city halls and are seeing young black attorneys in the courthouses. The South has always been one of the testing grounds for the nation's future. What happens there affects the tide of migration to the ghettos of the North, and the political balances in Congress, the dark stage of history where blacks and whites have always struggled for new definitions.

It has been said that the civil rights movement of the sixties moved in the seventies off of the streets and into the voting booths. Southern blacks are beginning to learn that the political system can be a major vehicle for peaceful social change in a democratic society. That some of their sons and daughters who were swept up in the sit-ins have now come to think of the law as a career can only advance that movement toward involvement in the processes of government.

This report challenged the institutions of the South to refocus their perceptions sufficiently to accommodate the changing ambitions of black students. The first steps had been taken; it had not been easy for the law schools or the students; there were serious obstacles ahead that would test commitments on all sides. But the first steps are often the most difficult and the schools could not turn back. The future would be determined by the quality of integrated public education, of higher education's adjustment to students' rising aspirations, and of whether there would be a continuing flow of black lawyers into southern society who would be a natural part of the terrain, free to defend the rights of all races seeking equal justice under law.

On November 3, 1992, at least three graduates of this program were elected to the United States Congress: Sanford Bishop from Columbus to represent the 2nd Congressional district in Georgia; William Jefferson, from New Orleans to represent the 2nd Congressional district in Louisiana; Mel Watt from Charlotte to represent the 12th Congressional district in North Carolina. There are scores of others—mayors, members of school boards and city councils, state legislators. In less than twenty years, on the most visible level, the U.S. Congress, the program is beginning to matter.

13

Southern Jews, Baptists, and Jimmy Carter

All during the 1976 presidential primaries, I tracked the reaction of Jewish, Protestant fundamentalist, and Catholic groups to Jimmy Carter's confession that he had once had a "born again" experience; my feeling was that Carter had been caught in a nexus of changing images among Jews, Roman Catholics, white Southern Baptists, and blacks about themselves, each other, and the South. Stereotypes crumble slowly, however, and when religion and race are involved we are all prisoners of our emotions and of history.

It was always an axiom of Jewish life in the South that racial trouble meant heated passions and a dangerous atmosphere that was "bad for the Jews." The opposite was true, too: if blacks were making progress, so were Jews. As the presidential campaign progressed that year, these and other lessons of growing up Jewish in the South came to seem more and more relevant.

One of the real secrets of Carter's appeal to blacks lay in his native ability to communicate in the idiom of the black church. Even with the tough talk after the second debate, Carter's style before black audiences remained the same. His soothing manner, the tones of his voice, his willingness to speak of love in a religious context—all marked him as a man capable of understanding. The southern accent when he talked politics may have grated on the ears of northerners so used to hearing bigotry in that accent, but in the context of the black church it was home talk from a familiar terrain of the heart. It stirred mixed memories for me.

My friends and I, southern teenagers, did what most other white boys did on weekends. Occasionally, on a Sunday night, we visited the rural black churches just to see the holy rollers shake and chant. It was a special experience for me to be able to immerse myself in a kind of Old Testament Christianity and to sing out spirituals about my heroes, Moses and Joshua, without fear. For one thing, no black preacher would try to convert a Jewish boy like me, because I was white; and, more important, there was no chance that any of my buddies, who were all Baptists, would get swept away and go down front to be saved and leave me as the only outsider at the service.

Looking back, I realize now that it seemed to me that the Jesus of the white man and the Jesus of the black man were gazing down at congregations whose needs and histories had created two distinctly different saviors.

While black Jesus was benign and comforting, white Jesus was strict and unbending. Black Jesus passed among the people as a friendly saint; white Jesus stood tall like an awesome soldier bent on retribution against sinners.

Because of the history of the Ku Klux Klan, Jews in the South have always judged politicians by their attitudes toward blacks. To Jews and Catholics in the North, ardent Christianity and the Klan have been joined as images—the burning crosses, the sounds of "Onward, Christian Soldiers" in the cow pastures, the lynchings. Jews in the South, more at home in the Bible Belt atmosphere, have learned to distinguish among politicians intuitively, and the race issue is one of the measures.

"It's like Andy Young said about blacks," a Jewish lawyer in

Atlanta told me. "As a Jew in the South, you develop antennae about politicians. For instance, when you're around Lester Maddox, who always mixed up God with segregation, you just knew he could be anti-Semitic at the drop of a hat. Jimmy is different. You just sense it."

To members of the older generation, with memories of Eastern European persecution, sawdust Christianity carries associations of narrow-minded, relentless suspicion of the Jews. But a Jewish shop owner in Georgia with a slight accent said: "No one down here can imagine Jimmy as a cossack on a steed. Hell, Carter won't destroy the shtetl. He comes from a shtetl."

But Jimmy Carter was not running for office in the South; he was running for president, and the major issue for Jews, north and south, is Israel. In that connection, the southern Jewish response was instructive, perhaps another example of the ignorance in the North about Southern Baptist attitudes. Jews in the South have felt that in a world of growing dependence on Arab oil they are more secure with a candidate whose commitment to Israel's survival is based on something deeper than a search for Jewish votes.

"We Jews are paranoid," an Atlanta doctor said at the time, "and for good reason. Given petro-dollars, we can't trust anyone. But Carter's support for Israel is biblical. It's deep. He doesn't have to be convinced there ought to be a Jewish state. He knows that in his heart." Jimmy Carter's statement that "I think God wants the Jews to have a place to live" was a moral and biblical justification, not a campaign invention.

Support for Israel is not only deep in fundamentalist prophecy, but became stronger politically as the Soviet Union began pouring arms into Egypt and Syria. Time and events translated it into southern myth—the appeal of the underdog, the respect for toughness and scrappiness, the admiration for military daring and bravery in the face of overwhelming odds. The exploits of the Israeli military have managed to crack through the Jewish stereotype and change the image of the modern Jew in the mind of the South.

"I always thought Jews were yellow," a filling station atten-
dant in south Georgia once said to me, "but them Israelites,
they're tough."

If the South has changed in the last twenty years in attitudes
toward Jews, Catholics, and blacks, then the Southern Baptist
church is changing also. Doctrinal disputes abound, but there
are deep psychological changes that were little noticed until a
Southern Baptist ran for president.

Before the Civil War, every church in the South with a
constituency in the North experienced a deep schism (including the Jews, who in the South feared for their safety and
wanted to remain quiet on the issue of slavery).

The Southern Baptist Convention was formed out of the abolitionist condemnation of the South, and slavery was banished
from its agenda. After the war, all the southern Protestant
churches that had claimed divine justification for slavery
turned inward. They abandoned for a hundred years talk of
social justice and embraced the notion of the "spirituality of
the church," maintaining that private witness and individual
soul-saving was the church's primary purpose and thus remov-
ing the church from any involvement in political and economic
issues. The opposite occurred in the black church. Born in
bondage, it cried out for freedom and grew into the heart of the
civil rights movement.

In the early stages of Carter's campaign when he seemed to
be speaking from a pulpit, it was Daddy King and Andy
Young—symbols of the black church—that gave him credibility in the North. When he spoke of the need for "simple
justice" in his acceptance speech, it echoed what he had said
in his men's Bible class in Plains, Georgia, an episode that
made front-page news across the South. Perhaps the more vital
issue for Jews and Catholics was not the narrow influence of
the Southern Baptists on Carter but the profound impact of
Carter on the 34,902 Southern Baptist congregations. To the
mass of Baptists, Carter was becoming something of a church
folk hero.

Carter's challenge as a Southern Baptist in the White House, with integrationist pride and black support, was to begin to build bridges between the black and white churches in the nation on the "public sins" of racial discrimination and urban blight.

The Klan is as great a historical burden for Southern Baptists as slavery is for the South as a whole. Perhaps Jews, evangelicals, mainline Protestants, and Catholics, recognizing the new southern realities revealed by the political campaign, could begin a dialogue aimed at mutual understanding beyond outdated stereotypes on all sides. It would be fitting, indeed, if the black church, with its common links to the Old and New testaments, could be the catalyst for the first steps toward building new trust and communication among the major American faiths.

It is fascinating that in 1992 another Southern Baptist, Bill Clinton, ran a campaign without the religious rhetoric or fervent born-again confession that so characterized the Carter campaign. But Carter was running as an outsider in the aftermath of Watergate, when people were disgusted with scandal, cover-up, threats of impeachment, and abuses of government. Gerald Ford was a classic Washington insider, a career congressional leader who was elevated to the presidency after Richard Nixon resigned. Ford promptly pardoned Nixon, thereby enveloping his presidency in a cloud of complicity and mistrust. I recall a conversation with a friend who said during the Democratic primaries of 1976 that "America is looking for a combination of a Boy Scout and a savior."

Carter's religious confessions began in North Carolina when George Wallace was a formidable obstacle to his nomination. Subsequently, his "I'll never lie to you" campaign of trust and honesty in government was an intended counterpoint to the suspicions about Ford. And his open religious affirmation cut deeply into the moral majority campaigns that were making headway in the fundamentalist white churches in the South.

In contrast, Bill Clinton's 1992 campaign against George Bush was so anchored in a failed economy that from the beginning, he muted any distracting themes. And there was much to be lost by any reminders of the presidency of Jimmy Carter. In fact, during one of the presidential debates, when Bush was comparing interest rates and inflation in 1992 to the "last southern democrat governor in office," Clinton promptly complained that Bush "wants to run against Jimmy Carter or anyone else other than me."

With Ronald Reagan's 1980 words "Are you better off now than you were four years ago?" still lingering in the voters' minds, it was important for Clinton not to remind voters of Carter's economic record, even to the point of carefully avoiding that same ringing question to Bush that Reagan used against Carter in 1980. Subliminally, however, with similarities in accent and geography, it was inevitable that the economic hardships of the Carter years would become part of the Republican litany of charges against Clinton. Religious talk, to a man like Clinton who does not teach Sunday school or a weekly men's Bible class, or even wear his religious beliefs on his sleeve, would have struck a false note in any case. Even bland fundamentalist rhetoric by Clinton would have caused a negative reaction (as it did for Carter in 1976) among Jewish voters who were upset with Bush for pressuring Israel during his four-year term, and among ethnic Catholic voters, who were part of the Reagan Democrats that Clinton sought to lure back to him by appealing to their concern over the economy. (Clinton received more than 80 percent of the Jewish vote.)

Seeing the economy as a losing issue, the Republicans and Bush walked into a right-wing trap of their own creation, structuring a 1992 Republican convention around "family values." Speech after speech at the Houston convention railed against abortion, homosexuality, gun control, and pornography, and advocated prayer in the schools and parochial school choice. Convention managers even allowed Marilyn Quayle to attack Hillary Clinton for being a working mother. Bush would later

complain that "the Democrats left G-O-D out of their platform," but at a time when more than seventy percent of the
country, in national polls, were concerned about the economy,
most voters dismissed such talk as a transparent ploy to avoid
the real issues. With Ross Perot reminding voters of Bush's
responsibility for the deficit, the Clinton campaign's strict discipline in avoiding sideshow issues paid off in a resounding
victory in November, bringing into office with him a Democratic Congress with a mandate to move forcefully on economic
issues and the potential to change policies and directions in
almost every domestic policy area.

14

The Natural Superiority
of Southern Politicians

When Richard Nixon learned that Senator Sam Ervin of North Carolina would be chairman of the special Senate committee investigating the Watergate break-ins, he moaned on tape to John Dean, "Goddam it . . . Ervin works even harder than most of our southern gentlemen. They are great politicians. They are just more clever than the others. Just more clever."

Nixon had watched the southern establishment at work in the Senate for decades. He knew that, when matters of the Constitution are at stake, "the club" of southerners in the Senate asserts its historic responsibilities. The White House had a battle on its hands—and it wasn't just *The Washington Post*, the CIA, the FBI, and the courts that would have to be manipulated. Now Nixon would face the United States Senate Incarnate and Corporate, with its collective conscience stirring from deep within southern history, biblical and titanic, righteousness from southern fundamentalism come to summon them all, sinners and investigators, to the marble halls of the lawmakers for justification and judgment.

Any southern writer can wax ecstatic about such a scene, but David Leon Chandler's chauvinism runs rampant in his

1977 book *The Natural Superiority of Southern Politicians.* His thesis is that "the South has produced the pre-eminent geniuses of all American political history," a contribution unrecognized by the nation because "conquerors, not losers, write history." Chandler charges that the major universities, newspapers, magazines, and broadcast media in the North have "written and lectured and preached for Northern audiences. . . . Harvard University traditionally focuses on the New England contribution to the American Revolution. . . . The Southerners are treated more or less as footnotes."

The author seeks to set the record straight with an analysis of American history focusing on the lives of Thomas Jefferson, Patrick Henry, Richard Henry Lee, John Randolph, George Washington, James Monroe, and James Madison; then on to Andrew Jackson, John C. Calhoun, and Jefferson Davis; and finally Woodrow Wilson, Huey Long, Sam Rayburn, Richard Russell, Tom Connally, Wright Patman, Lyndon Johnson, John Stennis, Herman Talmadge, and Sam Ervin.

"During the past two hundred years," he writes, "Southerners have invented the Declaration of Independence; the world's first written national constitution . . . the concept of judicial review . . . and that unique body, the United States Senate." He adds that southerners also "invented" other American political institutions such as the two-party system, the filibuster, the seniority system, and the leadership that passed the New Deal, the United Nations, and the Great Society. "And yet," he argues, "this staggering array of accomplishment has gone without credit. The Southern mind and culture . . . has instead been given the image of an outlaw camp; impoverished in goods and ideas . . . quick to shoot, quick with the rope, having no principle other than its own miserable survival."

The book is a presentation of southerners without warts, a song of praise to the South *in excelsis Deo.* It depicts a leadership that is always cloaked in first principles, that is the protector of tradition and stability—the very embodiment of the Constitution.

It's a puzzling argument, since no one who suffered through the bicentennial some years ago could have detected any lack of tribute to the founding Virginians who gave the nation life. Nor have Andrew Jackson or Woodrow Wilson been overlooked by the proclaimers of greatness. What seems to be bothering the author is the reluctance of the nation to acknowledge the wisdom and contribution of the congressional leaders of the past forty years and to link them to the legends of the colonial era as products of the same ground and tradition.

Lord knows, every southern senator believes it. But another book could have been written calling the southern-dominated Senate obstructionist, filibustered to the point of ineptitude, arrogant, and the cynical protector of white supremacy until the sit-ins and the civil rights movement finally forced Congress to act.

Yet, in this premise of southern superiority there is a grain of truth, which may be characterized as southern shrewdness. The author calls the Senate "a country legislature picked up and removed from the 1800s and given a place in our time." The northern and western states may grow in industry and population, but in the Senate the states are equal, and the senator of the smallest state can become head of the most powerful committee.

"The secret is seniority," says the author. "It is a system whereby in 1975, an elderly, conservative collection of self-employed, small-town lawyers and farmers, mostly from the South and entirely white, share with the President and the Supreme Court the running of a nation which is largely liberal, city-dwelling, and salaried."

A senator elected from outside the South, for instance, might have arrived in Washington ambitious but largely alone and inexperienced, whereas a new senator from the South had home folks he could call on from at least eleven other states, as well as advice and counsel from the most powerful leaders in the Senate. Southerners approached the Senate as a region and controlled the Senate to protect the South from federal interference. They developed what the author calls "the protégé tradition," whereby young southern lawmakers were informally "adopted," taken under the wing of the wise old leaders, and steered into positions of power. So John Nance Garner from Texas "adopted" Sam Rayburn, who was the patron of Congressman Lyndon Johnson (who as senator was the protégé of Georgia's senator, Richard Russell), who "played the role to platoons of incoming Senators and Congressmen" including Senator Sam Nunn of Georgia.

Chandler rarely mentions the southern senators whose politics ruled them out of "The Club"—Tennessee's Estes Kefauver and Albert Gore, Alabama's Lister Hill, Texas's Ralph Yarborough, North Carolina's Frank Graham, and South Carolina's Olin Johnston—progressives whose careers gave a measure of credibility and authenticity to the candidacy of Jimmy Carter, the first southern president in a hundred years.

In *The Ethnic Southerners*, George Brown Tindall, one of the South's foremost historians, has written a series of essays in which he puts forth in vigorous prose some unconventional ideas about the South.

Tindall proclaims that the farewells to Dixie have been so frequent in the last hundred years that "the Vanishing South will have staged one of the most prolonged disappearing acts since the decline and fall of Rome." He believes that the "enduring spell cast by the South" stems from "Southern ethnicity," and that the South has survived because it has "embodied the purest Americanism (with overtones of nativism and fundamentalism)" when most American values are under siege. He quotes North Carolina newspaper editor Jonathan Daniels: "For good or ill, being a Southerner is like being a Jew. And indeed, more needs to be written about the similarity of the minds and emotions of the Jew, the Irishman, the Southerner, and perhaps the Pole, as a basis for the better understanding of each of them and of them all." Tindall believes that the experience that has bound southerners and other ethnics together is "the migration from a peasant background into the mills and towns. It has been to bear a common stigma as the perpetual outsider, yet for that reason to be fascinating to other folk."

What the South seems to lack, Tindall almost suggests, is a Norman Mailer, a Betty Friedan, or a Malcolm X to write visceral essays about second-class citizenship. Instead, there was H. L. Mencken, the villain of these essays, who raised South-baiting to a high art. Tindall calls him "the hatchet man from Baltimore"; during the Scopes trial and after, Mencken sold the nation the myth of the "yowling yokels" and the "Homo Boobians" in the "miasmic jungles" of the South.

The Jewish-southern-Irish-Polish analogy breaks down when one considers how much authentic material Mencken and other critics had to work with. Injustice and exploitation were rife in mill villages, and on chain gangs and tenant farms. The Ku Klux Klan was a reality, as were the Scottsboro trials, Bilbo and Rankin, Emmett Till, the Birmingham bombing, Bull Connor's dogs, Orval Faubus and later the murders of Medgar Evers, Michael Schwerner, and James Chaney, among others. Southern outrages followed one after the other as the poor whites reacted violently to their crumbling order in the way that history dictated they must. It's not easy to be a loser in a land that glorifies success, to be poor in a land of plenty, to be guilty in a country that celebrates its innocence.

Moreover, Tindall's "Southern white ethnic" does not guzzle beer and cuss the Yankees in a vacuum. As the author points out, "Three and a half centuries of confrontation upon the Southern soil have marked the culture of both black and white. The experience of each, while different, has touched the experience of the other. Like other aspects of ethnicity, this becomes most apparent when either group moves North and encounters the selfsame response that greeted earlier migrants from the Hapsburg and Romanov empires. . . . Southerners white and black share the bonds of a common heritage, indeed a common tragedy, and often speak a common language, however seldom they may acknowledge it."

During the 1976 election a Catholic newspaper claimed that "Jimmy Carter thinks he's a Southern Jack Kennedy but he could end up a Baptist Al Smith." Could an outsider Democratic coalition of Jews, Catholics, blacks, and rednecks hold together for a white southern governor? A Carter radio ad that played across the South was designed to appeal to the pickup-truck vote. It said: "We've been the butt of every bad joke for a hundred years. Don't let the Washington politicians keep one of *us* out of the White House."

That's a familiar refrain to urban minorities, which suggests that northerners might better understand the mood of the South today if they could picture southerners as ethnics like themselves. A justifiable suspicion still exists among many Americans who perceive so many inconsistencies about the region— the lazy South and the fighting South; the segregationist South and the liberal South; the booster South and the populist South; the rapacious urban South and the land-worshiping rural South; the black South and the white South.

Even in 1992, the nation's prejudice toward the South and its suspicion of southern politicians have presented a constant dilemma for Bill Clinton. There are many reasons. He is, after all, from the state that gave the nation Orval Faubus and the Little Rock crisis of 1957 (when Clinton was ten years old). All through the primaries in the North, his accent nonetheless generated a flood of bad images from southern history, even when he offered progressive and carefully articulated views. The press continued to call him "slick Willie." When he sounded more moderate and showed himself to be capable of complex analysis and subtle thinking, as any Yale Law School graduate and Rhodes scholar was trained to be, to those in the press who were cynical and searching for sound bites or to the ordinary voter accustomed to easy answers who found him evasive and long-winded, he appeared to be just another Governor Foghorn. He was trapped in a prison of southern history—literature, films, television news, and entertainment images. These visceral ghosts of racism have shadowed every southern candidate for president, from Estes Kefauver to Lyndon Johnson, from Jimmy Carter to Bill Clinton. But the story is complicated, as are the characters in the long-running drama of southern politics, because the region has been transformed in the last thirty years, especially by the civil rights movement, the courts, the empowerment of millions of black voters since 1965. The campaign of 1992 determined that these old images will not endure and that the New South has made the transition into the mainstream politics of the nation. And the Clinton-Gore years in Washington will test, one more time, the bold premise of the natural superiority of Southern politicians.

Part III

The Past and the Future

15

Presidential Politics and the
Democratic National Conventions:
1964—1976

I have been to every Democratic National Convention since 1964 but have only written about 1964, 1968, 1972, and 1976, because in those years I was loosely affiliated with the North Carolina delegation through Terry Sanford. Sanford announced his candidacy for the presidency twice—in 1972 and 1976—but was never able to break through into national awareness. He was elected governor at the age of forty-two in 1960, and was prohibited by the state constitution from serving beyond 1964. After becoming president of Duke University in 1969 and serving for sixteen years, he was elected to the U.S. Senate in 1986 and served only one term. Open-heart surgery in the middle of the 1992 campaign cost him a double-digit lead in the polls and he lost his seat and the opportunity to serve in Congress during the Clinton-Gore administration.

1964: Atlantic City and Big Brother Lyndon

The boardwalk at Atlantic City, in those pre-gambling days, was seedy, splinter-ridden, gray, and weathered, evoking a by-

gone era in its mood. Walking for miles up and down its long
vistas, seeing the delegates strolling in their campaign hats
mingling with blue-haired elderly ladies, one had the feeling
that it absorbed the people and paraphernalia of politics in its
neon doorways and from its souvenir barkers as easily as it
blended the latest fad in hula hoops or glow-in-the-dark brace-
lets. This was Lyndon Johnson's revenge on the Democratic
party. He had been shunted aside for what he regarded as the
upstart Kennedys at the 1960 convention and was now running
alone for his party's nomination without a vice president on the
buttons to share in his reflected glory. The image of his half-
smiling visage loomed large over the convention hall and along
the boardwalks, as impressive as any Big Brother in an Or-
wellian future. The last night, the outline of his face literally
covered the sky, etched in red, white, and blue fireworks.

I was there as a former aide and speech writer to Richardson
Preyer, the defeated candidate for the Democratic nomination
for governor, who had been Governor Terry Sanford's choice to
succeed him. The North Carolina delegation was divided—
half had been appointed by outgoing Governor Sanford and
half by Dan Moore, the victorious gubernatorial nominee who
was supported by the textile plutocracy and was keeping his
distance from the national ticket. Sanford had bolted the Johnson wing of the party in 1960 to nominate John F. Kennedy for
president, so the Kennedy connection in North Carolina was
emotional and direct. Oh, what a glorious feeling of participation and inclusion had shot through the Sanford wing of the
party in 1960! There was the young governor, Terry Sanford,
nominated at age forty-two, who had abandoned the old guard
of Lyndon Johnson and was standing before the convention and
on national television to nominate the young prince of Camelot.
A joint campaign would lead to a victory for the Kennedy/
Sanford ticket that fall. Now at the end of his term, Sanford was
attending this 1964 convention to watch the same Lyndon
Johnson claim the victory he lost four years earlier. (Evelyn
Lincoln, President Kennedy's secretary, would later write that,

just before the assassination, Kennedy had told her he had decided to drop Johnson from the ticket in 1964 and pick Sanford as his running mate. Whether this was true or not, Johnson would ultimately not only forgive Sanford but embrace him as a close political associate).

It was my first convention, and I roamed around the hall with all the curiosity of a country mouse newly liberated from a bag of flour into a vast new barn of fresh scents and images. In the backstage part of the arena, and in the bowels beneath it, were the trailers and trucks representing the eyes and ears of a nation and a world in attendance. Behind a curtained area along a vast labyrinth were the rat-a-tat-tat world and half-eaten sandwiches of the *New York Times* and the *Washington Post*, *Time*, and *Newsweek*. The logos of the networks and of the signs leading to the Japanese, German, and British broadcasting services lent an air of worldwide importance to what history would view as a rather cut-and-dried convention, with LBJ's tortuous dangling of the vice presidency to Senator Hubert Humphrey dominating the convention gossip and providing the only tension of the week.

There were, of course, what most delegates viewed as the "troublemakers" in the wings and on the convention floor. Out on the boardwalk, it was widely rumored (photographs dominated the front pages) that feminists were burning bras in protest. It was a sensuous thought to those of us confronting militant feminism for the first time—not the bras so much as the brazen public display of bras in the hands of speakers with bullhorns.

And there was the attempt of the Mississippi Freedom Democratic Party delegation, led by Fannie Lou Hamer, to challenge the all-white delegation of the Democratic party of Senators James Eastland and John Stennis that the Johnson-Humphrey ticket would need in 1964 to carry the state. I remember seeing Fannie Lou in action for the first time and being overwhelmed by her imposing presence. This was a re-markable woman from the tenant-farming soil and rural poverty of Mississippi. With her memorable eyes and a moral authority to her manner, she was like a black Joan of Arc, plumper and less heroically garbed but nevertheless storming the barricades of the uncomfortable establishment in Mississippi and thereby posing an embarrassing choice for President Johnson and the managers of the convention. The national Democratic party did not want to be seen by the world and by millions of black voters in the urban ghettoes expelling representatives of this moral crusade of excluded blacks in Mississippi. Besides, the Freedom Party delegation was integrated, and included such whites as Hodding Carter III of Greenville, the up-and-coming young editor of the *Delta Democrat-Times*, who represented another kind of future for the South. But neither did the president want to expel the friends and supporters of Jim Eastland and John Stennis, two senators with growing seniority who were part of Johnson's base in the Senate and who, in any event, were important symbols to millions of whites who would be needed if the ticket were to carry the South and defeat Goldwater in the fall.

Hubert Humphrey was dispatched to try to work out a compromise so that both delegations could be seated. (Over the next four years, Johnson would continue to use Humphrey in this role—as emissary to the liberal wing of the Democratic party—and it would slowly erode Humphrey's support and drain him of principle, drop by drop. By 1968 he was an apologist and "happy warrior" in behalf of the Vietnam War.)

This convention would also be remembered for its tribute to John F. Kennedy. Johnson's managers had postponed it until after Humphrey's nomination, out of fear that any appearance by Robert Kennedy would stir the delegates' emotions and force him onto the ticket.

They may not have been wrong. The film *A Thousand Days*, featuring Richard Burton's voice and words from the musical *Camelot*, filled a darkened hall, and swept all of us up in the memories of a fallen young king, killed in his prime, mourned by his beautiful widow and small children. "Ask every person if he's heard the story, and tell it strong and clear if he has not, that once there was a fleeting wisp of glory—called 'Camelot.'"

I looked around during the film. Everyone was crying unashamedly; hardened political operatives and delegates had tears streaming down their faces. One woman knelt in prayer in the aisles near the North Carolina delegation. A black delegate and a white delegate stood with their arms around each other's shoulders. The ten-minute ovation that followed when Robert Kennedy appeared was tinged with an anti-Johnson undercurrent; Bobby was the choice, without question, but these delegates were not going to challenge their party's president. Hubert Humphrey had already been nominated. A high point of the Johnson presidency—a landslide victory that fall over Barry Goldwater—would slowly sink into the jungles of Vietnam and set the stage for the 1968 convention.

1968: Chicago, Where the Streets Swallowed Hubert Humphrey

The excitement among the North Carolina delegation before the Chicago convention was very real, because former Governor Terry Sanford was considered by the national press to be a potential vice presidential candidate for Hubert Humphrey (who would certainly need a southerner to balance his ticket), or for Eugene McCarthy (who had even mentioned Sanford's name once when asked about a running mate), as he had been for Bobby Kennedy before the assassination. Sanford's closeness to the Kennedys would be considered an asset to a Humphrey candidacy, a means of uniting the party, and those of us who were with the delegation had even prepared "Sanford for Vice President" buttons and placards, in case lightning struck.

The deaths of Martin Luther King and Robert Kennedy had

turned American politics into something ugly and fearsome and had taken much of the joy out of "the game" for me and for so many others.

By 1968, I had been living in New York for over a year, but when a former gubernatorial aide to Sanford called and said, "We might need you," I could not resist and booked my trip to Chicago. I stayed in one of the rooms reserved for the North Carolina delegation at the Blackstone Hotel, which was directly beside the Hilton, on Grant Park, where Vice President Humphrey was headquartered. The elevators were jumping with the George McGovern campaign staff; the South Dakota senator had taken up the candidacy of Bobby Kennedy after the assassination, and a cluster of celebrity reporters, writers, and old Kennedy associates were dropping by to say hello. One of the staff, a mini-skirted woman with long auburn hair, aviator glasses, and the self-confident gait of a gazelle, drew particular attention in the lobby. Years later at a dinner party in New York, I would recall that time in a conversation with Gloria Steinem and ask why she never wrote about the McGovern campaign of 1968.

The Blackstone had a grand political history: Harry Truman had been staying there during the 1944 convention when he received the invitation from President Franklin Roosevelt to join him on the ticket. Maybe history would summon us, too.

From my window, I could look out on Grant Park. Chicago, that July, was not an ordinary convention city; tens of thousands of students, antiwar activists, yippies, hippies, radicals, folksingers, and underground journalists had descended on the city. The parks in front of the hotel were filled with people milling around small campfires, and by thousands of mounted police watching them; there were also scores of armed military police, who were guarding the entrances to all the hotels on the park. There were so many checkpoints that even getting a sandwich required delegates' credentials.

Several of us walked through the parks as if we were tourists, stepping over the sleeping bags, guitar cases, and sandwich wrappings and talking to the students, whose faces were unforgettable. They represented, to me, some of the best of their generation. The previous spring after the McCarthy campaign had run out of gas, I had worked on Long Island as a volunteer for Allard Lowenstein's campaign for Congress and had met many students who had been in New Hampshire working for McCarthy and then gravitated back to New York to be involved with a winnable campaign. Al was an old friend whose charisma and political talents had produced the national "Dump Johnson" antiwar campaign. The entry of Robert Kennedy into the race after Johnson had withdrawn had filled Al and many of the student workers he had recruited with dismay and confusion. I always felt that Al's decision to leave the McCarthy campaign and return to Long Island to run for Congress (he was successful) was a way to avoid having to choose between Eugene McCarthy, to whom he was grateful for entering the race after Robert Kennedy had refused his entreaties, and Kennedy, himself, who was truly one of Al's heroes.

The massive challenge of the antiwar movement was in full view in Chicago that week. Though the antiwar protesters had lost in the primaries to Lyndon Johnson's vice president, their presence was so threatening and Humphrey's need to dramatize his independence from Johnson so great, that the president whose face, image, personality, and policies had completely dominated the 1964 convention was almost invisible at this one. He could not even come from Washington to bid his party farewell.

As the week progressed, one could feel the tension and the anger growing. I had lunch with an old Yale Law School friend, Jerry Brown, who was part of the California delegation and was just starting his own political career. I was surprised to hear him say that he was going back to California early because the issues were all decided and he did not want to stay for the troubles or the crowning of Hubert Humphrey.

The Hilton Hotel became an armed camp after protesters charged the front door, broke a huge plate of glass, and threw a stink bomb into the lobby. The unsuccessful effort to clean it up left the rugs smelling for days like regurgitated milk mixed with cleaning fluid.

Coming out on the street on Wednesday morning, I introduced myself to Larry Spivak of "Meet the Press." "If Sanford is selected," he said, "tell him we would like to have him on." Suddenly, I felt a sharp pain in my eyes. I turned to see Spivak wince as he started coughing and reaching for a handkerchief. Tear gas. From Grant Park. I did not know then that it was the beginning of the violent confrontation that would forever mark the convention in the eyes of history.

I was out of my hotel most of the day of the presidential nomination, rushing around to see friends, going to state caucuses, attending a press conference at which Eugene McCarthy conceded. He was asked whom he would have selected to be vice president. "Oh, I don't know," he replied. "Maybe what's-his-name from North Carolina—Terry Sanford." It was a typical McCarthy comment—diffident, off-hand, self-mocking.

I ran into a former aide of Sanford's in the lobby who told me that Senator Ed Muskie of Maine had been selected for the ticket, and that Sanford was looking for me because Humphrey had called to ask Sanford to place Humphrey's name in nomination.

I finally caught up with Sanford late in the afternoon at the hotel and rode in a limousine with him for ten minutes while he outlined what he wanted to say. Sanford is an excellent writer when he has time, and he had already jotted notes on cards. He was very nonchalant about it. "If you can, just try to find something not obvious and give it to me at the convention; I plan to make it short." He dropped me off at the hotel. From the sounds coming from the park, I could almost imagine a great angry beast emerging from the bowels of the earth, its ugly growls building in intensity. The protests were beginning.

I was getting nervous. I had to leave for the convention hall almost immediately, so I rushed through the crowd in the lobby, waited an eternity for an elevator, changed clothes, grabbed a yellow pad, and headed for the Hilton next door so I could board the North Carolina delegates' bus.

Because the streets were lined with the National Guard and tanks, the bus was leaving very early for the trip out to the stockyards and the huge coliseum. Mounted police and troops equipped with helmets, plastic face guards, and billy clubs were everywhere as we wound our way through the streets, accompanied by motorcycle police with sirens blasting. We were later arriving than I had planned and the convention had already been gaveled to order when we arrived.

Even though the coliseum was isolated behind a huge fence, it did indeed seem, as we walked through the front doors and into the bright spotlights, as if the whole world was watching.

But I had a job to do, so I ran to find the CBS booth and a researcher I used to date in Washington. I asked her if I could see her file on Hubert Humphrey and if I could borrow a typewriter and a desk. Monitors were everywhere, and as I raced through the file of biographical data on Humphrey and sat typing out a draft of Sanford's seconding speech, I suddenly found myself watching the horrifying scene of Mayor Daley's police wading in on the student protesters out in Grant Park. There were dozens of monitors, and all the reporters, researchers, visitors, and CBS staff were mesmerized by the scenes. Typing away and occasionally looking up, I could see that the nominations of McCarthy and McGovern were moving along more quickly than expected and that I had to hurry. Then I saw in the monitors the face of Senator Abe Ribicoff of Connecticut, yelling directly at Daley to "call off his Nazi storm troopers," and the cameras picked up, for lip readers, Daley's beefy angry face and his distorted mouth replying, "Jew bastard." I was paralyzed at the typewriter. The seconders for Humphrey were beginning and I had not finished.

Eric Sevareid, whom I had met several times when my brother worked for CBS News in Washington, walked by, rec-

ognized me, and said, in a friendly but curious way to a very
intent young man bearing down on the typewriter, "Hello.
What are you doing?"

I was typing out something about how the plains of Minneso-
ta had nourished young Hubert Humphrey, and I really did not
have time to talk, even though I was looking up at a face and a
familiar shock of white hair that had been on the screen in
millions of living rooms perhaps thousands of times.

"Mr. Sevareid," I answered, "you really wouldn't believe me
if I told you."

I ripped the last page from the roller, ran for the door, and
rushed down the stairs that led to the convention floor.

The delegates on the floor of the hall were bathed in television lights. They were gathered in clusters around the TV sets
and were growling and screaming at Daley; they would point to
the sets and then at him, demanding that he acknowledge the
violence and stop it. They could see themselves on television
in the hall while they were watching television record the chaos
outside. It was a bizarre scene: the screens in the hall would
show horses and tear gas, then Walter Cronkite, then delegates; we would watch the violence, then watch ourselves
watching the violence. We were in the set, on the convention
floor, out of the TV set. It was real; it was surreal.

I began to run as fast as I could down the side of the hall
toward the rostrum, through this strange scene, to try to get to
Sanford before he stepped to the podium. A guard stopped me
because I had no special podium credentials. I begged him; I
showed him the typed pages. He must have felt sorry for me
because he let me go up the stairs. Sanford was standing there,
just offstage, ready to go on. I handed him the notes and
retreated to listen. He had written his own remarks and
skillfully folded some of my stuff in. It worked, smooth as silk.
I felt both relieved and pleased with myself. But, of course, no
one in the hall was listening and the world didn't give a damn
what was said. The nominators didn't even get broadcast. It

was what the world was watching outside the convention that counted.

Going back to the hotel, the bus at first raced with police escort and then inched along the streets of Chicago, through the helmeted police, rotating red sirens, fire engines, soldiers, and tanks, past parks drenched with spotlights and filled with national guard equipment. All was quiet, but it was like passing through a war zone. I will never forget the scene as we got off the bus and walked into the Hilton. The entry lobby, which had stairs on both sides winding up to a mezzanine, looked like a hospital ward. The young McCarthy kids were everywhere, with their heads bandaged, their girlfriends cradling them in their arms in an almost Pieta-like tableau. And they were murmuring something, like a mantra, over and over again, looking at delegates with pity and sorrow. I stopped to listen to the slow and measured cadence: "The party is dead. The party is dead. The party is dead."

Recent history might have been different had it not been for that evening. Vietnam and the Chicago convention (like twin volcanos spewing hot lava over a village) consumed the Humphrey-Muskie ticket. Sanford had been asked by Larry O'Brien, head of the Democratic party, and by Lyndon Johnson, before his withdrawal, to manage the reelection campaign; McCarthy had felt him out, through friends in Washington, for the same role; Humphrey would tap him again as chairman of the campaign that fall. But Hubert Humphrey never really recovered from the convention, and I always felt that he did not really deserve what he received. Richard Nixon was elected and the war went on for another six years. All the bitterness of Watergate and the years of bombing, death, anger, and pain followed. Politics was turning ugly and fierce and punishing.

Being at a convention, one forgets that there is a worldwide audience, and foreign reactions and exotic observations. Years later, a friend was in a remote part of the Soviet Union visiting relatives from his mother's family who had stayed behind when the others came to America at the turn of the century. He was ushered in the door, past relatives who looked just like him, into a back room where he found himself seated at a simple table in front of an old man with a white beard.

"We saw the films of the Chicago convention," the old man said in broken Yiddish/English. The Russians had shown the violent street scenes, the billy clubs, and the galloping horses in movie theaters as propaganda. "We noticed in the background a number of kosher butchers. Tell me, do many Jews keep kosher in America?"

1972: Miami—All Night Long with George McGovern

I flew down to Washington to attend the Terry Sanford announcement in 1972, because I wanted to be there when he launched his first campaign for president. His two books— *Storm Over the States* and *But What About the People?*—had been minor successes, and he had three years as president of Duke University under his belt. There was a good turnout of press and friends. Some of the national press wondered not about how Sanford would do against Nixon nor his position on the war but whether Sanford could beat back the challenge in his home state primary of Alabama's governor, George Wallace.

It was an unusual campaign, and most analysts believed that Sanford would have won had it not been for a maverick showing by Shirley Chisolm, the New York congresswoman eager to make her mark as the first black woman to run for president. Without her there, Sanford would have faced Wallace alone, in a battle for the soul of the state. Her presence played into Wallace's racial tactics, took away black votes from Sanford and generally exacerbated the racial rhetoric in the primary. Sanford lost his home state to Wallace, who only got 50.2 percent of the vote. (Chisolm later apologized to Sanford.)

It was a humiliating night in North Carolina, but Sanford gamely conceded, telling me it was well worth the effort to try to stop Wallace in the South. Everyone assumed that Sanford was really running for vice president, trying to appear viable to whoever the Democratic nominee was going to be. It was not true. He was serious about running for president, not vice president, but no one took him seriously.

I took leave from the Carnegie Corporation to go to the convention, because Sanford had decided to go all the way through the process—rent the trailer, play the game, be nominated by three speeches (which he asked me to write). The three nominators were Hodding Carter III, the editor of the *Greenville Times* in Mississippi, whose father had been a lonely voice of good sense in Mississippi in the thirties and forties; Howard Lee, the black mayor of Chapel Hill and a respected leader in the North Carolina black community; and Andrew Miller, the attorney general of Virginia.

This was George McGovern's convention, with mandated black and female participation in each delegation. As an antiwar candidate, he had many young people with him, including his campaign manager, Gary Hart, who was an old friend of mine from Yale Law School. We met on the convention floor; I was in a coat and tie and he was in shirt sleeves and jeans with a wide western belt, very calm and in control, talking quietly into a walkie-talkie in the center of the cyclone.

There will never again be two such nights back-to-back in a convention. On Tuesday, the convention took up the platform issues, and it was the greatest conglomeration of celebrities and delegates, alternates and hangers-on ever gathered. It lasted all night, and I vowed to stay up, sitting on the floor with my back against the podium, until the very end. It was a strange mixture of celebrities—Norman Mailer, Gloria Steinem, Sonny and Cher—and people were milling around, talking and moving through the crowds as if it were a giant cocktail party.

When the last plank came up, a woman approached the

podium and said, "I am a Democrat, I am a woman, and I am a lesbian." It was the first time a sexual preference plank had been offered in national politics. Had anyone been awake to hear her it would have been earthshaking, but my watch said five in the morning, and someone next to me turned and whispered, "Larry O'Brien, you're a genius."

The next night, the schedule got tangled up in presidential and vice presidential nominating speeches (Sanford's included), and McGovern did not get to deliver his acceptance speech until two in the morning. It was the best speech of McGovern's career—"Come Home, America"—and yet few people stayed up across the country to hear it. It was symptomatic of McGovern's organizational problems that the convention was so loosely managed, almost chaotic, and it was a bad omen for a national campaign.

His maverick campaign against the war brought many first-time delegates from all over the country to the convention, among them young women and men who were activists in various causes. Black, Asian, Hispanic, and white, they were intense, committed, and self-confident. I remember it as the most rousing and high-spirited convention ever. The antiwar constituency, beaten and clubbed in 1968, triumphed in 1972. The night of the debate about the feminist plank on the platform, Bella Abzug, the congresswoman from New York, stormed up and down the rows of the New York delegation in her picture hat, bumping people aside, telling the male delegates waiting to vote on the women's plank to "move your ass" to make way for the female alternates. And there was Congresswoman Shirley Chisolm at the black caucus, young black women standing on chairs yelling for her. When she said, "I ran because no man had the balls to do it," they all screamed as one, "Yeah!"

The outcome was foreordained, and I went to the Sanford trailer to be with Terry for the vote count. In some ways, he was pleased with the outcome. A couple of votes came in unexpectedly, and he ended up with 83-1/2 votes.

More important, though no one knew it then, in his own mind he had gone through a full dress rehearsal for 1976 and would be back. But as it turned out, Jimmy Carter, supported by the Coca-Cola wealthy and Georgia pride, would be the southern governor who would captivate the party. Under-funded, Sanford was forced to drop out in February, before the New Hampshire primary. Carter would go on to defeat a crippled George Wallace in North Carolina and Florida, thus setting the stage for his nomination—and election—as a southerner with black support.

1976: A New Coalition

Going through the Mill   In 1976, when Terry Sanford got off a plane in North Carolina after having spent four days in a Massachusetts hospital because of chest pains, his wife Margaret Rose told reporters at the airport, "Terry's a strong person. But the primaries are killing the candidates."

Whether Sanford withdrew from the Democratic race because of health, lack of money, or organizational problems is only part of the point. What the American people have to ask themselves is whether the system we've stumbled into for selecting candidates for the presidency produces the best leadership for the nation or just people with the stamina to get through the experience.

More important, does the selection process have much to do with being president?

The new finance laws expanded the length of time of the presidential campaign because a candidate has to raise money from more contributors. And that additional time means that it costs more than ever before, because running means setting up and staffing an office, traveling, hiring researchers and pollsters, and compiling extensive mailing lists.

With thirty-one primaries and no organization, a candidate

deciding whether to go through the process has a lot of ground to cover and usually must spend several years. Unfortunately, the burdens of candidacy do not coincide with the attention span of the American people. So candidates for president have to beg an awful lot of people for an awful lot of money at a time when most Americans are not even thinking about the next election yet.

Therefore, a candidate must have a job that gives him freedom to travel and research and staff help, but with no institutional pressure, like those of a university, pressing him.

Senators and congressmen and governors have a job designed for full-time politics, so the system more than ever before is weighted against non-officeholders.

The most distressing part of the Sanford candidacy, in my view, was the press's lack of interest in substantive issues. For six months, the only issues that interested them regarding any candidate were fund-raising and organization. In Sanford's case, that meant whether or not he could qualify for federal funds and could field a campaign. The lack of depth and interest by the press so frustrated him that, characteristically, when he did qualify, he refused to hold a news conference announcing it. He thought other issues were paramount.

But the media did not. Talk shows have to draw audiences and are more interested in celebrity and glibness than in deeper questions concerning the future of the country. National Sunday TV shows only have the appearance of enabling the candidates to meet the press. With four questioners, any answers longer than a couple of sentences make a candidate look as if he's filibustering.

The truth is that we have no forum for probing in depth the qualities of mind of presidential candidates. Thus a candidate like Sanford, who has written books on American government and comes from the more thoughtful world of the university, gets mangled in the nonstop motion and superficiality of the presidential sweepstakes. He's not a "serious" candidate because the press does not take him seriously; if he's not serious, he can't raise the money. It's a tragedy. Wisdom just doesn't sell in a razzmatazz age.

In the future, the men and women from business, the academy, the arts and sciences, will not be running for president. In the system we've developed, they haven't got a prayer. The irony is that once in the White House a president has no problem getting news media coverage or raising money. Can anyone suggest that a campaign tests anything else—say, honesty, character or, heaven help us, a grasp of the issues?

It seems that all a candidate needs is a repetitive speech he's been giving for a decade, or something the media call charisma. The staff works up a fifteen-second spot on nuclear weapons, a punchy statement on the environment, and a little something for minorities.

So the Terry Sanfords withdraw or don't run to begin with. And as the novelist R. M. Koster said in *Harper's*: "Terry Sanford may be the best qualified of all the candidates to handle Presidential problems, but certain of his qualities—his refusal to deal in catchy oversimplifications, for example—largely disqualify him as a vote-getter. Sanford is the kind of man who ought to be sentenced to serve four years in the White House—for our good, not for his. We use a different system, though."

We surely do, and we ought to ask if it keeps too many good people out.

Seen from a 1992 perspective, Sanford's withdrawal in 1976 merely set the stage for the rest of his public career. As André Gide, the French philosopher, remarked, "It is one of life's laws that as soon as one door closes, another opens." Duke University was that door for Sanford. He took a good university and made it a great one. And one of the ways he did it was by opening its admissions and its faculty to the very best, regardless of race, gender, or religion. At the time he retired, Duke had a student body that was truly diversified, about a quarter Jewish, a quarter Catholic, with a faculty open to all.

When Sanford's sixteen years at Duke ended in 1986, an editor of the *Washington Post* wrote that "Terry Sanford has committed his career . . . to the pursuit of excellence . . . [He] was in 1972 and 1976 by far the most distinguished, experienced and thoughtful candidate in either party. He should have gotten the job—he deserved it—and it is the Nation's loss that he did not."

But Sanford was not ready for the rocking chair or the fishing hole. The brutal 1984 campaign of Jesse Helms against a popular governor, Jim Hunt, shattered the spirits of the Democratic party, and Sanford decided to try to lead his state back from the precipice of far-right extremism to his mainstream vision of national leadership.

And on election night in 1986, two years after North Carolina elected Helms, Sanford's ideological opposite, to its other Senate seat, the young governor of 1960 won only his second election and became, at age 69, a seasoned senator. He was destined, however, to serve only one term. Health problems cost him his seat in 1992 and the chance to serve with a southern president who had admired him and publicly stated that he modeled his years in Arkansas after Sanford's record in North Carolina.

In assessing his political career in North Carolina, one must think of Terry Sanford in generational terms. Returning from European duty in World War II where he was a paratrooper in the Battle of the Bulge, Sanford became the heir to the legacy of populist governor Kerr Scott, and Dr. Frank Graham, the revered president of the University of North Carolina who served in the U.S. Senate in the late 1940s. Sanford built a political organization of returning veterans that won the governorship in 1960 and became the progressive force in the state for the next thirty years and beyond.

I am certain that Sanford regards his years as governor as the most creative of his public career and his contributions there the most satisfying. As the first New South governor to cast his future with a vigorous program of progressive policies on race and education, he has been cited as an inspiration and a role model by Jimmy Carter and Bill Clinton and dozens of other leaders who saw him in action.

His record as governor was extraordinary: by the end of the first two years, teacher pay raises averaged 22 percent, and almost 3,000 teachers were added to the system. By the end of his four-year term, Sanford had increased public-school budgets by 50 percent and university and college budgets by 70 percent. He started a system of community colleges that put every person within close proximity of an inexpensive higher education; he built experimental schools for underachievers and gifted children; he established the first state-supported school of the arts in America and pioneered by creating the first state antipoverty program in America—a local action program which Lyndon Johnson later adopted as the model for the war on poverty. He was the first southern governor to call for employment without regard to race, and then marshaled state and private efforts to end discrimination and carry out that pledge. It is no wonder that historians have rated him one of the ten best governors of any state in this century.

As governor, Terry Sanford saved North Carolina from the racial violence that engulfed the region in the 1960s. One must remember that he served in the era of Faubus of Arkansas, Wallace of Alabama, Talmadge of Georgia, and Barnett of Mississippi, in a state forging a path between the "massive resistance" of the Byrd machine in neighboring Virginia and the demagoguery of Strom Thurmond in South Carolina.

Breaking his state out of its regional parochialism and blunting the forces of reaction and extremism, inspiring it to reach out and embrace the future rather than fear it, especially with regard to race relations and education, giving North Carolina a progressive sense of itself and bequeathing the South a leadership model for the generation of southern governors that followed him—that is how Terry Sanford will be remembered, that is his legacy.

The End of the Line for Wallace   Jimmy Carter's victory over George Wallace in the North Carolina primary in 1976 represented the resolution of a historic conflict in the South and the end of the Wallace movement as a significant national force. What happened that Tuesday in a southern state could not be dismissed as just another event on the year's political calendar, for, in one way or the other, George Wallace had been the dominating force in southern politics for almost fifteen years, defining the issues and casting the arguments in simplistic racial terms.

Jimmy Carter was the perfect southern opponent for George Wallace. A moderate Deep South governor, he gave the "anti-Washington" voters an alternative to Wallace. An attractive campaigner with an easy manner, Carter played the gentleman in the briar patch, radiating all the New South confidence that permeates Atlanta and Charlotte and the other major cities in the region.

Carter was the new face that voters wanted to know; Wallace, the old face that voters were tired of. Carter's racial moderation contrasted with Wallace's record of extremism. Slumped in his wheelchair, Wallace seemed a pathetic shadow of the fire-eater of old. He was a throwback to the past, as unable to move politically as he was physically, subdued now but still ranting about the blacks on the school bus, reminding everyone of the old days of bayonets and fire hoses and the National Guard. Carter's charisma and newness made Wallace seem even more drab and outdated.

In 1972, the country was divided, and Wallace used his characteristic rhetoric in the primaries. He had stood in the schoolhouse door; he was a symbol of opposition to federal intervention and busing. "Send them a message" was his theme, and he was asking for support not in order to be elected president, but so he could influence the final choice and the party platform.

By 1976, though, the abuses of the Nixon years had pumped disgust and disillusionment into the national body politic. Wanting to capitalize on this loss of faith, Wallace decided to run in 1976 as a real candidate for president, to visit Europe

like a future head of state, and move toward the mainstream—
in short, to run to win. In so doing, he planted the seeds of his
undoing.

I had spent time in North Carolina during the 1972 primary
when Wallace won 50.2 percent of the vote against the former
governor, Terry Sanford. Voters were buying Wallace's "message" campaign. But did they want him to be president? "No,"
a waitress said, "I don't want his hand on the button." "Of
course not," replied a barbershop operator, "but Ole' George
will tear 'em up at the convention." The polls verified that
Wallace was a protest candidate, not a real choice for the
presidency. Nobody wanted him to be president; they just
wanted to vote for somebody who would tell off the Yankees.

But four years later, charming the Yankees seemed to be
more in order. Carter's early victories made southerners proud
to be represented outside the region by him; his smile projected a more graceful South than did Wallace's sneer. Thus,
the North Carolina primary wasn't a campaign between Wallace
and a favorite son (which had been part of Wallace's advantage
over Terry Sanford in 1972) but a battle between brothers over
who could best represent the South to the nation.

Because all the other southern candidates had dropped out,
Carter was even able to assume Wallace's usual underdog role,
a favored position for southerners ever since the Confederate
foot soldiers faced northern cannons. Wallace, ridiculing his
opposition in the fall of 1975, began to look more like a bully
turned loser than would have been the case had there been no
southern challenge to his self-constructed bandwagon. In biblical terms, the brother of light bested the brother of darkness.

Carter cut deep into Wallace support in another way, as well.
He came from a fundamentalist Christian background, and he
preached the politics of love and faith. The Wallace movement
had had a religious fervor from the beginning; now Carter's
campaign was reaching out to the true believers and offering
the southern church vote honesty and decency in the Oval
Office.

The tragedy of the Wallace movement was that his third-party escapade took millions of believers away from the mainstream into ineffectual protest. They were not bad Americans—as populists, they distrusted banks and the oil companies; they were victims, most of them, of technology and urbanization; they lived close to the land or worked in the mills and worried about their jobs (so many were on welfare and unemployment that Wallace dropped his "welfare chiselers" line altogether in North Carolina). They had been exploited by Wallace for his own aggrandizement for over a decade, but never again. The branches and leaves of brutal, direct racist politics would wither now that its southern roots had been cut.

It was no wonder that the liberal press in the North was suspicious of Carter, since the distorted image of George Wallace had represented southerners for so long. But Wallace was the last of the southern demagogues, the end of the line going back to Pitchfork Ben Tillman, Eugene Talmadge, and their "moderate" counterparts, Ross Barnett and Lester Maddox.

History will record that Wallace could turn on the yahoos, but in the end it was the South itself that shut him off and rejected him.

New York City and the Carter-King Revival   I was deeply ashamed to be a white southerner that April night in 1968 when Martin Luther King, Jr., was assassinated; I experienced a nauseating, profound humiliation over what was not just another race killing but the cruel crushing of a dream. I felt despair for the South, for the madness of the last hundred years preceding King's death. The hatred had reached its zenith, and the years of sit-ins and civil rights protest were temporarily overcome with brutal white vengeance. The faith of blacks and the hope they shared with many whites shattered with that bullet, and America spun into the abyss of chaos and disillusionment.

In the days that followed there were scenes of Robert Kennedy, dead, too, only sixty days after he pleaded with a ghetto audience for calm; menacing looks from Lester Maddox's highway patrol in Atlanta, as thousands of mourners filed past the state capitol; the funeral at the Ebenezer Baptist Church and the outpouring of sorrow, as the soothing home tones of the black church immersed in lamentation the King family in the South and blacks throughout the country. It was a stirring service of faith, and if they could still hope, could I?

And in Chicago that year at the Democratic National Convention, violence continued to stalk the political process—it somehow couldn't stop. What had been Lyndon Johnson's 1964 Texas-size landslide of support was torn apart by the politics of war and bombings, nightsticks and tear gas. In the bitterness that followed, with a nation searching for redemption turning almost in desperation for a way out of the miasma, who else was waiting in the wings but "the New Nixon," matured, they said, by years in the wilderness?

All of this was washing over me at the 1976 convention as I watched Martin Luther King's father, "Daddy" King, command absolute silence for his delivery of a soaring wrap-up benediction that endorsed Carter and gave his national congregants a taste of Sundays in Atlanta; Congressman Andrew Young, the closet King aide, nominate a white Georgia governor for president of the United States, and the widow Coretta King present the plank on human rights, while the King children, now almost grown, greeted the crowd.

The images that emerged from the convention echo in memory: Jackie Onassis at her first convention since 1956; Amy Carter, at age eight the first little girl in the White House since Caroline Kennedy; Lillian Carter, the feisty, straight-talking former nurse who ministered to the poor of Plains (Rose Kennedy was the last mother of a candidate to captivate the nation with her faith). These were subliminal assets throughout the fall campaign, triggering memories from a storefront in Harlem and from a trip long ago to Mississippi, in a little shack near Meridian, and in the nameless shacks across the state—three photographs still hanging together—Martin Luther King, Jr., flanked on each side by a murdered Kennedy brother.

Many say that John F. Kennedy won the 1960 election with a

phone call to Coretta King, but Jimmy Carter was the candidate the Kings had blessed this time. Without the help of
Martin Luther King, Sr., and Andrew Young, he would have
been stereotyped in the North as just another moderate southern governor. Such shifts can change history and the leadership of nations. For there was surely a direct link between
Martin Luther King, Jr., and Jimmy Carter—two Souths
merged in Atlanta and come together to produce a candidacy
built on Bible Belt fervor and the faith that has bound southerners of both races to each other.

But they would not have been together had it not been for
another South represented on the platform at the convention.
The threat of George Wallace forged the Carter-King coalition
in Florida where victory moved it north as a giant killer. Eventually, the vanquished old Alabama firebrand, trapped in his
wheelchair by a would-be assassin's bullet, gave in to his regional pride and supported Carter. As he said on the first day
of the convention, it was "because the party hierarchy always
looked down their noses at the Deep South." Many people
around me squirmed uncomfortably at seeing him on the platform with the Democratic standard bearer.

When I attended the University of North Carolina in the
1950s, no student politicians I knew talked about the presidency. The law school was filled with future candidates for
governor, honing a style that was based on gracious southern
manners and constitutional arguments laced with grits and
gravy. The only real role models we had for national leadership
were Harry Byrd, Orval Faubus, Strom Thurmond, and other
bitter-enders who knew how to bait the Yankees and strut their
stuff. The success of the Carter candidacy had an impact on the
South that was profound beyond prediction. Just as Martin
Luther King, Jr., inspired activist ministers like Andrew
Young and Jesse Jackson, a quiet-spoken white southerner
with black support and integrationist pride would have far-
reaching influence on the young people of both races who were
listening and watching.

No doubt participating and learning that night was the young future southern president from Arkansas. President Bill Clinton owes a historic debt to Carter, because Carter's victory in 1976 broke a stereotype that enabled another southern governor to win the presidency sixteen years later without the regional dead load of racial discrimination and injustice around his neck. Carter and Clinton were New South governors liberated from the burden of southern history by a newly enfranchized black vote that forever has altered the politics of their states and their region. Both spoke passionately of tolerance and racial reconciliation. It is indicative of how far we have come as a nation that Clinton's origins were more of an asset than a liability in 1992, because it enabled a Democratic ticket with hometown appeal in the South to begin to put its old coalition back together again and recapture the presidency.

But there are important differences between Clinton and Carter; the Arkansas president does not have Carter's religiosity, a parochial style, or an insular staff. In fact, in endorsing Clinton, the *New York Times* noted his "capacity to attract first-rate people." Clinton has another asset that was muted in the fall campaign, because it was distorted in the primaries. In the example of Hillary Clinton, America will discover a professional role model for young women around the world. Her commitments in the last fifteen years as a public interest lawyer in behalf of children and education will make her a presidential partner unlike any previous first lady in history.

America now knows that it was a sixteen-year-old Boys State visitor to Washington in 1963 who shook hands with John F. Kennedy in the White House, an encounter which stirred the ambitions of the teenager from Hope, Arkansas. But historians will surely note the Carter-Clinton linkages that enabled two deep-South governors to assume the American presidency in the last quarter of the twentieth century, and close the chapter that had excluded southerners from national leadership since the Civil War.

16

A New Generation Takes Over

It has been widely heralded that the outcome of the election of 1992 signaled the elevation of the baby-boom generation to leadership in America. The truth is more complicated than that because a generational profile is so complex and multi-layered.

Theodore White pointed out in 1960 that the Kennedy election brought to power the junior officers who had fought and won World War II. Seeing former Lieutenant John F. Kennedy ride down Pennsylvania Avenue with former Allied Commander Dwight D. Eisenhower, it was obvious something like that had happened.

On January 20, 1993, Bill Clinton's trip to the U.S. Capitol for his oath of office with sixty-eight-year-old George Bush at his side will be equally reminiscent, evocative, and dramatic. America, at that inauguration, will bid farewell to the World War II generation of junior officers who have dominated national politics since 1960.

But the 110 new members of the 1993 Congress, as well as the old faces on Capitol Hill, and the new administration will also be peppered with those who were born in the 1930s and

1940s, too young for World War II and too old for Vietnam, whose memories and maturation were shaped by the 1950s.

The politics of the 1992 election will not have been the first glimpse of those differences in the character and experiences of the postwar generation. In fact, "generational politics," so successful in 1960 and 1992, was tried in a previous election—the Democratic primaries of 1984. That story, like 1992, had its genesis, ironically, in New Haven, Connecticut, in the excitement of an earlier generation of law students inspired by the Kennedy campaign and presidency.

During my second year at Yale Law School, I advised two first-year students in their moot-court competition. Neither Gary Hart nor Jerry Brown was an ordinary law student, and they had a lot in common in 1962. Both had unusual personal histories, grounded in theological training. Jerry had been in a Jesuit seminary in California, and Gary was fresh from a small Oklahoma church school and two years at the Yale Divinity School. Both were so earnest, hardworking, and thorough, finding in the law an outlet for their preaching, that even then it was not hard to see that they might both have larger pulpits in mind.

By the 1970s and 1980s Hart and Brown emerged as the two most successful practitioners of "generational politics." But in the 1984 election, neither was of the generation they were said to lead. Like me, they came of age in the fifties, as members of the "silent generation"—conventional, respectful of our elders, elusive. Little has been written about our complexities. We have been overlooked and misperceived as a valley of calm between mountains of turbulence and war.

Our own memories are different. Our lives were permanently changed at the moment we learned America would forever be just a few minutes from doomsday. The last generation to grow up and share in a deep-rooted, purely American sense of security and invincibility, we were also the first to have had that security removed at an impressionable age. This loss of innocence was a pivotal psychological event. It separated us not only from the generation that landed on the beaches of Normandy, won World War II, and continued to believe in America's superiority and invulnerability, but also from the generation that was born following the dawn of the nuclear age.

Nuclear annihilation—vividly imagined during civil-defense drills in school—was not our only fear. A legacy of insecurity was also passed on to us by our parents. Deeply traumatized by the Great Depression, they taught us about the dark side of economics: every boom was suspect, every dollar earned at risk.

We considered ourselves a new generation, never dreaming that an even newer one was about to rise up so quickly behind us. We, after all, were not really part of the postwar baby-boom generation whose revolutionaries and flower children imprinted their images on the 1960s. We had been born in the first flickers of recovery from the Depression: we were symbols of hope for our parents. We did not fight in the war but, instead, as small boys we hung from tree branches, pretending we were parachutists floating on a breeze behind German lines. And when the second world war ended, we celebrated too, but we were nine-year-olds celebrating the end of a war we had followed only through newspaper photographs and radio broadcasts. Hiroshima and Auschwitz were the twin nightmares of RKO-Pathe newsreels in darkened movie theaters.

When the Russians exploded their first bomb, we, like our parents, were shocked. When American troops were ground down in a "limited war" in Korea, we felt unsure. But the most critical events of our adolescence were the 1954 Supreme Court desegregation decision, which changed race relations in this country, and McCarthyism, which asserted that there were dangers in being out of step with prevailing ideas. So we were silent but we were not self-absorbed. Stirred by the first television president to practice "generational politics," we knocked on doors and manned the phones. The Kennedy years were a great liberation for us, opening up the country, we felt, to new ideas and hope. Vietnam and the assassinations would quickly put an end to our great society, but by the time the protests of the 1960s erupted, most of us were several years into establishment careers.

Thus, we easily blended in attitude, aspiration, even in dress and hair styles with those who preceded us. Because a generation is usually defined in thirty-year cycles, we have been lumped together with the generation that preceded us or with the one that followed. Yet I think that there are a number of distinctive characteristics that we, who missed America's wars, share and, as a new generation takes over Washington in 1993, bringing more of us into prominence as well, it may be time to pay attention to just what the differences are.

Perhaps our greatest legacy will be the way we served as interpreters of the rebellious young to our elders. Of neither generation, we had, in many ways, been called on to build bridges between the generations on either side of us. Those who came after us confronted their parents and challenged their values while we were already young aides and entry-level managers in establishment institutions: in law firms, corporations, and government. Indeed, when Jerry Brown and I had lunch together at the 1968 Democratic convention in Chicago, it was on the delegate side of the police barricades. And when, four years later, I saw Gary Hart again at the 1972 convention, he was, despite his open shirt, dungarees, and wide Western belt, the quintessential insider—the manager of a presidential campaign. Although deeply stirred by the revolution of the 1960s, it remained something we could understand, almost envy, but not embrace.

In the election of 1992 Bill Clinton and Al Gore gambled their party's future on the most blatant strategy of generational change since the Kennedy election of 1960, albeit with much more of a Southern accent. This turning point in American history has all the attributes of a watershed election.

With a world already in transition from the end of the cold war, it is somehow appropriate that the generation that fought

World War II and postwar communism will now give way to the young, pragmatic leaders of a new generation, including those shaped by the 1950s. The challenge for President Clinton is to reconceive America's role for the next century, rebuilding its economy and inspiring hope and confidence in the American people for the uncertainties that lie ahead.

And what of those who stumbled in 1984 and 1992—Gary Hart and Jerry Brown?

It is fascinating that Gary Hart's candidacy was destroyed by the same kind of charges that Clinton survived, perhaps because he challenged the press so blatantly to catch him and was the first candidate ever to be confronted by the press about "womanizing." Unfortunately, Hart's major contribution to American politics has been to open up the private life of national candidates to public scrutiny. But for 1992, the year of political surprises, even a sitting president has not been immune to similar charges—but the American people just don't seem to care either way this time.

And the pundits are still shaking their heads in disbelief that Jerry Brown's following grew throughout the 1992 presidential primaries with a new age message, an 800 number, and an astonishing capacity to speak the language of the young. However, Brown's future is always surprising, and for its direction, one only has to return to a prescient cartoon from the 1970s. It showed an entranced Jerry Brown as "Governor Moonbeam" sailing off in a spaceship with the caption: "I will be back."

17

Lincoln and Kennedy
Bound by Fate and History

The continued reverberations in films and books of the John F. Kennedy assassination is reminiscent for historians of the decades of questions and theories that followed the assassination of Abraham Lincoln. A visitor can turn from the flickering flame at the Kennedy gravesite in Arlington to look across the Potomac at the temple where Lincoln sits. What can the story of Abraham Lincoln's assassination tell us on this twenty-ninth anniversary of John F. Kennedy's death? Consider the two men, taken on Fridays almost a hundred years apart, bound together by fate and history, by the sense of national loss, of great deeds unfinished, dreams unrealized.

In 1865, an innocent nation was beyond imagining the violent act that dramatized the human fragility of its president. Lincoln was struck down in the final springtime of the Civil War, on Good Friday of what came to be called "Black Easter." "I mourned," Walt Whitman wrote, "and yet shall mourn with ever-returning spring." Thousands of sermons were preached that Sunday, almost all of them drawing parallels between the assassination and the crucifixion. Typical was one which declaimed: "Jesus Christ died for the world; Abraham Lincoln died for his country." The timing and circumstances of his death almost immediately elevated Lincoln into American sainthood, made him a martyr who sacrificed his life to his struggling country in a Civil War passion play in which John Wilkes Booth was called "The American Judas."

"Now he belongs to the ages," Secretary of War Stanton is supposed to have said, at the moment Lincoln breathed his last. As Lincoln's funeral train worked its way north and then west for three weeks, the myth of Lincoln gathered strength. No television eulogy bade him farewell, but the long good-bye was a national spectacle that touched almost every home and heart in the nation. Millions of ordinary people lined the railroad tracks to see his crepe-decked train. When it stopped for orations and prayers, they filed past the casket as Lincoln lay in state in Washington, Philadelphia, New York, Cleveland, and Chicago. The canonization of Lincoln was beginning.

It is often said that Kennedy in office harnessed television as no previous president had; what is less often realized is that Lincoln was president at the dawn of the age of photography, the first president whose photograph was circulated nationwide. After his death, the emancipated slaves and the families of Union soldiers and the plains farmers tacked his photograph to the walls of their homes. They felt attached in a deep personal way to his somber visage. While Kennedy's death provides a contemporary frame of reference for understanding the national mood of 1865, in many ways the public's feelings for Lincoln were distinctive because Lincoln had been a wartime father figure. His death was a horror occurring on the brink of victory; it was as if Franklin Roosevelt had been shot in 1945 by an assassin who might have been a German spy, or a political operative.

"It is odd," wrote poet John Berryman, "that Dallas cannot after their crimes . . . criminals protect or Presidents." Booth, like Lee Harvey Oswald, was killed, and thus his testimony was silenced; after 1865, rumors of dark plots reverberated for decades. Almost immediately, the Confederate leadership was accused, and later, four other conspirators were tried and hanged. As time passed, the event began to devour everyone it touched. Charges tumbled over one another; there was guilt, it was whispered, in high places. Secretary of War Stanton, Secretary of State Seward, and other radicals in the federal government had despised Lincoln's policies of reconciliation toward the South; President Andrew Johnson, who, it was publicly stated, had the most to gain from the assassination, was rumored to have engineered it; the shadow of suspicion spread as far as the Vatican; there were even hints of international conspiracies by bankers.

The literature surrounding Lincoln's death and the long post-assassination period reveals a shocking and terrible time in American history. It has been called the "age of hate," of "wild rumor and suspicion," when everyone in power and all institutions seemed to be accused of complicity in the assassination of the president. Both assassinations generated for decades a continuing stream of books and essays reinterpreting the evidence and generating new conspiracy theories.

In November 1963, our living rooms were transformed by television, first into amphitheaters where we witnessed a terrifying event, and then into a vast nationwide church, where families gathered about the electronic hearth during a sad weekend of aftershock and shared mourning.

The anniversary of the assassination of President Kennedy heightens the emotional memory of the half of the nation old enough to remember, but it has also stayed immediate for everyone, even for those born afterward, because it was filmed—it is a permanent part of our shared visual vocabulary. Lincoln's assassination was captured by artists, and the scene at Ford's Theater remained real to a people conditioned to experience the war and other events through the artist's eye. What is extraordinary is not only the way in which the Kennedy assassination lent insight to the grieving of an earlier generation of Americans, but how it brought the first assassination of an American president so powerfully back into the national consciousness. For black Americans, especially, Kennedy's commitment to civil rights struck deep and responsive chords that linked him to Lincoln, and this connection was reinforced by the subsequent deaths of Robert Kennedy and Martin Luther King, Jr.

"Death immortalizes," a poet wrote of Kennedy, and so it was for Lincoln as well. The drama of the assassinations has enlarged the personalities of both men, so it is as if each of them could have saved us from the troubled history that followed their deaths. Had Lincoln lived, many historians believe, his generous spirit would have labored in peace, as mightily as it had in war, to heal the nation's wounds, and perhaps much of America's tortured post–Civil War history would have been different. After Lincoln's death, a profound despair seized the nation, along with a deep bitterness that lasted for years, but America endured and the process of governing and nation-building went on. Had John F. Kennedy lived, Robert Kennedy once told a reporter, the 1960s would have been different because he would have listened more sensitively to the young. It is somehow reassuring that even in the desperate hours after each assassination, a shaken nation, gripped with near-panic, gathered its will, looked to its Constitution, and reasserted political order.

But there is a dark side. With the Lincoln assassination, a beast was loosed upon democracy: there followed the deaths of Garfield and McKinley; attempts made on Theodore Roosevelt and Franklin D. Roosevelt; two Kennedys and King dead; attempts on George Wallace, Gerald Ford, and Ronald Reagan. Today, a videotape of the Dallas motorcade plays in our heads during open-air speeches by presidents, and candidates wave from bulletproof limousines. An eight-year-old tells a national magazine he looks forward to seeing presidents shot on television. Thirty years later, there are both hopeful and disturbing lessons from history, but one thing is certain: the terrible events of November 1963 and April 1865 will echo in our nation's future in a thousand ways for years to come.

18

Reflections in a Mirror

There are two ways of spreading light: to be the candle
or the mirror that reflects it.

Edith Wharton

In the struggles for freedom that we have witnessed around the
world over the past few years, other countries have looked to
America for a pathway to the future. In China, a model of the
Statue of Liberty was erected as the symbol of the hope for
freedom, until it was toppled by the tanks and helmeted troops
of repression. For Vaclav Havel, the playwright-president of
Czechoslovakia, the United States was an inspiration through
all his years of dissent and imprisonment. The great documents
on which our country is based, he declared when he visited the
U.S. Congress, "inspire us all. They inspire us despite the fact
that they are over two hundred years old." And Nelson Mandela, freed finally after more than a quarter-century in South
African prisons, in his speech before Congress stated, "We
could not have known of your Declaration of Independence and
not elected to join in the struggle to guarantee the people's life,
liberty and the pursuit of happiness."

But even as the rest of the world declares a triumph for the
American revolution, it is rare to hear, in our own country,

such eloquent expressions of our nation's higher ideals. The honesty and passion of Havel, Mandela, Lech Walesa, Andrei Sakharov, and so many others in prison cells and in the streets recall a spirit that has all but vanished from political dialogue in America. They see in our system a vitality that, when we search for it in ourselves, seems to have been consigned to the dry pages of history.

Trying, like so many, to explain the contrast between the caliber of leadership that has emerged under oppression as compared with our own system, *The New Yorker* observed that "the individuality of a Havel or a Mandela can survive oppression by brutal regimes, but it's doubtful whether it could remain recognizable through a successful American Presidential campaign. Our economic system has triumphed, but the very market values that are vindicated by this triumph have undermined and corrupted the political climate."

As others have sought to emulate our system, over the past decade many of our own political leaders promoted the attitude that government itself was the "enemy." A fundamental distrust of government was enshrined as public policy, calling into question the notion of the common good and the legitimacy of a government role as active partner, regulator, and protector in many aspects of American life. For the most vulnerable segments of society—the poor, minorities, children, the sick, the aged—this disengagement has had devastating effects. But the impact stretches farther still. From the gigantic and ever-growing savings and loan bailout to toxic waste to the dismal disrepair of our bridges, roads, and water and sewer systems, we will be paying the price for this philosophy of neglect and indifference for a long, long time.

Noting the importance of the American model to the revolutions of Eastern Europe, Felix Rohatyn, chairman of New York City's Municipal Assistance Corporation, asked in *The New York Review of Books* "whether the American system is all that they think it is, or whether they are seeing the light of a dis-

tant star which, some time ago, may have ceased to shine so
brightly."

The contrast between ideal and reality, though perhaps never more dramatic, is not new. In 1960, I visited the Soviet
Union for the first time, as a student tourist, and spent hours in
Red Square talking to students. At that time, not many Americans traveled to Moscow, and the students flocked around me
to practice their English and ask some simple but profound
questions. I kept a diary to remember:

> "Is it true that unemployed people have to beg in the
> streets?"
> "Why do you still treat the Negro like a slave?"
> "Do the poor really have no place to go when they are
> sick?"
> "Why do you deny some people freedom of speech?"

The Russian students I met had obviously been well schooled
in the flaws of capitalism, but their questions were not asked in
an argumentative tone. It was as if they suspected their own
propaganda and genuinely wanted to believe in America. Yet
they were sincerely bothered by the inconsistencies between
American ideals and realities. Rereading the questions thirty
years later reminds me of how frustrated and upset I was at the
time. There were answers, of course, in unemployment insur-
ance and Social Security; in housing and health programs; in
democratic elections and the Supreme Court; in the facts and
figures of America compared with other countries. But I was as
idealistic as they were, and in my heart, I wanted America to
be the perfect answer. I realized then that others around the
world would always hold up the mirror to us and ask us why we
could not rise to our own self-proclaimed image as the standard
for the world. In all that followed—from Bull Connor's dogs
and fire hoses to Martin Luther King's "I Have a Dream"
speech; from the assassinations of the 1960s to the placing of a
man on the moon; from the plight of the homeless to the mira-

cles of American science—after that encounter on the streets of Moscow, I have always thought about how people in other countries viewed America.

While disillusionment may be fashionable in contemporary America, it is extraordinary to see the power that American history holds for other nations. Perhaps the question for the 1990s is whether the vision of America reflected back to us by the mirror abroad will strengthen our resolve to attack with deeper determination the problems we face here at home.

The tremendous outpouring of support in America for the remarkable leaders who had been prisoners of conscience demonstrated the abiding power of hope and the hunger for leaders people can respect, who are willing to suffer for their beliefs and press on in spite of personal hardship. The problems we face are complex and deep-seated, and change will require not just one heroic leader but a whole new generation of leaders who not only have vision but are willing to hammer at the anvil for long years to come.

John Gardner, as president of the Carnegie Corporation and founder of Common Cause, brought the subject of leadership to the forefront of foundation and national concern. In his new book, *On Leadership*, he expresses alarm at the apparent loss of commitment in America and of "our capacity to gather our forces and act" for what he calls "the visible future" of the next century. Despite tremendous and urgent problems threatening the well-being of society—drugs and crime, terrorism and the threat of nuclear conflict, ozone depletion and AIDS—he writes that "we give every appearance of sleepwalking through a dangerous passage of history." He sees a glimmer of hope for new leadership in that "free societies have clear advantages in the task of continuous renewal . . . to create a climate favorable to problem solving, risk taking and experimentation."

Is such leadership possible in America, a mature democracy with all the tensions inherent in a free, pluralistic society, or are we naive to wish for it? In some respects, perhaps it is unrealistic to expect the kind of leadership borne of suffering and struggle, of lives in opposition, and dedicated to an ideal still in the future, that is now emerging in other countries. But it is not unreasonable to look for leaders with ideals, integrity, and the vision of a new world, leaders great enough to inspire others and humble enough to be inspired by something larger than themselves.

We need to broaden access to the system for the visionary leaders Gardner calls "pathfinders" and look to new pools of talent that have previously been shut out. The last decade has not been sympathetic to young people interested in public service. The prevailing winds have taken them in other directions, toward private gain and personal advantage, even as government has cut back most avenues to public careers. It is essential that we tap the strain of idealism and commitment that is very strong in America. We must find ways to encourage our most idealistic and talented young people to enter the fields of public interest law, education, human rights, and women's leadership, or other fields—and help build the next generation of what one young person described in a recent letter to me as "social artists," who are both "outside and included in the collaborative process, compassionate and creative thinkers." Rich sources of leadership, ranging from community-based organizations to unions to local government to the arts must be sought out, sustained, and strengthened.

We must reinforce the changes in the political landscape that have brought new kinds of leaders into office, providing fresh perspectives and enhancing the representativeness of government. For example, in 1965, there were 75 black elected officials in the South; in 1990, twenty-five years after the Voting Rights Act enfranchised two million new voters, there were 3,855, including a black governor in Virginia, a black congressman in Mississippi, and candidates for major office in several states. Nationally, there were in 1990 more than 7,370 black elected officials, including 326 mayors. After the Voting Rights Act was extended to cover Hispanics in 1972, the number of Hispanic elected officials in the Southwest increased from 1,500 in 1976 to nearly 3,360 in 1990. And in 1990, 10 women ran for governor, 5 for the U.S. Senate, and more than 40 for the House of Representatives (24 of them incumbents). Nationwide, more than 16,000 women are serving as elected officials, including mayors, municipal council members, and county board members. But these figures are only a beginning: in 1990 minorities still constituted fewer than 2 percent of all elected officials, and women roughly 14 percent at the local level and fewer than 6 percent in Congress. The underrepresentation of minorities has been exacerbated by the 1990 census, which shifted representation from urban areas, where there are large minority populations, to the mostly white suburbs and to the Sunbelt states.

Much more needs to be done to open the way for committed, imaginative men and women. The demands of running for office—the vast amounts of money required, the intense scrutiny of private lives, the debasement of ideas in campaigns that are designed for "sound bites," the constant assessment of polling results that undermines creative leadership— discourage too many talented people from entering the field. The need for ever-increasing amounts of money to fuel the election machinery has given such enormous power to the special interests that large numbers of people feel elections do not matter (and U.S. voter participation rates are the lowest of any democracy in the world). The special interests are most powerful where large sums are necessary for expensive media time, particularly at the level of statewide office and presidential politics. Once in office, elected officials facing interest-group pressures are too often unable, or unwilling, to make difficult decisions, permitting many problems to be ignored until they reach crisis proportions.

The continued vitality of our political system requires not only changes in the way politics are conducted, but greater participation by citizens as both voters and candidates in the future. In the wake of dramatic world events and the legacy of domestic problems that have gone too long untended, the need for creative leadership is more critical than ever.

Foundations can play a role by helping to search out, develop, and inspire leadership from both traditional and new sources. At their best, foundations represent pluralism and diversity, alternative sources of funding, ways for a fresh idea or a nonconforming theory to persist and gain support. Possessing a rare degree of independence, foundations can assemble the best minds that will take the long view and nudge traditional institutions in unorthodox directions. On a scale beyond any country in the world, the American system of taxation and governance has encouraged the creation of foundations of all sizes and interests; there are now more than thirty thousand. They are in a unique position to try to improve the climate and context of political debate, to help stimulate citizen participation, and to keep government accountable by monitoring its actions and reporting to the public on behalf of constituencies without power.

While watching the swiftly moving events of the recent past, I have been drawn over and over to a framed photograph of my home-state hero, Dr. Frank Porter Graham, on the wall of my office. "Dr. Frank," as he was affectionately called by thousands of students and alumni of the University of North Carolina, where he served as president from 1936 until he was appointed to the U.S. Senate in 1949, was a gentle-hearted man with a loving spirit and fearless courage when it came to the great issues of his time. In his first Senate speech, at a time when the United States was gearing up for the Cold War, he told his colleagues that "America . . . must rely more upon the ideas of freedom . . . than on economic and military power. The freedom and dignity of the human being, democratic ideals, and moral idealism are the ultimate weapons in the global struggle." Although no one could have predicted it, the revolutions of 1989 have demonstrated the enduring power of American values.

If Frank Graham were alive today, I'm sure he would celebrate the cycle he recognized in a later speech, in North Carolina in 1961, when he said of the civil rights movement that
"the ideals of the American Revolution have gone around the
world and have come home again." I believe he would declare
that America should not be smug at this fragile and pivotal
moment in the great march of history down freedom road, but
should respect the enormous sacrifices that dissidents of total-
itarian regimes, gathering in "the meetings that had no name,"
have been willing to pay for the principles of democracy in
their own countries. He would urge us to embrace their lives as
models of persistence, faith, and dignity and to be inspired by
their passion for social justice. The faces we see in the mirror
are the millions of Czechoslovaks, Poles, Russians, black
South Africans, and Chinese students, as well as many others
to come who cherish the American ideal.

We must not fear to hold up the mirror of history to ourselves
and accept the challenges of a mature democracy that is worthy
of inspiring a new world and to rededicate ourselves to building
a society that fulfills the hope that others see in us.

Part IV

Israel, the Holocaust, and Jewish History

19

The Jewish Secretary of State in Israel: A Diary of the Kissinger Shuttle

Seventeen years later, one can look back with new insights at the summer of 1975 in the Middle East. That year, assigned credentials from an American magazine, I spent six weeks in Israel as a correspondent covering the culmination of the shuttle diplomacy of the secretary of state, Henry Kissinger. Kissinger "shuttled" between Jerusalem and Arab capitals, acting as a go-between and deal-maker, negotiating with leaders who refused to see each other. In Israel at the time, one could sense the historical importance of the result, but it is only in retrospect that we can see beyond its immediate impact, which resolved the disputes between Israel and its neighbors in the aftermath of the 1973 Yom Kippur War. This high-profile personal diplomacy broke a logjam, set new standards for high-level interaction, and profoundly changed Arab-Israeli relations. Kissinger's effort laid the foundation for Anwar Sadat's landmark visit to Jerusalem and the later personal intervention of President Jimmy Carter, which led to the Israeli-Egyptian peace treaty. It established a new norm of personal involvement by future United States secretaries of state and blazed a trail that would be followed by Cyrus Vance, George Shultz, and

James Baker. And it was the high point in the career of Israel's then prime minister, Yitzhak Rabin, who led his party back into office in 1992 to face a new world after the Gulf War and the end of the Cold War, in a Middle East without Soviet arms and mischief-making.

Covering the Kissinger shuttle was one of the most exciting experiences of my journalistic career because of the whole spirit of the time and place. Several hundred journalists from all over the world were covering the shuttle, and it was fascinating to sit around at meals or in the bars talking about Middle East politics with a reporter from the Israeli press or hearing the latest rumors from a correspondent who represented a major newspaper and had talked to Kissinger that day. There were daily briefings at the foreign ministry by Israeli spokesmen and bizarre visits by celebrities such as Elizabeth Taylor and Sonny and Cher. When the Israeli government organized a trip to the Suez Canal and the Sinai desert for a *Time* magazine photographer and writer, I went along for a look at the scene of the war. Tired of being cooped up in a hotel, a number of us also traveled all over the West Bank, interviewing Palestinians, Jordanians, and Israeli settlers. I went to the Knesset (Parliament) and spent a day talking to members and a memorable hour interviewing the leader of the opposition, future prime minister Menachem Begin. I watched as angry members booed Prime Minister Rabin, and I talked to a wide variety of lesser-known political figures. I attended street demonstrations and roamed through the Old City of Jerusalem.

It is extraordinary, looking back now, in 1992, how little the personalities have changed. Still in power are King Hussein in Jordan, Hafaz el Assad in Syria, Saddam Hussein in Iraq, Yasir Arafat at the PLO, and the Saudi royal family. Only Anwar Sadat is gone. And the acting secretary of state, after James Baker was called into the White House in August 1992 to rescue George Bush's faltering campaign, is Lawrence Eagleburger, who served on the National Security Council when Kissinger was in office and later joined Kissinger, Inc., the international consulting firm.

I decided to keep a diary for possible future publication, because of the unusual reactions I was hearing from ordinary citizens of all types to the fact that Henry Kissinger was Jewish and would probably have perished in the Holocaust had his family not fled from Germany just before the war. Improbably, here he was as the American secretary of state, traveling between Jerusalem and Arab capitals trying to arrange an Arab-Israeli peace treaty.

The interim agreement negotiated by Kissinger represented a new turning point not only for the Middle East but for the United States as well. It was the first agreement between Israel and an Arab state involving a separate agreement with the United States. Moreover, it was the most complicated agreement negotiated in the area up to that time, involving not only the two countries, but United States guarantees as well, for Israel's military, economic, and energy needs.

Under Henry Kissinger's guidance and tenacity, the United States gained momentum as the major power in the area, enlarging its economic and political influence among the emerging new Arab oil power bloc and enhancing its military position by neutralizing Soviet influence in the more extreme Arab states. It laid the groundwork for the Sinai peace agreement to come, an agreement that would be shattered by the Lebanese War, the assassination of Anwar Sadat, and the intifada or uprising of Palestinians on the West Bank. The key was to keep the Arabs interested in diplomacy rather than war and oil embargo; to do that, the United States had to convince Israel that further concessions were in its long-term interest. The full cycle of that reality would not be realized until 1992 when Yitzhak Rabin would be swept back into power, after years in a kind of political wilderness, to usher in a new phase of Israel's relationship with all of its Arab neighbors.

I was in Israel that August in 1975 partly as a tourist but mostly as a journalist, recording conversations, impressions, and experiences. It was my fourth visit but my first since 1967, after the Six-Day War. When Kissinger announced that he would resume the shuttle in late August, I joined the international press corps covering the event.

Several things struck me about the experience.

First was the role of the press itself, since a shuttle is a high-wire act requiring the attention of an audience to make it work. Second was the degree to which the average Israeli was caught up in the event. Israel may be the most interesting country in the world in which to do man-in-the-street interviews—everyone has an opinion, often an informed one, and is anxious to share it. Most fascinating, though, was the dominating presence of Dr. Henry Kissinger, the ex-professor and German immigrant who served as the American secretary of state.

The subject of Henry Kissinger's personality had been one of overwhelming interest in the worlds of Israeli politics and public opinion from the time he took over as American secretary of state. "There has never been so much curiosity about the personal life of any American," said an Israeli editor. The Israelis saw him initially as a positive figure, though always with the suspicions that Jews hold toward any other Jew in a position of power, especially power over questions of Jewish survival.

"I am an American, secretary of state, and a Jew, in that order," Kissinger is supposed to have told Golda Meir. "That's all right," she is said to have replied. "We read from right to left."

But Kissinger was not just another American Jew. To Israelis he was a fifteen-year-old Jewish boy who had escaped Hitler's Germany, a man who had lost a dozen members of his family to the inferno called the Holocaust—the event that convinced the world that in the name of justice and life, there must be an Israel. "He was," said one Israeli writer, "the only American who could get through to the Israeli leaders, because they thought he understood them."

This Jewish man, not a noble figure physically (he is plump, wears glasses, and speaks with an accent), stepped down from a plane on Arab soil and was greeted with traditional Arab welcomes—the embrace and the kiss. The shock reverberated.

"As soon as Sadat called him 'My brother Henry,'" observed one Israeli journalist, "the argument that all the Arabs wanted to drive us into the sea because we were Jews and holy enemies didn't hold. If they could talk to Kissinger, maybe they could talk to us." Israelis tended to overlook the fact that the plane Kissinger arrived on was Air Force One, and that he represented to Arabs an elevation of their concerns to the level of the presidency itself, raising hopes (some said exaggerated hopes) that something would be done about the Middle East.

Kissinger's shuttle in August had to be played against the background of the 1973 Yom Kippur War, when Egypt crossed the Suez Canal in a surprise attack and won new respect in the Arab world, though its army was saved by Russian and American intervention. It was a war that shook Israeli confidence and drained the arrogance from the Israeli swagger that had been so apparent after the lightning victory in 1967.

"The Arabs remember the first three days and we remember the last ten," pointed out one wise man in his seventies. But for Israel, the reality was that the big powers would never let them win a war with the Arabs. The joint Russian-American ultimatum on October 22 had, in the minds of the Israelis, deprived them of any resolution of the conflict and made them understand how firmly their future was held in the hands of others. The ease with which Europe acquiesced to Arab demands, the denial by West Germany of permission for American planes to land during the war for refueling, and the break of diplomatic relations in Africa after decades of aid and support fed the Israeli despair. There arose, intoned Israeli novelist Amos Oz, "the haunting fear that Israelis are once again just Jews with no control over their fate." Moreover, in the period after the war, the spector of the Palestinians loomed more menacing—terrorists who bragged of their violence against athletes, women, and children seemed celebrated for their exploits, and Yasir Arafat, pistol on display, was brought as an honored guest to the UN, where a statement calling for the end of the Jewish state was greeted with a standing ovation.

For the young Israelis, fighting in 1967 had been a legendary feat; fighting in 1973 was a nightmare.

"The 1973 war renewed interest in the Holocaust for my generation," said a twenty-four-year-old graduate student who fought in the war. "It brought home the possibility of annihilation, which was fed by the panic of our parents. That panic is always just beneath the surface for the older generation. But we were supposed to be the new generation, starting anew. But the private fears in our roots were exposed by the war."

"After 1973," said a girl in her late twenties, "we were a shtetl [a village] again. The whole world was against us. For those in my generation, we had to admit the existence of an anti-Semitic world and that we were all alone—the UNESCO resolution, the refusal to condemn terrorism—all unjust. There was no rationality anymore. Just do anything to get the Jews."

Given such circumstances, one could only imagine the Israeli reaction if the secretary of state had been a Rogers, a Rusk, a Dulles, or an Acheson. Jews had survived out of stubbornness, after all, and the Rogers plan never got off the ground. From the American perspective, it was difficult to picture any of those men, so preoccupied with the dignity of office and American morning-coat diplomacy, energizing an exercise as complex and with as many personal risks as a shuttle. Then why does Kissinger do it? Israelis asked. Did he really see himself as Israel's "savior," as he had told a *Boston Globe* reporter on August 6 just a few weeks before he left for the Middle East?

Israel was looking for hope when Kissinger entered the Middle East. He was direct and original, with more power to commit American influence and arms than any secretary before him. Vietnam had not yet crumbled, thus destroying his credibility all over the world and shaking Israeli trust in any Kissinger-contrived solutions.

"There was admiration for Kissinger," said an Israeli journalist, "but there was also fear. Fear that he comes from us and therefore knows us—knows how we work. That's why his statement that he was 'our savior' received such publicity in Israel. All the messianic movements were led by Jews who knew of our dreams of the messiah. And they manipulated us with that knowledge. Thus, we fear he will trick us in the end, just as he did the South Vietnamese."

After several weeks of interviewing people on the subject, I could see that how an Israeli felt about Kissinger as a Jew was a kind of Rorschach test on how he or she felt about Zionism, assimilation, the Holocaust, intermarriage, Judaism as a religion, and the relationship between the Jews of Israel and the Diaspora (the Jews outside Israel). All of these questions crystallized around the Kissinger shuttle. The answer varied from generation to generation, between sabra and East European, between Zionist pioneer of the twenties and thirties and survivor of the Holocaust, between religious Jews of Jerusalem and the nonreligious Israelis in Tel Aviv and on the kibbutzim. Kissinger's insistence on an agreement caused Israelis to confront the fundamental issues of relations with the Arabs, to face the implications of a deepening relationship with the United States and the politics of pressure, and to ponder the position of American Jews—to face the fear that Israel could be alone and abandoned once again, its survival placed on a scale by blindfolded judges who would weigh the cost of supporting it against oil, détente, and the possibility of an American-Russian nuclear war. In sum, Kissinger, as a Jew and as a symbol of American pressure and power, raised the most profound questions in the Israeli soul.

Thursday, August 14, 1975

The early morning light casts a rose hue over the Judean hills as the car winds its way from Jerusalem toward Beersheba, from which we will aim straight across the Negev into the Sinai desert to our destination—the much-discussed Mitla and Gidi passes less than twenty-five miles from the Suez Canal. Now we are in the farming section of the West Bank, and suddenly the windshield is splashed with rain—rain! In August, in Jerusalem—not in fifty years has such a phenomenon occurred. The clusters of green trees on the hills are glistening with the reflected drops, radiant emeralds in the brown dryness of the desert.

Kissinger is due in a week, and the Israeli army has agreed that it might be a good idea to take some journalists down to see the passes in Sinai that lead to the Suez Canal. But just now, it is the rain that occupies our attention. The driver laughs out loud as he flicks on his windshield wipers. Rain in August, in Israel . . . is it a sign, some foreboding omen for the Kissinger visit?

The desert begins to reassert itself after Beersheba as the car cuts straight toward the expanse of Sinai. Four hours to the Suez Canal by car—longer by tank tracking on sand. It's not difficult to understand why the Israelis want this empty desert between themselves and the Egyptians.

We stop for gas and a sandwich at Refidim, the largest Israeli base in Sinai. Just north of the passes, it is a major factor in the negotiations, since giving up the passes will make this base less secure. Refidim was the major Egyptian base before 1967, the place from which Nasser announced two days before June 6 that "the time has come to revenge 1948 and 1956; the time has come to drive the Jews into the sea." The base extends across three to five square miles, it seems to us driving through it, but the only signs of the camouflaged Israeli air force that must be present are the several jet streams in the sky. I have been on a number of American bases both in the states and overseas, and this falls far short of them in terms of permanent buildings or size. Americans can think of reconstructing a base like this, but Israelis have trouble thinking on such a scale. To them, Refidim is one of the largest bases in the country.

The passes themselves are unimpressive, only significant

strategically. They are the two slender passageways through rugged mountains that extend for several hundred miles north and south along the Suez front, the mountains being natural barriers to the movement of materiel and men of an invading army. The most surprising aspect of these narrow roads is length; they wind through the hills for twelve to fifteen miles. Somewhere, I had gotten the impression that they were short little corridors no longer than a mile or so that could be raced through (the very word "pass" suggests an informal slice through the hills, not a long winding road through a major obstacle). No wonder the Israeli military is reluctant to withdraw from them.

The passes played a crucial part in both the 1956 and 1967 wars, as bottlenecks to the Egyptian armies retreating from the open desert of Sinai. I flew over the passes in August 1967, the last time I visited Israel, when the Israeli government allowed tourists to fly over the Sinai at low altitudes while a guide explained the various battles that made up the six-day victory. I'll never forget the awesome expanse of burned-out trucks, tanks, and weapons—miles and miles of rusted equipment, over $2 billion worth—the burned wreckage of the Egyptian army. Some of that still exists near the Mitla pass, nothing like what I had seen earlier, but still a grim reminder of the fierce amount of violence that must have heated up those hills.

The action in 1967 had taken place in the foothills at the entrance of the passes where, under the new agreement, the Israelis will be stationing troops. Our guide, who had taken several dozen trips with journalists, said, "I could give my regular speech on how losing the passes would mean the destruction of Israel, but frankly, I would feel a little silly." He pointed out, however, that Israel was a country with a small standing army and a large reserve. "Our strategy must be calculated to position a smaller force so that it can hold off a large invasion for enough time to enable the reserves to mobilize," he said. The bottleneck topography of the passes limits the amount of firepower a large army can assemble, giving a smaller number of Israelis the position they need, if the agreement allows Israeli troops to remain close enough to the mouth of the passes.

The army will not take us up to the radar stations at Umm Kheisheba, but they point out the peaks to give us an idea of its location. In 1967, from the air, one could easily see its importance—beyond the passes lies almost flat desert straight to the canal and beyond. A position on the peaks would give the Israelis a complete view of Egyptian army movement all along the canal and, with sophisticated radar, all the way to Cairo. (Still, one has unsettled feelings about the debate over the early warning stations; the Israelis had radar equipment at the Bar-lev line in October 1973 and saw every move the Egyptians made. But they didn't believe what they were seeing.)

Two soldiers come out of tents along the road through the Gidi pass and we ask them questions. "Do you think that Israel should give back the passes?"

One of them answers bitterly, "Let Kissinger and the politicians do it. I'm fed up with it." We ask him to say more. "There are the politicians, and there is the army. If the politicians say pull back, we pull back."

The widespread opinion in military circles is that the Israelis are best as mobile desert fighters and were mistaken in 1967 to get wedded to a line that they had to dig in and defend. "Of course," said one former soldier who fought in Sinai, "when you ask 436 men and three tanks to defend the entire stretch of the Suez Canal against thousands of Egyptians, it's not much of a line." During the negotiations, Foreign Minister Yigal Allon alluded to the "return to the classical doctrine of movement," pointing out that "it will be recalled that in the past, Israel achieved results in the Sinai expanses."

The loss of the passes has been difficult for the Israeli public to accept for psychological reasons, since they played such an important role in two wars. But one longtime observer of Middle East affairs pointed out that "the question is not the psychology of Israeli public opinion but of Egyptian public opinion. The Mitla pass was a graveyard for the Egyptian army in 1956 and 1967. It is a symbol of humiliation they want to regain and they will feel far more secure with Israel out of the passes than we will feel safe with a few troops in there. After all, we are still closer to Cairo than they are to Tel Aviv."

A veteran of three wars sits in a café drinking beer and scooping up humus with chunks of pita bread. "We have to give back the passes so that we'll have something to capture in the next war. Otherwise, what can we do? Go to Cairo?" He has his own business now and likes the cold economics of the agreement. "We'll sell the passes to the Americans to give to the Egyptians. Then, I suppose, we'll have to win them back to sell them again."

A sixty-eight-year-old man is more sarcastic about it. "Kissinger would be very good as an oriental rug salesman. But he is turning the Middle East into a giant bazaar."

Tuesday, August 19

With Kissinger due on Thursday, the Likud or right-wing opposition calls for a special session of the Knesset to debate the agreement. It seems odd to debate an agreement when all the elements of it are not known, but the Likud opposes any concessions and wants to begin stirring up its constituency.

The Knesset building is glassed-in modern, not luxurious at all, but not inspiring, either. It's a satisfactory parliament building that should have been more beautiful with a $6 million gift from the Rothschild family of England and France. The main chamber where the 120 members meet is filled with symbolism: the chairs and desks are arranged in the shape of a giant menorah, the walls behind the speaker's table are suggestive of the Western Wall in the old city, and a photograph of Theodor Herzl hangs off to one side. Since the building was constructed before 1967, the wall has incomplete geometric shapes carved in bas-relief—half a triangle, a circle with a slice missing—to suggest a divided Jerusalem and an unfinished state. In the rear of the chamber is symbolism of a different sort—the public sits behind bullet-proof glass.

Almost all the members are in their shirtsleeves with open-necked shirts, including Prime Minister Yitzhak Rabin, who sits in the middle of a U-shaped table with all the other government ministers. He was chief of staff during the Six-Day War, the first sabra (Israeli-born) prime minister and a heroic figure to most Israelis, who associated him more with the lightning victory of 1967 than with the bitter recriminations of 1973. Rabin is calm, expressionless, and workmanlike on the floor of the Knesset. He always seems subdued and speaks to others without animation or gestures. He is flanked by the other members of the negotiating team—Defense Minister Shimon Peres and Foreign Minister Yigal Allon. Looking over the members assembled, I counted only nine women and two Arabs; in addition, there are fourteen skullcaps in the section where the religious party sits. The press sits in a balcony barely ten feet above the floor, and today it is crammed with the American network crews and the international press, arriving ahead of the Kissinger shuttle.

Menachem Begin, the leader of the opposition, starts off with a twenty-five-minute speech (the debate is in Hebrew but a reporter who went with us to Sinai translates). Unlike most of the others, Begin is wearing a grey silk suit and a dark tie, attire which rather belies his past as a head of the Irgun, the 1940s terrorist group that claimed credit for blowing up a wing of the King David Hotel in 1946, killing ninety-one people. Although he has a reputation as a dynamic speaker (some say demagogue), today he cloaks himself in a low-keyed rationality, asking for the resignation of the government, new elections, and a referendum on the agreement. No one seems to be listening. As they do in Congress, members slouch in their seats reading a paper or talking to a neighbor—the scene more nearly resembles a B'nai B'rith meeting in a Hilton ballroom than the site of the most crucial parliamentary debate since the 1967 war.

Rabin rises and slowly makes his way to the rostrum, which is on an elevated stage along with the desk of the Speaker of the Knesset. "Mr. Speaker, members of the Knesset. The policy of the government has been and is to exhaust every possibility of advancing towards peace." Rabin's speaking style is more like a drone—slow and ponderous, correct and gray. ("You, a foreigner, should not judge a man in Hebrew from his English," an Israeli vendor tells me. "Then how is Rabin in Hebrew?" I ask. "Terrible," he replies.) The opposition occupies one side of the hall, and one can sense their restlessness. Mentioning "interim settlement," Rabin says that "the nation gave us a mandate to work for this aim." Suddenly, a woman in the opposition rises and screams, "You don't have a mandate"; then the opposition erupts into fists waving and pounding desks and mutterings of "You don't speak for the people." Rabin stays cool and moves ahead in his determined monotone.

"Our purpose is to . . . strengthen the country's security and to consolidate our relations with the American people and government."

The chamber explodes again in voices from the right. "That's it," says one. "The American government . . . " screams another, "you're nothing but a puppet on a string . . . ." Outbursts come from the opposition with an undercurrent of scorn and objection; Rabin cannot go on for the sounds of disorder. The Speaker is pounding his gavel, asking for quiet. Finally he continues, mentioning the momentary arrival of the American secretary of state.

At the first mention of Kissinger's name, the hall explodes in opposition again. "Did the government invite Kissinger? Answer." And now it is time for Rabin's Labor colleagues to defend him. Both sides of the chamber are now on their feet and snatches from the supporters can be heard: "Be ashamed," says one. "You are acting like juveniles," shouts another. "I had questions for Begin but I let him speak," and the Knesset is now out of control.

Rabin smiles at the chaos all around him, but those of us

here for the first time are astounded at the lack of respect. An old-timer confirms that it was never like this with Golda Meir or Ben-Gurion, though the debates were often stormy. Perhaps I am overreacting, since it is also obvious that the opposition is quieting down, as if by signal. There are smiles all around over the noisiness, as if everyone realizes that this has gone too far.

"There are clauses of great importance on which agreement has not yet been reached," Rabin starts again. And the opposition interrupts again. "Why don't you tell us about it?" "To Egypt you answer; to Israel, you don't." When someone shouts, "You are a Don Quixote," Rabin can resist no longer. "Even if your policy is like Sancho Panza, you shouldn't make sounds like Sancho Panza's donkey," he says, and the entire chamber dissolves into laughter and fury. For five minutes, the noise continues, rising and falling, and yet, Rabin is pleased with himself. He finishes, leaves the rostrum, and the Speaker declares a recess; friends slap Rabin's back at just the right moment.

During lunchtime, the ministers mingle with reporters in the cafeteria downstairs, and a few of us corner Begin: "Would you say that the Rabin government is selling out Israel?"

Begin is once again true to the role he has chosen to play in front of the international press. "I never use such language. Everyone is entitled to an opinion. I simply say it is not good for the security of Israel."

But some of his colleagues are not circumspect. Geula Cohen, who looks like an Israeli Anna Magnani, replies, "I believe that it is the beginning of another holocaust for us."

Wednesday, August 20

King Hussein arrived in Damascus today to a greeting by thousands of Syrians chanting, "One people, one army, one flag." Syrian television switched live to welcome "the beloved guest to Damascus," and observers say that there will be some announcement before Kissinger's arrival about a joint military command.

It's difficult to believe that in 1971, Syrian tanks were massed in the desert north of Amman ready to strike against Hussein; that the Rabat conference in which the other Arab states dismissed him and elevated Arafat's PLO was just ten months ago; that Arafat's visit to the UN was on November 9, 1974—but here is King Hussein of Jordan, celebrated by the Syrians, with a triumphant welcome to Damascus.

Some observers see the "fine hand of the Saudis" in Hussein's comeback, an effort to rehabilitate one of the royal brothers—a visit by Sadat to Jordan in the spring, the first by an Egyptian president in history, and a visit to the king by Assad, the first by a Syrian president in twenty-one years. Syria is worried that the Israelis could simply bypass their forces in case of another war and circle toward Damascus in a pincer movement through their Jordan flank. Thus Hussein has defense to offer the Syrians, which is one of the reasons that military people say that Israel is opposing so adamantly the sale of the Hawk missiles to Jordan.

The timing is interesting, since Kissinger is coming soon, but Israeli sources are saying that Syria is trying to isolate Egypt, and that Hussein is playing along to restore his militant credibility on the West Bank. "There is a law in physics that explains it," says an Israeli source. "If Hussein goes up, Arafat comes down."

So the Israelis are not unhappy with Hussein's comeback, for it is widely admitted here that Israel made a major mistake just after the 1973 war in not reaching some interim agreement with Hussein after the canal and Golan settlements with Egypt and Syria. "We are responsible for Rabat and the rise of Arafat," said one Israeli dove, "because we humiliated Hussein by not giving him some foothold on the West Bank." If Hussein can be restored to respectability, the possibilities of an overall settlement that Israel can support are that much greater now that the Israelis have learned that the PLO is the alternative.

Not that the average Israeli has much respect for the soon-to-be-announced joint Supreme Political Command. "They will probably meet four times a year to have coffee," said one former tank commander who fought twice in the Golan. "The little king is amazing to have survived so long. He dashes between the raindrops, not just for one shower, but for twenty years."

Why is it that the Israelis seem to have more trust in the Egyptians than in the Syrians? I ask.

"It is the prisoners. The Syrians were barbarians with the Israeli prisoners—we found them shot, mutilated, cut into pieces—horrible. That's the main reason."

Because the Syrian tank assault during Yom Kippur was so successful, most military men think that Syria will try again. In 1973, 1,400 Syrian tanks broke through the lines being held by fewer than 180 Israeli tanks and could have gone all the way to Haifa had they not suspected a trap. They simply lacked the confidence to believe their success. And with so many Russian arms being stuffed into Syria, most Israeli military think restraining Syria, even by their Russian sponsors, will be difficult.

"Besides," said a shoe store owner, "the Russians make plenty money off the war. They get paid for guns with petrodollars; and when the price of oil goes up, so does the price of Russian oil. And the Arabs get blamed. It's good business."

Thursday, August 21

In an interview with *Le Monde*, PLO leader Yasir Arafat threatened to "shake up the Middle East" if the expected Israeli-Egyptian pact does not respect the decisions taken at the Arab summit at Rabat. "Important events and upheavals will take place both on the official and popular levels."

There are more roadblocks than usual today because of Kissinger's arrival, and the police are snarling up traffic with careful inspections. "I can live with it," says a Hebrew University professor of the increasing number of searches since the bomb went off in an empty refrigerator in Zion Square six weeks ago, killing thirteen people and injuring seventy-two. "If you're European-looking," he stresses, "they wave you through. It's the Arabs they search."

I went down to the Allenby Bridge over the Jordan River this morning, and I counted more than one hundred Arab taxicabs waiting to be searched before crossing the bridge. They will wait five or six hours, an Israeli soldier said.

The headline reads, "Watchman Foils Bomb Attempt in Jerusalem Bus." The story is about a "sharp-eyed watchman" who spotted a "suspicious blue plastic bag" on the number 12 Jerusalem bus as it stopped in front of the education ministry near the old city. "The bomb squad arrived minutes later," the story continued, "and safely dismantled the charge—300 grams of plastic explosive wired to a watch and a 1.5 battery."

I ride the number 12 bus almost every day back and forth to Zion Square.

Kissinger arrives tonight and the security is as tough as any I've seen since the 1972 Democratic convention in Miami. The street in front of the King David Hotel, where Kissinger will be staying, is blocked off for three long blocks, and at checkpoints all over the city cars are stopped and searched, questions asked. The PLO has vowed to disrupt the negotiations, and the right wing has announced that it will greet Kissinger's arrival with demonstrations, so extra precautions are being taken. Everyone is on edge—the March shuttle that failed last spring brought terrorists by boat down from Lebanon to shoot up the Savoy Hotel in Tel Aviv; in 1974 the Syrian shuttle saw the killing of eighteen civilians at Kiryat Shemona and twenty-two children at a school in Ma-alot settlement in the North.

It takes a press card and a passport to get into the King David the first night, and that's after the Israeli Shinbed (secret service) has removed the lens from your camera to check for a hidden pistol, looked at your photograph on the identification card and stared intently into your eyes before waving you through. The men from the secret service are all over the hotel and can be easily identified by their burliness, the earphones tucked into their ears, and the blue blazers that cover the lump of firearms under their armpits.

The hotel lobby is alive with television and news photographers, mostly, lounging around with enormous amounts of sound and light equipment. Nikons or television cameras slung over their shoulders, they sit around playing cards and talking. For them, the job is hours and hours of boredom interrupted by moments of action, such as Kissinger returning to the hotel, or going out to cover a demonstration.

Tonight, reporters are asking each other where the demonstrations are, and rushing all over town to watch and report. A foreign network producer says, "Thank God for the demonstrations. It gives us something to shoot." But the first night is disappointing. Only two hundred demonstrators dancing in the streets; there is some police activity, but a British reporter sighs, "I've seen better riots on a quiet night in Belfast." Still there's an ugly, personal, anti-Semitic tone—"Jewish Traitor," says one sign. "Hitler saved you to finish the job" and "He killed six million but he was not a Jew" read others.

The few guests in the lobby start to gather for Kissinger's return late that night; the place is packed with onlookers, security, photographers, and press. Perhaps he'll say something, probably he won't, but still we're all there just in case.

A woman tourist behind me says, "Kissinger, the chutzpa— he marries a shiksa and took the oath on a New Treatment—he should eat pork with nails." (It was a Yiddish expression I had not heard before.)

A murmur of expectation rushes through the crowd as the time approaches for Kissinger's arrival (he is traveling by helicopter to a soccer stadium nearby). There is a look of concern on the faces of the secret service men, now bunched and poised all over the lobby. Nineteen soldiers come through the door one by one in full battle gear, and the hotel puts up velvet ropes to make a path to the elevators. The few guests climb on tables and chairs to look over the photographers, who by now have tested their meters in the floodlights. Suddenly there is the sound of motorcycles and the glitter of a black car; the foyer of the lobby is bathed in lights and in walks Kissinger, followed by six men in suits with briefcases, as well as a group of better-known American network correspondents and big newspaper journalists. To the applause of the crowd, Kissinger strolls over to the photographers where microphones are shoved into his face. "We had constructive talks with the Israeli negotiating team . . . ." It would be the first in a long series of meaningless statements from him during the week.

Friday, August 22

On the morning after his arrival, Kissinger visits Yad Vashem, the memorial to the six million who died in Europe. It is Kissinger's third visit to the memorial—he went once on his first trip and a second time with President Nixon. The *Jerusalem Post* reports that "observers felt that Kissinger thought the visit might soften public opposition in Israel to the interim accord," but every important visitor is taken to the memorial, and it is difficult to see how he could turn down an invitation without offending Israeli leaders.

Yad Vashem, the Hebrew words meaning "hand" (or memorial) and "names," is a tasteful monument carved into a hillside, simple in color and impression with large boulders topped by concrete. It stands near Mount Herzl, where Theodor Herzl is buried. It is a fitting proximity, since Herzl gave voice to the idea of a Jewish state; the Holocaust and the determination by Jews to have a state for the refugees from Europe brought it into being.

The central part of the memorial is divided in half. To the right as one enters is a display of photographs and documents from 1931 to 1939, the period of the tightening noose when the Nazi regime came to power, passed laws, distributed anti-

Semitic pamphlets and posters, and issued identity papers. The other room covers the period from 1940 until the end of the war—the trains, the death camps, the painful scenes of slaughter and brutality that have become so familiar that we are numb to their meaning. The language describing the photographs is spare, without adjectives, straightforward description of pictures that speak for themselves.

In a slide presentation entitled "The Jewish Community That Was," slides flick by depicting shtetl life in Eastern Europe—faces of a shoemaker and a tailor, of little children in school, of a marriage—smiling faces unaware of the impending doom.

Nearly half of the exhibit is devoted to the Resistance— detailed displays from the Warsaw ghetto including pistols, pipes, makeshift weapons, and maps of the sewer that was the communications system for the uprising. Outside, a Pillar of Heroism has been erected in honor of the Resistance fighters.

The memorial has a document room with forty-five thousand volumes of testimony, periodicals, Nuremberg war records, and diaries. The directors have gathered documents from Kissinger's village, Furth, such as the restrictions on travel and emigration and the published directives that Jewish doctors could serve only Jews and Jewish shops could sell only to Jews. Kissinger was shown photographs of the synagogue, now destroyed, that he presumably studied in and told the statistics on the declining Jewish population: in 1933, 1,990 Jews; in 1941, 600; in 1944, 23.

Without reporters, Kissinger visits the Hall of Remembrance, a special building that contains a dark slate floor with the names of twenty-two of the largest concentration camps inscribed on it. In one corner, a single flame flickers in a broken bronze cup over a vault containing the ashes of "the martyrs."

"When I guided the secretary of state, Dr. Kissinger, on his visit to Yad Vashem," said Gideon Hausner, chairman of the memorial and former chief prosecutor in the Eichmann trial, "I pointed out to him that our considerations and misgivings regarding the political proposals on the agenda stem also from the bitter experience of the Holocaust." Speaking to delegates of the United Jewish Appeal visiting Israel, Hausner continued: "What happened to European Jewry serves as a grim reminder to the state established by the remnant. If one keeps proclaiming today that there will be no second Holocaust, this can only be true thanks to the existence of the state of Israel strong enough to defend itself. The heritage of the Holocaust, to my mind, is that Israel must never be isolated and exposed to her enemies' hatred. I was told by Dr. Kissinger that Israel will never again stand alone."

Police Minister Shlomo Hillel announced today that in checking out over ten thousand reports of suspicious objects and people since the beginning of the year, the police have dismantled twenty explosive devices. Of the sixty-five explosive devices deposited in Jerusalem since the first of the year, he says, thirty-two others have exploded without injury and thirteen have failed to go off for technical reasons.

With the aid of police girls, the report went on, police in Jerusalem have stopped more than fifty thousand vehicles and searched more than fifty thousand people in routine security checks. Security activities amount to almost half of the activities of the police, the police minister said, because the "terrorists design to undermine co-existence in the city."

A woman whose parents also escaped from Nazi Germany explained, "You have to understand the Zionist premise to understand our reaction to Kissinger. Out of the ashes of Europe, Am Yisrael Hai—the people of Israel—live. The events are linked. Kissinger survived those ashes, too. It is inconceivable that he not be one of us. Yet, he must placate the Arabs to show Americans and Arabs he is not one of us. So we trust him and we don't trust him. It's a dilemma."

Her brother added, "And we had our troubles with Kreisky to remind us who we can't trust." It was not the first time I had heard Bruno Kreisky and Kissinger mentioned together. Two

years ago, Kreisky, the Jewish premier of Austria, had acquiesced immediately to terrorist kidnappers' demands over three
Russian emigrants seized on a train to Vienna, and closed the
halfway house for Soviet Jews at Schonau Castle. The action,
particularly by a fellow Jew, outraged Israelis.

I had never been to Masada, the enormous fortress ruins on
a mountaintop that rises majestically out of the harsh desert
plain south of Jerusalem near the Dead Sea. In eleven months
in 1965, thousands of volunteers from all over the world had
come to Israel in mounting excitement over the archaeological
finds uncovered there, for Masada had been so inaccessible for
the last two thousand years that most of the artifacts were
undisturbed by desert robbers or anything else except the sand
and the wind, and thus everything found could be reliably
dated.

Masada has been transformed by Israelis from an archaeological site into a symbol. For it was here in 70 A.D. that a
group of 967 religious zealots held out against the Romans for
three years, before they decided to martyr themselves in a
mass suicide rather than live in slavery. "Charitable execu-
tioners," Joseph Flavius, the historian, calls them, describing
how "everyone lay down in close embrace and bared their
necks to the blades." The last man "set fire to the palace and
impaled himself on his own sword."

Kissinger has been taken to Masada, and the message hasn't
been lost on him—the stand of the few against the many, the
weak against the strong, death rather than submission. Together with the Holocaust and the Warsaw ghetto, Masada has
become one of the crucial symbols to young Israelis. A guide-
book points out: "'Masada shall not fall again!' has become one
of the cherished watchwords of the new state of Israel. . . .
While the hitherto mysterious mountain has lost some of its
mystical quality since the excavation and restoration, it still
remains the most dramatic symbol of Israel's Tank Corps, who
swear their oath of allegiance high above the wilderness and
the azure of the Dead Sea."

Later today Kissinger leaves for Alexandria, and the differences in status among members of the press corps become apparent. Kissinger travels with seventeen reporters on his plane, and the rest of us, about one hundred, I was told by the Israeli press representatives (it seemed more like about two dozen), stay and read the wire service reports in the hopes of picking up something through the Israeli newspapers, which have good sources inside the government.

The daily 11:30 briefings by the press attaché of the Foreign Ministry mostly consist of international journalists reading stories and speculation from the Israeli afternoon papers for the government to deny or confirm. The ground rules are that a story can quote the spokesman as a "government source" unless he specifically says a statement is for "background" or is his "private view." He will also indicate when he is speaking officially, and the press on those occasions can quote him as a "government spokesman."

It's an even more intricate process, because the press is an intimate participant in the hammering out of an agreement, or at least in the portrayal of the conflicts in negotiations. The spokesman, in this case the number-two man in the press sections of the Foreign Ministry, Benny Avi-Lea, is in telephone contact with his number one, Benny Avon (they are known as the two Bennys), who is sitting outside the room where the negotiations are going on. Inside, the Israeli negotiating team knows that it is talking not only to Kissinger, but to Israeli and world public opinion, and that part of its performance is the managing of information. Through this briefing and other informal meetings with the press, the Israeli leaders must respond to the pressures of what is being said about the debates going on behind closed doors.

Yes, he can confirm that the number of manned stations on Umm Khesheiba is still under discussion; no, the *Newsweek* report sounds farfetched that Israeli intelligence is checking out a castle outside Vienna for a possible meeting between Sadat and Rabin; yes, Israeli cargo will be passing through the canal under the agreement, but not an Israeli ship under the Israeli flag nor will Israeli crews be allowed. He will check and tell us later whether the Americans will rule out any recognition of the Palestinians as part of the agreement. Sometimes he will say, "I cannot discuss the specifics of the agreement, but I suggest you check Monday's *Jerusalem Post.*" It's a nerve-wracking performance for Avi-Lea. "By 1:00 P.M.," he says, "when the wire service reports come in, my stomach is in knots."

In private discussions, sometimes lasting several hours after the briefing, the press spokesman is known to be more open and informative. Then, he admitted to me, he is making individual judgments about the reliability of the reporter, the kind of paper or magazine he or she is writing for, the nature of the question. These are background discussions and can range from history to economics, from Arab politics to gossip. Avi-Lea will check any information you've heard or gathered. At that point, reporters are honing individual stories, and the Israelis want themselves well reported.

A short time after the briefings are over, one can sit around the newsroom and listen to the stories being filed on one of the seven telephones to London and New York. It's early morning in both cities, and there's something eerie about the immediacy of words, conversations among us, the tap-tap of typewriters in the press room and feedback to the world. A Swedish journalist may be feeding a morning radio report and an American reading his own analysis, fresh from the briefing, into a telephone for the afternoon papers we will all be absorbing in a day or so. On the telex in a small room behind the check-in desk at the King David, a journalist types out his code numbers to his paper in London; he types out "Are you ready?" and a cryptic set of fingers halfway around the world answers, "Go ahead."

Kissinger, the American officials admit, gets a roundup several times a day of all important press reactions to his trip, and we know they are being digested and calculated for impact on the negotiations. It's sobering to think that these same stories are being read in Moscow, Damascus, and Cairo, that the press is a part of the shuttle as surely as the negotiators themselves. Kissinger and the Israelis know that a scrap of information will be eagerly reported. It's one of the ways the Egyptians and Israelis communicate with each other. But during the first rounds of the shuttle between Jerusalem and Cairo, there are no leaks, almost nothing.

"It's a good sign," says one reporter who has covered all eleven shuttles so far. "When they are negotiating seriously, both sides are quiet and intense. It's only when things start to come apart that each side wants to protect itself with its own version of events."

Saturday Night, August 23

Today must have been a backbreaking one for Kissinger—five hours of talks in Cairo on Saturday morning, four hours of talks in Damascus in the afternoon, and arrival back in Jerusalem for another three hours of talks with Israelis, all while still fighting the jet lag from his arrival in Jerusalem less than two days before.

We were told that Kissinger was meeting with the Israeli negotiating team in a guest house near the airport, but later it turned out to be a hotel on the outskirts of Jerusalem. The secrecy is obviously to confuse the demonstrators—meetings, the press now knows, can be held at the prime minister's office near the Knesset, at the prime minister's home several blocks from the King David Hotel, at the King David Hotel itself in the Kissinger suite, and now at two new sites, a guest house north of Tel Aviv or another hotel in Jerusalem. In addition, they will not be announcing the time of Kissinger's arrival at the airport. It's disturbing to think of an American secretary of state having to use such tactics, but Israelis understand what's at stake in keeping Kissinger safe from both militant Israelis and Palestinian terrorists.

The rest of us have been waiting around since 7:30 P.M. for Kissinger's arrival, which will not be until after midnight. The conversation runs to past shuttles and curious points of interest: Kissinger rarely spends the night in Damascus (only once in the thirty-five-day Syrian disengagement in 1974), it is rumored, because Nancy can't rest there and the secret service objects; the flight from Damascus is less than forty minutes long; Kissinger talks to Sadat in English but Assad speaks only Arabic, and therefore a four-hour talk in Damascus is really just two hours of conversation; he never asks the Israeli negotiators to work on the Sabbath but always manages to be somewhere else working himself; Nancy likes Sadat's lavish guest house in Alexandria and will probably stay behind and relax in the sun (thereby avoiding the demonstrators).

Most of the reporters based in Jerusalem, serving as stringers for various publishing and news services, carry portable radios and listen to the news every hour for the latest events. A number of the reporters who do not speak Hebrew will tape the broadcasts so that they can translate them at leisure later. In the hotel bars and restaurants the same thing happens, except that during dinner, four or five waiters come over to listen, too.

Reporters and photographers simply do not mix at all during the waiting. The conversations differ—reporters invariably talk shop about politics and the agreement; photographers talk about girls and booze and how much their Hasselblads cost. Reporters wear trousers and shirts, but photographers always wear faded jeans outfits with Nikons and light meters around their necks. They are relaxed tigers, sprawled around the lobby waiting for the action. They resent the fact that David Kennerly, the White House photographer, has full access to the negotiations and an inside track on the prize photographs of the mission. To reporters, Kennerly is another sign of Kissinger's confidence in the success of the shuttle, since candid photographs will turn it into a personal triumph. The other photographers feel professional jealousy.

The strenuous character of the first round is reflected on the faces of the plane reporters straggling in behind Kissinger's arrival from his first talks with Sadat. They have a dazed, beat-to-hell look as they drag their luggage, cameras, or portable typewriters. Except for familiar faces such as Bernard Kalb of CBS or ABC's Ted Koppel, they could easily pass for a returning group of big UJA givers just off the bus from a tour of the new Negev settlements.

Bernard Kalb, with his brother Marvin co-author of a book on Kissinger, is covering his first shuttle for CBS because of Marvin's illness. He is surprised by the stress of travel and the pressure of negotiations on Kissinger and the press as well. "He's not got the silhouette of an athlete," says Kalb with a degree of admiration, "but he has the stamina of the long-distance runner."

In the press room, Bernard Gwertzman of the *New York Times* has agreed to talk to five or six reporters about the mood on the plane. "My impression," he is saying, "was that he was not unhappy with his meeting with Sadat. There are only narrow issues now, not principles, and Kissinger seems relaxed." Someone asks about Kissinger's schedule. "He said he could go back to the States for his speech September 2 and come back again if necessary." He notices two reporters taking notes and says, "Don't quote me. This is just background and I don't want to sound like some government spokesman." And then he asks, "What has Israeli radio been saying?"

Sunday, August 24

The *Jerusalem Post* and all other newspapers are publishing detailed descriptions of the agreement, and reporters arrive at the 11:30 briefing asking about an unexpected reference that reads, "The U.S. undertakes not to recognize the Palestine Liberation Organization nor to hold political talks with it." The press spokesman says he cannot confirm or deny it but will check on it during the day. When there is no word by late afternoon, we all assume its validity; another source has told a reporter, however, that the clause will probably have an "unless they recognize the existence of Israel" condition attached to it.

Because so many details seem locked up, everyone is saying that Kissinger had the agreement in his pocket before he came, but that both sides needed to make the bargaining look tough to prepare the political and military opposition in their countries for the announcement. Moreover, some reporters are saying that the publicity will polish Kissinger's tarnished image from the failure last March and lend new validity to the shuttle idea.

Even though all but a few territorial details seem completed, Kissinger is still trying to get political concessions from the Egyptians (which requires further concessions from the Israelis), and therefore he is back in the middle of this fascinating game. It's a tricky business and dazzling to think about—Kissinger flies to Alexandria already knowing what Israel has agreed to; he can withhold that knowledge until he gets Egypt to agree to something if the Israelis give in; in fact, the Israelis have already conceded the point but Sadat thinks he has won it. On his return, however, Kissinger uses the Egyptian concession (which he knows but the Israelis do not) to get another Israeli concession on a new point. It's a three-handed card game; only one of the players is looking at all three hands. There is a simultaneous game going on between the Israelis and the Americans, which is producing concessions Kissinger can use with the Egyptians. He can describe a suggestion as American, rather than Israeli or Egyptian, to save face for both parties. With more than fifty clauses in the American-Israeli agreement, as well as hundreds of small issues involved in the public and "secret" agreements, the process must be a chess player's delight. It's no wonder that at the end of a shuttle the story resembles Lawrence Durrell's *Alexandria Quartet*—four versions of the same event. The Israelis, the Egyptians, and

the public have three different versions of what took place—
only Kissinger, the smiling Buddha-cat in the middle, knows
how it really happened.

An editorial in *Ha-Aretz*, a leading Israeli paper, condemned
the language used by the demonstrators.

"The demonstrations staged by Gush Emunim and the Youth
Section of Heruth represent a combination of violence and
childishness, and what is worse—crude anti-Semitism. Although no stage managing can hide the fact that national consensus regarding the agreement is lacking, the initiators of the
demonstrations must not tarnish Israel's reputation by using
anti-Semitic slogans, reminiscent of Der Sturmer, against Dr.
Kissinger."

Not only territory is being given up, but a source of oil as
well. Since the 1967 war, the Abu Rodeis oil wells out on the
Gulf of Suez have satisfied over half of Israel's internal fuel
needs, estimated at a cost of between $300 million and $400
million a year. The Israelis are giving them up for the guarantees of oil from the United States in cases of peacetime embargo or wartime emergency.

Some critics of the agreement contend that Israel received
nothing tangible from the Egyptians for this concession, and
that giving it up will only add another large import burden on
the already gaping trade deficit. Moreover, they argue, the
Shah of Iran's recent visit to Egypt and his appetite for more
power and prestige jeopardize current sources of supply (widely known to be the Iranians) and leave the Israelis vulnerable to
a prolonged war and a decision by the Shah to withhold shipments.

In all probability, American guarantees that will calm Israeli
fears will be revealed in the "secret" agreements; already,
there is a confirmation that the aid package will include the
building of underground storage facilities for a one-year supply
in case of war. Since Abu Rodeis is a fragile and undependable
source of oil in case of war anyway, this is a clear gain for

Israel. And the widespread rumor in Israel is that Abu Rodeis was only a few years away from drying up anyway, and that it was better to face it now than later.

An Israeli afternoon paper features a large front-page photograph of Sadat planting a kiss on Kissinger's cheek.

An East European immigrant who came to Israel before the war observed, "Kissinger is the energetic, ambitious boy who wants to be first in his class and is. Always in the yeshiva, that is the boy you want to fall flat on his face. Call it envy toward the one who points up your own failure, call it insecurity, but when you combine the brilliance and success with the power and the pressure, it's bound to cause resentments."

The demonstrations are taking a violent turn, and the police reaction reported on television is shocking the Israeli public. Israel is not a country used to heavy-handed police action, and because of a history of injustice by the authorities in Europe, any violence ("Jews beating Jews," as one Israeli friend of mine said in revulsion at the television scenes), receives large attention in the Israeli press. One front-page eyewitness account by a *Jerusalem Post* reporter is already stirring up demands for investigations and sanctions against the police: "Police last night swung their clubs indiscriminately to disperse demonstrators. . . . As the demonstrators crowded on traffic islands, the police moved in swinging clubs and hitting innocent passers-by, including women and youngsters. One policeman swung his truncheon at this reporter as he was taking notes. Another deliberately broke the rear window of a car parked next to a traffic island—its driver standing next to it—without warning the driver to move on."

The demonstrators are mostly of the young Gush Emunin ("Movement of the Faithful"), a youth movement of the right-wing religious parties, and so far, there have not been more than five hundred at any one demonstration, usually much fewer. They frequently sing and dance the hora, but are sometimes capable of real mischief. On the night before Kissinger arrived, three demonstrators climbed into Foreign Minister Allon's house in the old city; at 4 A.M. on Friday morning, a car with loudspeakers blaring appeared in the vicinity of the King David Hotel, and the papers reported that lights went on near Kissinger's suite.

The coming of the Sabbath even brought a little charm into the protest movement—a "pray-in" at the prime minister's home on Saturday morning, complete with prayer shawls and Sabbath songs, and the 3 A.M. arrival of a red tractor pulling a cart carrying three calves, shivering and mooing in the Jerusalem night, which a dozen or so kids said were symbolic of the slaughter that would come if the people did not rise up in opposition with a mind of their own.

The newspapers are carrying photographs of all this, but there is something too visually sophisticated about it, more America in the sixties than Israel in the seventies. Moreover, many of the signs are in English, and it's not difficult to hear American accents among the demonstrators. The Israeli reporters confirm that there has been a large American immigration since the 1967 war, many of them Orthodox young people living on religious kibbutzim or attached to yeshivas throughout Israel. These are kids who were raised on American television (in Israel, television is only five years old, and even today, doesn't start until eight o'clock at night), who watched the Vietnam protest movement in the states. "Moreover," said another reporter, "they cut their teeth on the Soviet Jewry demonstrations in New York, so they are not amateurs."

The papers are carrying headlines that Richard Burton and Elizabeth Taylor will arrive at the King David in a few days to check out locations for a new movie, parade their reconciliation, perhaps even be married here. "After all, Elizabeth is Jewish," Burton volunteered, but the papers point out that the rabbinate will oppose such a marriage since Burton is not Jewish and a mixed marriage cannot occur in Israel. An Israeli sitting next to me on the bus says, "It gives Elizabeth and Henry something to talk about; they both married non-Jews."

A young Israeli woman of twenty-eight, a sabra, asks what

American Jews think of Kissinger, and I answer that American Jews are proud that a Jew is serving in such a high position.

"Here," she answers, "we are not so proud. In Israel, everyone is Jewish and we don't judge ourselves by achievements in the Gentile world."

I ask if she did not think that Kissinger was brave to be flying to Egypt and Syria and meeting face-to-face with Arab leaders.

"No. It is a Jewish trait to be brave, to face danger if you have to. Yours is ghetto thinking. In Israel, Jews are brave and we don't have to prove it."

What did she think of the slogans in the demonstrations?

"He's not so Jewish, so we should not treat him as if he is one of us. Judaism is a state of consciousness and you have to live it in some way. If he does not want to be so Jewish, we should not keep reminding him of it. He's just the American secretary of state, and he represents American interests, not ours."

But don't Israelis think of all Jews as one people, as half-Israeli?

"Yes," she says. "But your obligation is to help us, not to tell us what to do. When the new immigrants start to complain, the common answer is, 'Did you serve in the army?' It's easy for you to talk about concessions to the Arabs on Jerusalem and the West Bank. You don't have to stay here to fight them."

An Israeli correspondent for a European news service who came to Israel after the 1967 war is writing a book on Jewish identity.

"Sure the sabras understand him. They are religious and can separate religious feelings from their feelings as Israelis. They project this attitude on Kissinger, who they naturally sense can separate his religious feelings from his loyalties as secretary of state. They think of themselves as new Jews, separated by history from the syndrome of the suffering in the past. They grant Kissinger his right to escape his past as well.

"Kissinger also appeals to them as a historian, for they study the Bible as history and literature, not as a religious document only. They sense in him the intellectual's detachment from the emotional impact of Judaism as a religion. And since he is like them in that way, they judge him less harshly.

"But he doesn't love the land the way we do. He wants to give it back and it hits them hard."

Friends arrange a conversation for me with an Arab intellectual in East Jerusalem, an ex-patriot who was raised in Aman and studied in England.

"This is a blood quarrel," he explained in an impeccable British accent. "Arabs can nurture resentments for generations. The West can't understand that because you externalize hurts and release resentment; but resentment smolders in Arabs for generations. You and the Israelis are Western and believe time heals all wounds. To Arabs, time deepens wounds."

But what of the Israeli hospitals, jobs, medical care, and training of Arabs? I ask. Won't life be worse for Arabs if there is a Palestinian government?

"In a tribal conflict, that kind of thinking isn't applicable. It doesn't matter that the hospitals and schools will be worse if we take over. That's Western thinking. We resent the fact that they are living better now on our land, even if we left it fallow for thousands of years."

But that's not rational, I say.

"When Hussein's prime minister was assassinated at the Arab summit in 1971," he answers, "his assassins, Palestinian terrorists, bent down and licked up their victim's blood off the steps of the Sheraton Hotel. Does that sound rational? We're not dealing with rationality in the Middle East; we're dealing with primal passions."

An Israeli student tried to explain the psychological and Old Testament roots of the conflict. "When Sara saw she cannot have a child," she began, recounting the biblical story, "she asked Abraham if he would give a child to Hagar, Sara's servant girl. Thus Ishmael was born, and even though he was the elder, Isaac, who came later to Sara after the visitation of the three angels, was the chosen son. Then Ishmael became a fighter in the desert and began the Arab people. You see, with the Arab concept of dignity, they must face the humiliation of the un-preferred son. That is the reason many psychologists see aspects of sibling rivalry in the conflict."

Then she laughed. "I remember in school, once, talking to Arab friends. One of them recounted with great accuracy the story of God's test of Abraham's loyalty over the sacrifice of his son Isaac. Only, in the Arab version, at the last minute, Ishmael sneaked into the brambles and stole the lamb so Abraham had to go through with it."

Monday, August 25

Kissinger told a network news correspondent that an agreement was "quite close" and that he hoped to wrap things up in time for his return to the United Nations on September 2, a week from today, for a major address. This focus on the United Nations underscores American concern over the Arab effort to expel Israel from the UN, and Kissinger obviously feels that he can pull the rug out from under the more extreme Arab states if he can return with an agreement in hand. At the same time, Kissinger's making public his intention to return to New York next week puts more pressure on the Israelis to yield on various issues this week.

Five months ago, there was a front-page gossip saga about a nineteen-year-old Israeli female soldier who had hidden in the back of one of those white UN vans driven by her twenty-five-year-old boyfriend, an Austrian UN corporal, and driven into Syria for a weekend in a UN camp and in Kuneitra. Today, the military court let her off with a suspended sentence because of the emotional turmoil involved—it seems the corporal has returned to Israel with a promise to marry her, but that he is already married to a girl in Vienna; in addition, the Israeli papers now report that the girl is expecting his child.

At a party in Jerusalem, an Israeli friend laughs. "I always thought the UN was impotent."

It is reported that at a rally in Haifa there are two hundred demonstrators holding a huge banner declaring in English that "A False Messiah Can Only Bring a False Peace." The reference is to an interview that Kissinger gave to a *Boston Globe* reporter early in August, which quoted him as saying, "The Israelis do not appreciate that I am their real savior."

No one can help but be struck by the personal nature of the demonstrations against Kissinger as a symbol of the agreement. The "Jewboy, go home" epithets, a reference to a quotation from the Nixon tapes used by demonstrators to upset Kissinger last March, have been denounced by the newspapers as extreme and indecent.

"To attack him as a Jew is the ultimate futility," declared an editorial in the *Jerusalem Post*. "He comes to us as the U.S. secretary of state and nothing else. We do not have to accept his—possible joking—claim to be our savior, but we owe him all the courtesy to be extended to a statesman of his rank. To pile abuse on him as a Jew is disrespect to the right of every Jew to choose his own way in the world."

The afternoon Israeli papers are flagging headlines quoting the "Senior U.S. Official" (as Kissinger is always called when he speaks from the airplane) as having expected that Egypt would demand to advance beyond the current buffer zone into Israeli-held territory. Since the Israeli public is unprepared for Egyptian troops any closer than the buffer zone (having been sold for eight years the concept of Israeli withdrawals only if it resulted in a demilitarized Sinai), this newest revelation is a bombshell that has the press anxiously awaiting the end of the negotiating session that night at the prime minister's office after Kissinger's return to Israel.

Late at night, Allon and Kissinger walk out of the prime minister's office into the glare of lights and microphones.

Asked about the movement of Egyptian troops, Allon says, "There may be one change in this buffer zone when they will be permitted to go south along the Gulf of Suez, a certain distance within the zone . . . " Kissinger turns to Allon in surprise, seeming almost to glare at him. Allon, with the secretary at his side, is leaking a major point in the negotiations.

A reporter asks Allon, "Why did you agree to that as an exception?" Kissinger then interrupts, "Look, excuse me. I really do not feel that I can be a party to this discussion now . . . "

Later that night, according to a wire service report, Kissinger is asked about the new lines and says "acidly" (according to the report), "I don't want to deprive others who will no doubt feel the need to talk before the night is out on every possible subject."

What we were seeing was the Israelis withdrawing a major card from the Kissinger deck. The press reports were only partially correct, we found out the next day. There would be movement by the Egyptians beyond the buffer zone, but it would be only two or three kilometers *south* where there is a network of roads around the city of Suez, not east toward the passes, as the original news story suggested. Allon and the negotiators felt they had to minimize the concession before the Israeli public could react. But given that Kissinger is constructing a complex house of delicately placed cards, we don't know what the impact in Alexandria will be of a withdrawal of a card at the foundation of the house.

It's one o'clock in the morning and things look calm on the streets. Fourteen soldiers are talking across the barricades to two girls.

Tuesday, August 26

The role of the press on the plane is becoming more and more apparent as the drama of the week unfolds. Major American newspapers and magazines are represented: the *New York Times*, the *Washington Post*, the *Los Angeles Times*, *Newsweek*,

and *Time*; the wire services, the networks, and photographers
are also there, and they are filing stories after every flight.

The ritual, I was told, is almost always the same. After
takeoff, Kissinger, in his shirt sleeves, wanders back for patter
and jokes, always light and usually personal, often about
events. "It's the illusion of shared confidences," said one reporter on his first shuttle. "He tells us stuff as deep background that was in the press the day before." At some point, he
summons everyone up to his cabin in the 707 for an exchange,
usually with a tape recorder or two on the desk in front of him
so that reporters who cannot hear for the roar of the engines
can check his quotations later on. For sustenance, he keeps a
bowl of Hershey kisses in front of him.

"The role of the press is overrated," says Bernard Gwertzman of the *New York Times*. "If he didn't talk to us on the
plane, he would talk to reporters once he was on the ground."
Gwertzman admits the press plays a part in that "he does use
us to control the parameters of speculation. The Israeli press
is given to excessive rumors, particularly the opposition
press, and Kissinger can shoot things down before they gain
currency."

The more subtle question is their informal impact on the
parties themselves, who do not see each other, and are hungry
for news about what's going on in the other countries.

"When we get off the plane in Egypt," says Marilyn Berger
of the *Washington Post*, "they want to know what it's like in
Israel—the mood, the tone, what's being said. The journalists
and officials on both sides know we talk directly to Kissinger so
they figure we have some inside information to give them. And
there are things we suspect that we don't write. So we are
having an informal impact that can't be measured."

The press is sensitive to the charge that they are being
manipulated and not critical enough of Kissinger.

"It is said," confessed one reporter who asked not to be
identified, "that Kissinger plays the press like an accordion to
reflect an upbeat mood for the negotiations and influence the
countries involved. But our job is to assess and weigh and

balance with contacts in Israel and Egypt. Still, it's tough, because we're running all the time—helicopters, buses, stories to file, exhaustion to fight. It's diplomatic theater, and one part of our job is to quote the major actor accurately and watch his mood."

Reporters tonight are predicting that Kissinger will have the agreement all wrapped up by Friday, in time for the cover stories of *Time* and *Newsweek*. Some of the writers who have covered all the shuttles caution against too much optimism.

Time magazine arrived today and reports that Israel will receive the coveted Lance surface-to-surface missile, which can deliver either a conventional or a nuclear warhead over a seventy-mile range. *Time* also reports that "the Israelis are believed to possess at least ten nuclear bombs with a 20-kiloton yield—the size of the U.S. atom bomb dropped on Nagasaki."

In a conversation with friends in Jerusalem, I ask how they feel about nuclear weapons in the Middle East.

"It's frightening to think of a country like Syria or Libya with atomic weapons," said one of the young men, who, although he is under thirty, has already fought in two wars. "But it was the nuclear balance of terror that pushed the Soviet Union and the United States to learn to coexist. Maybe it will happen here too."

At a press conference with the president of Mexico several days ago, Rabin was twice asked by Mexican journalists about reports of Israeli nuclear weapons. Rabin said, "Israel is not a nuclear weapons country. We will not be the first to introduce nuclear weapons into the Middle East."

Still, ever since the building of a nuclear reactor at Dimona in 1960, there has been speculation about possible appearance of nuclear weapons in the Middle East. Dr. Yair Evron, a Hebrew University lecturer on strategic problems, took up the knotty problems of nuclear deterrence in an article in the August issue of *The New Outlook*, a publication committed to cooperation between Jews and Arabs, which publishes mostly liberal opinions about the Middle East.

He points out that the superpowers are no model for the Middle East because they reached "their present degree of stability only after years of developing and studying nuclear weaponry." He asserts that the Middle East, where leaders are known to "resort to an irrational course of behavior," can have years of "tension and anxiety before adopting forms of conduct" dictated by nuclear weapons.

Moreover, Dr. Evron states, "The complex of relations between the United States and the Soviet Union is characterized by the fact that there are only two sides . . . . Should nuclear weaponry appear in this area, the problems of planning and control over it will be a thousand times more complicated." He suggests that "since some of the Arab countries are sharply hostile to one another, one can imagine situations in which one Arab country will try to precipitate an exchange of nuclear blows between Israel and another Arab country."

Dr. Evron warns of the "small number of targets in the Middle East" as being too tempting without the development of "second-strike capability" with silos and control mechanisms, which are too expensive. He also points out that "it is possible to imagine that a nuclear power friendly to the Arab states might even threaten to use nuclear weapons against Israel."

Wednesday, August 27

The problems with drafting the agreements are reflected in the complex nature and status of the documents themselves.

There are at least six or seven different levels of the agreement, as well as other informal assurances that must be considered part of the overall package.

First is the public agreement between Israel and Egypt.

Second is the public agreement between Israel and the United States.

Third is the public foreign-aid agreement between Egypt and Israel through the United States but not to each other.

Fourth are the annexes to each of the agreements that define clauses therein—maps, timetable, and definitions.

Fifth are the military protocols, which are to be worked out on exactly when and in what sequence military pullbacks and troop movements are to take place and how.

Sixth, and most important, are the so-called "secret" or non-public aspects of the agreement, also worked out in specific language but not yet known. In addition, there may be "private assurances" which are not in the agreements at all.

"Secret" doesn't mean that promises will never be known. It really refers to the time when the agreement will be made public. It is improbable, indeed (though not impossible), to think that after Watergate and Vietnam, Kissinger could keep anything of substance from the Congress, especially with President Ford seeking a more "open" image in contrast to Nixon.

But there may be aspects to the agreement that will not be made known until Kissinger appears before congressional committees to plead for passage of the package.

The negotiating strategy then revolves around the differing status of the agreements: for example, the Egyptians want to put as little into the bilateral agreements with Israel and as much in the "secret" agreements with Israel as possible, because to reach a bilateral agreement at all with Israel implies recognition, and "secret" agreements between Egypt and Israel directly might exacerbate beyond any rationality the extreme Arab states. Thus, even after Egypt agrees to the easing of the economic boycott, the passage of canal cargoes, or the clauses on reduced propaganda, the two countries bargain as to what document they will be stated in.

For the Israelis, the problem is not only to get an agreement with the Egyptians, but, since they are trading territory for promises, to get as much of it in the public agreement as possible. And if the Israelis want a public statement on cargo, would they give up something else to get it (say five hundred yards further from the mouth of the Mitla pass)? The Egyptians, having once agreed in the first place, would like all of their concessions downplayed in importance, either by having them stated as a promise to the Americans (not Israel) or made part of the "secret" documents.

In the Arab world, the very presence of "secret" agreements suggests all kinds of possibilities. Sadat met alone with Kissinger for fifty minutes the first day—how might Sadat describe such a conversation to the Syrians? "Don't worry," he might tell Assad of Syria, "I have told my friend Henry that if the Israelis don't give up every inch of the Golan Heights, this agreement will be void, as well. And he has given me his private word that he will press the Israelis with all the power at his command."

In a kibbutz at mealtime, I asked an eight-year-old Israeli girl if she knew who Henry Kissinger was. "Yes," she answered proudly, "he's president of the United States."

The Burtons are arriving at the hotel tonight and the place is alive with expectation. The hotel guests are out in full force, tired of Kissinger and ready for Liz. The ordinary precautions are available all around but are not activated; there are secret service smiles at the circus and a little concern at who might sneak through in the confusion. The reporters have a kind of cynical toleration of the way the Burtons are using us to personal and commercial advantage, though it is clear that a publicity machine is neutral—Kissinger or the Burtons—it's all the same.

The same faces are out to cover the arrival, and all of us are trying to top each other with quips. "They're going to get Henry to arrange an interim agreement," says one reporter, "renewable every year." "We gave them Sinai, and they sent us Cleopatra," says an Israeli journalist. "At last," says a third, "not actors posing as statesmen, but the real thing."

Their entrance is a caricature of the Kissinger arrivals, except that without the secret service to keep things orderly, the lobby turns into a chaotic camel market. The press is aggressive and the photographers have reverted to their paparazzi instincts, climbing on each other's shoulders and packing the Burtons so tightly together that they can barely move through the lobby.

The next day, Elizabeth (called on Israeli radio by her Hebrew name, "Elisheba"), accompanied by dozens of press people, visited the Wall ("Taylor at the Wailer," one British writer called it), and of course the Kissingers invited them up for a drink. Liz managed to walk through the lobby in a Kissinger T-shirt signed by the secretary himself, and she and Nancy went shopping together. It's clear that the Kissingers don't mind a little extra publicity themselves, but there's something profane about it. I suppose it's the intrusion into this deadly serious process in which two countries are coming to an agreement that involves war, peace, and survival; with Israel and Egypt at a crossroads, in waltz the Burtons to turn the event into something else—a self-promoting, camera-hogging show.

"London radio just called and said to hell with Kissinger. They want Liz and Dick." In the next three days, the reporter told me later, he filed one story on the negotiations and eight on the Burtons.

The Russians have been quiet since Kissinger arrived, and the silence is beginning to deafen some American officials. By the King David swimming pool, one of the American diplomats talks about his concern: "The Russian silence must mean that they just don't know what to do. Americans think of Russians as all-knowing but they have lapses of uncertainty, too. Maybe since they are going to lose something over this, they just don't want to call attention to it—you know, they'd rather fall out of a two-story window than a nine-story."

He continued, "When the Russians began the movement to reconvene Geneva and sent emissaries out there, it didn't take them long to see what a can of worms they were getting into. So they learned a lesson. Now they prefer to sit back, stay uninvolved, and take targets of opportunity. They can be like sharks when they see blood but there's nothing fresh for them to feed on out here now."

A cartoon in *Ma-ariv*, the afternoon paper, features a big policeman with a club over a very small Kissinger at the entrance of the King David Hotel. Kissinger is trying to get into the hotel. The caption reads: "My name is Kissinger. Richard Burton knows me personally."

Moshe Dayan has announced that he will vote against the agreement when it comes before the Knesset.

"It will strengthen Dr. Kissinger but it will weaken Israel," the former defense minister said, "which will have less to give in future negotiations."

Dayan favors an overall settlement which would include "a total withdrawal from Sinai and a settlement with Syria with whatever price we have to pay." The agreement he would favor, says Dayan, "would have to include a termination of the state of war with Egypt and Syria, with U.S. and Soviet agreement. It would be impossible to expect a total end to belligerence unless a similar status were also created with Syria."

Though Dayan has lost almost all influence in Israel after the 1973 war ("Israel's Pearl Harbor," a writer has called it) and the official inquiry afterward that placed some of the blame on him, the Israeli press has for sometime now been saying that Dayan is the only political figure in the country that Rabin fears.

"Rabin seems to see Dayan's shadow everywhere," said one Israeli journalist. "It's irrational. Dayan is finished and Peres is Rabin's only rival. It would take a national disaster for Dayan to regain even a foothold."

The reason for Rabin's concern, according to some observers, is that the Jewish community in the United States knows Dayan far better than Rabin and associates Dayan more with the 1967 war he led than with the 1973 war he stumbled in. It's as if Rabin rather envies Dayan's flamboyance, sensing instinctively that the eyepatch is more a symbol of tenacity and victory than it is of nonpreparedness and stalemate.

Beyond personal jealousies and rivalries for public favor, there is particular anger among Labor party leaders over Dayan's position on the agreement. Dayan, in 1971, was the first Israeli leader to advocate piecemeal negotiations separately arrived at with Arab countries because an overall settlement was impossible on any terms that Israel could accept. They suspect, according to one report, that Dayan wants to be suspended from the Labor party, to set up a new faction of his own.

The Israeli afternoon papers are unloading on Dayan for his opposition. A pro-Labor paper says that "Moshe Dayan, who has become an opposer of the proposed agreement, cannot expect his stand to be considered a bona fide opinion, since he himself was among those who initiated the idea of an interim agreement. Dayan is trying to make the public forget that he bears the chief responsibility for the present situation, which forces Israel to accept the agreement under given conditions. Dayan is aiming at a political comeback carried on waves of Likud and Gush Emunin hysteria. Dayan's gimmicks should be exposed."

I am invited to lunch with old family friends in Jerusalem, where Dayan and Golda are the center of conversation.

"Since 1967," said one man, an American who immigrated to Israel fifteen years ago, "the government should have been made to watch soccer games every day. Then they would have learned that you can't score goals sitting on your ass."

"But Golda tried to reach agreements with the Egyptians," protested his Israeli wife, "and nothing happened."

"Not true," said a student who is studying political science at the university. "The only possibility was an agreement that would have opened the canal. The Americans wanted the canal closed because of Vietnam."

"What do you mean?" I ask.

"The shortest route of Russian resupply for North Vietnam was through the canal. As long as the canal was closed, the Russians had to send supplies nine thousand miles overland and by ship from Vladivostock. It's the end of the Vietnam War that has made this agreement possible. The Americans want the canal open and flowing to pacify the area, the Russians want it open so they can put their warships into the Indian Ocean, the Egyptians want it open for money, and the Israelis want it open because Sadat is less likely to make war over a thriving canal than an empty one. That leaves the Syrians, and we'll have to count on the Russian interest in the canal to restrain them in the Golan."

Al Ahram, the leading Egyptian daily, is reporting the details of the agreement, according to the Israeli papers, "fully, fairly and accurately." The Israeli leaders are said to be pleased that the official report in Egypt is that the United Nations Emergency Force will be renewed annually and that "the United States will stress to Israel that it expects the agreement to remain in force for no less than three years."

Observers are saying that Sadat is under heavy and mounting pressure from Arab hard-liners, and for this reason would like to conclude negotiations with all possible speed.

Ilan Peker, who is Israel's leading astrologer and who predicted the Yom Kippur War, made his latest predictions today:

"In three months' time, Anwar Sadat will be out of a job.

"An earth tremor, plague, or just plain epidemic will wreak havoc throughout Egypt.

"Riot will rock both Egypt and Israel as opposing factions bash each other's teeth in.

"Henry Kissinger is due for some sort of accident, at about the same time as Anwar is booted out of office."

He shrugged when asked if he was certain. "It's in the stars," he said.

One of the afternoon newspapers reported under the headline "When is Rosh Hashanah? asks Kissinger" that during the six-hour negotiations yesterday, Kissinger asked when the Jewish New Year was, and then "explained that it was his intention to invite to a festive dinner new members of the Israeli delegation to the United Nations and he didn't want to do it on Rosh Hashanah."

An Orthodox rabbi comments, "It's our own fault. We don't educate Jewish children, so God is punishing us by sending us one of the products of our own neglect."

Kissinger left today for Alexandria at 4:30 in the afternoon.

Since the Likud opposition has called for its members from all over the country to meet at the Western Wall at 6:30 for speeches and a march through Jerusalem, the press suspects that Kissinger's departure was more a matter of avoiding the demonstrations than of talking to Sadat. The Likud has promised to turn out the largest crowds it can muster, using buses to transport demonstrators into Jerusalem from yeshivas and religious kibbutzim in the North. Most of us in the press, craving a change of pace, are looking forward to the evening.

At the airport, Kissinger says that "if possible, I would like to be back tonight (Thursday) because of the Sabbath so that we can work tomorrow during the day and leave then for Egypt. There are some things to be done on Saturday."

Crowds are moving through the winding streets into the old city for the demonstrations, heading for the broad plaza in front of the Wall. "This is already provocative," says an Israeli reporter friend looking up at the Arabs peering from their windows at the people below.

There's a sea of people in front of the Wall, and it's a young and spirited crowd. Kids in their mid-teens are dancing the hora in concentric circles in the middle of the demonstrators, banners and signs are waving—it seems more like a pep rally at Ohio State than a protest march. Several of us estimate between ten thousand and fifteen thousand people, which would make it the largest demonstration in Jerusalem's history.

These are mostly religious youth, boys and girls from the religious kibbutzim, the boys wearing colorful silver-dollar-sized yarmulkes pinned to their heads. As we move among the crowd, we see a sprinkling of some very religious boys in black fur hats and long coats, as well as a number of adults—even a few members of the Knesset mingling with their constituents.

One sign says, "God . . . Save Me From My Friends"; another shows Kissinger in an Arab headdress; another portrays him pushing a figure labeled "Israel" down steps labeled "Sinai," "Golan," "Jerusalem," and finally the sea.

I ask a girl what her sign would say if the secretary of state were Rogers. "Him," she says, "we could call an anti-Semite." "Why are you meeting here?" I ask another. "Because this is the heart of Israel," a young man answers. "If he will make us give back Sinai, he will give back the Wall." Another adds, "How much can an unreligious Jew care about Jerusalem?"

A placard reads: "Kissinger, your parents would be ashamed!" "Do you really believe that?" I ask a young bystander. "No," she says. "It's better than being a doctor."

Several of us corner Joachim Fried. One of the founders of the Gush Emunin, he is in his early thirties, bearded and over six feet tall, very soft-spoken and polite. While we talk, the speakers in the background are turning on the crowd with references to "treason" and "Munich in 1938." A rabbi calls Rabin "Yitzhak Chamberlain" and says that the agreement could lead to "another holocaust."

We ask Fried why he believes that Israel has been put in this position.

"To a religious Jew," he says, "there are no accidents. Perhaps God has sent Kissinger, the Jew, to test our love of the land." He believes that Kissinger is putting special pressure on Israel because he is not a good enough Jew. "He had to ask when Rosh Hashanah was," he points out. "That's the kind of Jew he is. And he spends every Shabbat in an Arab country, and took his oath on a New Testament, and married a non-Jew. Nancy—that's where it always ends. It gives us special pain."

The crowd hushes for Assa Kadmoni, the former Israeli soldier who returned his Medal of Valor to the government the first night Kissinger arrived. Kadmoni, a handsome blond in a tight dark T-shirt, has become an important ally to the religious group opposing the agreement. He speaks with the authority of a hero who fought at the Suez Canal in the 1973 war, getting his medal for holding off three hundred Egyptians for several hours. But he is a dull speaker, with neither inspiration nor coherence. His speech wanders into issues like the lack of discipline in Israeli life and the cheating in business and taxes. He receives his most respectful applause when he charges at the end of his speech that "Kissinger helped Formosa and Vietnam to their grave and it will happen to us."

The crowd begins to break up for the march through the city over to the major auditorium near the Hilton where they will hear more speeches. It's an impressive sight to see them march through Zion square past the television cameras and the lights—rows and rows of young demonstrators with arms around each others' shoulders, maybe thirty in a row across the street, trotting past in rhythm to slogans and songs. "Kissinger dye, Am Yisrael Hai" ("Kissinger enough, the people of Israel live").

One of the Israeli radio stations had a one-hour discussion tonight on the subject of Kissinger's dilemma as a Jewish secretary of state. An Israeli journalist, who is also interested in the subject, took extensive notes.

The discussion pointed out that "a Jew shouldn't hold a high position in a Gentile world. Kissinger must prove his objectivity by putting more pressure on us than any Gentile would." The moderator asked how a Jew like Kissinger can serve American interests and Israeli interests without a conflict of interest. The answer, according to one member of the panel, was, "For him, there is no conflict. It is very convenient for the United States to get a non-Zionist Jew like Kissinger to do its dirty work for them; for him there is no dilemma. America's interest is Israel's interest. And this non-Zionist will tell us Zionists what to do."

"But," said one panelist, "how can a survivor of Germany be a non-Zionist?"

"Because he is secretary of state and very powerful. But American Jews will learn, including Kissinger, that what happened in Nazi Germany can happen in America. Only the existence of Israel, which Kissinger is undermining, can save them."

Another complained that "Kissinger fled to America instead

of coming here where he could have been head of American relations in the foreign ministry and helped the Jewish state."

One Kissinger supporter defended him by comparing him to Mordecai in the Purim story of Esther—the important Jew in the non-Jewish world using his position to help the Jews. "America's interest is indeed Israel's interest," he said, "because the United States is the only friend we have in the world." He criticized as "unjust" the way the government "dragged Kissinger to Yad Vashem and to Masada," and he condemned "the disgusting use of anti-Semitic slogans against Kissinger."

Friday, August 29

In *Israel Digest*, which comes out weekly, Nissim Rejwan, an Israeli writer who monitors Arab publications and broadcasts, writes, "It is interesting to note that Dr. Kissinger's Jewish ancestry is never referred to in Arab writings and pronouncements about him. The nearest any Arab leader came to this is said to have been the late King Faisal of Saudi Arabia in an anecdote which is probably apocryphal but which gained some currency during one of Dr. Kissinger's shuttle missions.

"'I welcome you here.' Faisal is said to have told the secretary of state, 'not as a Jew but as a human being.' To which the quick-witted professor retorted, 'Don't worry, Your Majesty. Some of my best friends are human beings.'"

Naomi Shemer, the singer and songwriter who wrote "Jerusalem of Gold" just after the 1967 war, has written a new song for the demonstrators, entitled "The Shark." "A little sardine met a shark at the beach of El Areish," the song goes, "and what does a sardine say to a shark? 'Shalom' [Peace]."

"He gave his tail in exchange for peace and then his two eyes in exchange for peace, and then his stomach in exchange for peace. The sardine said, 'I will give everything for peace' . . . Now the shark swims alone."

At the morning briefing, members of the press living in the

King David Hotel show up in bathing suits or jogging outfits with tennis rackets, relaxed and on the way to the pool or the courts. After the briefing we all gather at the bar to compare notes. Everyone is sure Kissinger will find a way to work things out.

We have all become "the boys in the bar" by now, interviewing each other to find some new angle to report. A woman, who several people tell me later is a major Israeli gossip columnist, is chasing around after the Burtons for *People* magazine. She tells a group of us how she cornered Defense Minister Shimon Peres at a cocktail party. "He told me, 'If there's no agreement we'll have a war,' so I told him, 'You'll have a war anyway so why give up strategic positions like the passes?' He answered me, 'The passes we can capture back. In the meantime, I'd rather have the money and the arms.'"

By now, we've all grown tired of writing the same story. While Nancy is sitting by the pool in a long red-and-black caftan talking to the major writers she knows from the plane, I'm having a hamburger with an English writer covering his first shuttle. "I've never been so bored on such a big story," he says.

A European wire service reporter complains, "This whole shuttle was an unnecessary charade. It was important only for Kissinger to justify the validity of shuttles and get publicity for the agreement. But it all could have been done from Washington just as well."

Phillip Gallon, who writes features for the *Jerusalem Post*, has written a day-by-day report of the agreement as seen on Israeli television. It's entitled "Emerging Street" and points out that "there was a time when we could sneer at the Arab countries because of the power of the street, could point out that no Arab leader would dare to negotiate such and such a deal because the street would not allow it, and he would be in immediate danger of being torn to pieces. Now Dr. Kissinger has to be defended by vast numbers of policy and security men, not against the danger of assassination by El Fatah terrorists, but against those Israelis who oppose his ideas of peace. It is a curious thought that in Cairo and Alexandria he can walk unmolested and almost unguarded through the bazaars."

What Gallon did not mention is that, just as Israelis and Arabs on the West Bank can watch Jordanian television every night (and some have aerials that can receive Beirut and even Cairo), so is the opposite true. Moreover, the Yom Kippur War was the first television war for Israel (and the Arabs), which surely must have some relationship to the degree of participation that the population at home experienced. The global village has come to the Middle East as a major factor in shaping things to come.

"It's as if we can watch them watching us," said one student.

After this week, Israel can expect more and more of its politics to be played out through the mass media. The success of the demonstrators in galvanizing public opinion will surely encourage the believers in future causes of all types to go directly to the public, and the country may find itself generating more and more leaders who know how to exploit the media.

Saturday, August 30

At a small Sabbath luncheon, a leading Israeli psychiatrist and the editor of a newspaper opposing the agreement discuss the Kissinger personality.

"After Kissinger was appointed as a presidential advisor," says the psychiatrist, "I respected him enormously for adapting to the pragmatic demands of Washington politics—he was the first European intellectual with such power and he used it skillfully in dealing with China and the Soviets. Mostly, I respected his wisdom in seeing the complexity of his being a Jew and therefore the necessity to leave the Middle East to Rogers and the State Department.

"But two months after he became secretary of state, the October war broke out, and a new Kissinger was unveiled—an exhibitionist on a global scale. He seemed to love the attention, the accolade, the manipulation. Where did the need for attention come from? No American before him, no English diplomat ever allowed such hugging and kissing by the Arabs. It was undignified."

The editor, who is in his mid-forties, broke in, "The German Jews always looked with condescension on the East Europeans—their Judaism was rational, analytical, and intellectual; ours was mystical, emotional, Bohemian, and Hasidic. I'm sure Kissinger sees Israel as too excitable, too hot-blooded—not controlled and, if you please, German-Jewish enough."

"Yes," says the psychiatrist, "it plays out in everything he does. He is 'Dr. Kissinger' and they are 'Yigal.' He is teacher and they are his students—Allon was a former student at Harvard, you know—he is the worldly German Jew with great power, they are the narrow shtetl leaders to whom he will explain how the world works. Only he knows. We can't tell him anything."

I ask about the quotation from the Kalbs' book on Kissinger. ("My life in Furth seems to have passed without leaving any lasting impressions," the Kalbs report that Kissinger once told a German reporter. "I can't remember any interesting or lasting impressions. That part of my childhood is not a key to anything. It is fashionable now to explain everything psychoanalytically, but let me tell you, the political persecutions of my childhood are not what control my life.")

The psychiatrist, who has had a great deal of experience in dealing with survivors, shakes his head. "No man can be unaffected by such an uprooting. Either he is repressed or he is lying. Either way it is neurotic."

The editor adds, "The people of Furth were assimilated. It was a town that was 70 percent Protestant and only 2 percent Jewish. They were religious Jews but not Zionists."

Then how does a German Jew with such a background relate to Israel? I ask.

"For any non-Zionist Jew," says the psychiatrist, "Israel is a profound confrontation—with history, with personality, with his soul."

The editor continues, "At the least, his worldview is very pessimistic. He has seen disaster. That's the reason he moves about with such urgency and is in a bigger hurry than the parties to the agreement are. If the only alternative to an agreement is a catastrophe, then any agreement will do."

"The problem is," says the editor's wife, "we don't know how much pressure is coming from the American public and how much from Kissinger himself. We suspect that he is putting more pressure on us than the American public is."

Someone at the table suggests that the pressure is from President Ford, who needs a concrete foreign-policy achievement to get reelected.

"But if so," points out the editor, "there will be powerful elements in the American political system, ordinarily friendly to Israel, that will want to undermine the agreement. If we are asking America to make real sacrifices for us, we can't expect Jewish interests alone to carry the day. We will need to develop new friends."

How do you make the case to these new friends? I ask.

"Moral arguments alone will not do it. Only pragmatics. Kissinger told the editors in his off-the-record briefing that in his travels, Americans ask him why, and that we must help him convince them."

Another guest interrupts. "I was disappointed the agreement with the United States said nothing about an American base at Haifa, or that the fuel we will store up could be used by American ships."

Has it been talked about?

"It was mentioned during the Turkey-Greece mess in Cyprus," the editor says. "At least then, we could answer the question of why the United States has a stake in Israel."

And what of the long run?

"I'm sure this agreement fits into Kissinger's grand design," says the editor, "of Iran, Egypt, and Saudi Arabia as the new oil superpowers in the new world—a new power bloc if you will—independent of the Soviet Union and the United States, but profoundly anti-Communist and dependent on the West. My problem with that is that it all depends on a few men, not the countries themselves. Sadat and the Shah of Iran could be assassinated tomorrow and big leftist movements inside those countries could take over."

Monday, September 1

Headlines today say that the accord will be initialed tonight, and that Israel has been outmaneuvered in a bid to have it signed by high-ranking diplomats from both sides. Sadat named his chief of staff, General Mohammed Aly Fahmy, as the signatory, since in Egypt, he outranks top diplomats. Thus, Sadat can still insist that the agreement is primarily military in character. Kissinger will carry the documents personally from Jerusalem to Alexandria, holding press conferences in both places.

Always suspicious of Arab motives, the Israeli press is watching how the agreement is being portrayed in the government-controlled Egyptian press. The *Jerusalem Post* points out that "the prestigious *Rose el Yousef* weekly yesterday informed the Arab world for the first time that Egypt has made a pledge with Israel through the U.S. not to attack each other under the interim peace accord."

There is violent reaction from the PLO leaders, who call it the "Sinai conspiracy," with Arafat vowing to obstruct "an American plot aimed at liquidating the Palestinian movement."

Two more terrorists were killed in the North, only thirty hours after three others were killed in a similar incident. Leaflets and documents they were carrying showed that they belonged to George Habash's Popular Front for the Liberation of

Palestine, one of the rival organizations to Yasir Arafat's Fatah, to which the earlier groups belonged. The press reports noted that Kfar Giladi, a northern kibbutz, "had been the apparent target of the gang, as the PFLP was yesterday claiming in Beirut that its men had succeeded in attacking Kfar Giladi and were holding 30 hostages. The PFLP went on to say that their men would murder one hostage every 15 minutes unless Israel released an unspecified number of imprisoned terrorists."

The signing of the accord is deliberately downplayed by the two sides. The private Israeli attitude is reflected in a Golda Meir radio interview: "You have to take it in proper proportions," she said, "not with fanfare, not with mourning."

After the stacks of copies of the accord had been signed in Jerusalem, Prime Minister Rabin turned to Kissinger and said with a smile, "I hope that, realizing the difficulties of the shuttle diplomacy, in the future you will encourage direct negotiations. It will save you lots of effort and lots of time."

President Ford, who telephoned Kissinger and Rabin in Jerusalem and Sadat in Egypt, was much less circumspect, calling the agreement "one of the great achievements of the world at this time." In his talks with Kissinger, Ford began, in his best post-Watergate etiquette, by telling his secretary of state that he was taping the call. "You don't have any objections, I trust," said Ford. "I guess it's for historical purposes."

After my luggage is searched at the airport, because of a chronic backache I ask the security person for help. She smiles and wrestles the bag a few feet away to be checked onto the plane. An old woman behind us, who is putting her grandchild on the plane, berates me.

"But she is a strong Israeli," I defend myself, "and I am a weak American."

"Of course," she replies. "If you were strong, you'd be living here in Israel."

20

Abba Eban at Columbia

I interviewed Abba Eban, former foreign minister and Israeli ambassador to the United Nations, for four hours over a period of several days in 1974 for this profile. I was to come to know him well several years later through the Revson Foundation's partnership in his public broadcasting series, "Heritage: Civilization and the Jews." At this first encounter, I soon understood why other journalists told me to take a tape recorder with me. One of the great spontaneous orators on earth, Eban shapes his language into poetry as he talks. Whole paragraphs emerge as elegant prose, so mesmerizing that it is easy to forget to listen with care to *what* is said because of *how* it is said. His mastery of language was one reason the immigrant generation loved Eban; he made them proud to be Jews, and because he was so articulate, the press loved to quote him, too. As a result, he has remained in the public eye for over forty years.

You can find Abba Eban at Columbia University on Tuesdays and Wednesdays meeting with his students up in the International Affairs Building on 118th Street. For the first time since he was appointed ambassador to the United Nations in 1948, the experienced diplomat is no longer a part of Israel's official family, and his personal style has changed accordingly.

"Professor" Eban wears blazers, sport coats, and loafers now, and he hustles cabs like other New Yorkers—it's a far cry from his limousine and pinstripe days in the UN corridors. Cast by events to the sidelines, he suffers the pangs of the retired quarterback watching his team's lackluster performance in the big game. When Palestine Liberation Organization chief Yasir Arafat made his dramatic appearance at the United Nations, Eban was meeting with his class at Columbia, and he says he received letters and phone calls "from Jews who said they felt very uncomfortable that I wasn't there to answer."

Eban wanted to be there to answer, but his long-simmering differences with Israeli Prime Minister Yitzhak Rabin bubbled up to public view when the new coalition was put together last May after Golda Meir's retirement, and Eban turned down a minor post for a private life of writing, teaching, and public speaking. He is working on his memoirs, hopes to turn his Columbia lectures on "multilateral diplomacy" into his fifth book, and will return to Israel before the first of the year to stir the waters in Israeli politics as a member of the Knesset and of the various Labor party policy committees. In the meantime, he crammed his teaching duties into two days a week so that he could undertake a backbreaking speaking schedule of more than forty lectures, which has carried him all over the United States.

His teaching schedule consists of a lecture on modern diplomacy on Tuesday evenings and an afternoon graduate seminar on Wednesdays titled "Case Histories on War and Peace in the Middle East." His research assistant says that more than ninety students applied, of which thirty-two were admitted. There are two Israelis, and a Palestinian, who said that he took the course to observe a major Israeli leader at close hand, and while he disagrees with almost everything said, he calls Eban "a very good Arabist and very kind as an individual." (Eban speaks six languages, including Arabic, Persian, and Hebrew.)

When Eban lectures, he sits on the edge of his chair like a frog on a lily pad, leaning forward for emphasis. His mannerisms—fidgeting with his pen, wriggling in his seat, always speaking eloquently, almost to a fault—remind one of his United Nations appearances. In fact, watching Eban at Columbia is much like seeing an old TV star on the "Joe Franklin Show" doing his thing again without scenery or a supporting cast.

In person, he radiates restlessness and mental energy. He wears thick horn-rimmed glasses that wrap around his face like goggles, with lenses that enlarge the eyes of a man who reads a great deal. He wheels in his chair as he talks, underscoring his reputation for pontification, and the words flow with such rapidity that it is easy to see why some Israeli leaders complain that a conversation with Eban is a one-sided monologue ("Easy to respect, impossible to like," said one American Jewish leader). He is reserved but has an engaging smile and a Cambridge wit that cannot resist turning a phrase on every subject ("My wife likes Chinese food and I eat it with docility"). He considers Columbia a "well-earned interlude," and though he has been written off as a domestic political leader by almost every observer of Israeli politics, he describes his past and the internal shifts in Israel in ways that make him a logical choice for prime minister should the Rabin coalition collapse over internal issues. In fact, it seems that he is almost campaigning in America for the job.

"Whether I like it or not," he says, "most people, and especially most Jews, still think I'm responsible somehow for the destiny of Israel, and that I articulate its visions. People still stop me on the streets—what do I think, what do I not think, what's going to happen—half the people who speak to me don't even know that I've left office. Abba Eban is a kind of institution, and they ask me why am I not in charge."

He is more frank in his public utterances than ever before, he claims, and though he can burst into poetic soliloquy on any issue about the Middle East, he goes out of his way to answer questions with directness and candor, perhaps to dispel his image as an evasive and pretentious diplomat. He will even discuss his differences with Rabin.

"There were differences in outlook in which, during his position in Washington, he advocated a very hard line. . . . I was less attached to the status quo, I was for a less rigid attitude than he was." Rabin had offered Eban a newly created job as information minister, knowing, some say, that Eban would turn it down, since as foreign minister, Eban had opposed the formation of a similar post that would have created a spokesman's office separate from the responsible agencies.

"I didn't think I had any reason to accept a position that I thought was not compatible with my capacities or my prestige or my dignity," Eban says. "Being a minister isn't the be-all or end-all, and since the functions he suggested didn't appeal to me, I said, 'Thanks very much, I'll stay out.'"

To the American public, Eban and Moshe Dayan—the tongue and the sword—had been the two rising stars in Israeli politics, but Eban carefully separated his voluntary withdrawal from events that discredited Dayan after the 1973 war. "That's a completely different situation because he was involved in a report that found certain deficiencies in defensive preparations, and his chief of staff and leading officers resigned. Nothing like that happened to me. My ambassadors did not resign and I am not mentioned in the report."

To dramatize his differences with the hard-line military leaders, he even talked about the background of negotiations last spring, implying for the first time in public that the Israeli cabinet had voted down any concessions to King Hussein, even when an agreement seemed possible. (A few days ago an Israeli newspaper reported that Eban himself had met with Hussein in 1967 and 1968.) "We did explore very carefully with him—after the 1973 war—the possibility of compromise, but he was never able to make a compromise outside the volition of the Arabs as a collective unit. After the Yom Kippur War, it might have been better, after the Syrian disengagement agreement, to pursue the possibility of a Jordanian-Israeli agreement—even a limited agreement. I advocated that."

Eban reviewed carefully the 1974 negotiations with Hussein, seeming to validate Hussein's lament after the Rabat conference that "there was an opportunity" and underscoring the claim that hard-liners in the Israeli government are partially to blame for the emergence of the PLO. "Hussein made a proposal that was not acceptable—that Israel withdraw from the whole length of the Jordan. Some of us thought that although this was not acceptable, we ought not rule out a symbolic return of a single place to him, like Jericho, in order to establish that he is the addressee for a settlement and to suppress the movement toward the PLO. The Israeli cabinet did not ever adopt such a proposal, though I threw it out as a personal idea in an article I wrote for the Israeli press in July or August. Since I did say it, I don't see any reason not to admit saying it now. . . . It didn't happen, and in the vacuum of diplomacy, the Palestine revolutionary movement made great strides."

Eban believes that he cannot be written off as a future prime minister, especially because of his access to and popularity with the American Jewish community so crucial to Israel's survival. When asked if he would ever be elected prime minister, he replied, "Nothing in Israeli politics is impossible. At the moment, the whole prospect is obscure. All I can say is that I am not abandoning the political arena; that I am going back to it at the end of December, and then I'll follow its course. I don't want to say anything that will either preclude or commit the future." He said that no one can ever be ruled out, recalling that when he ran "into Nixon on the shuttle service between Washington and New York in 1965, he gave an impression of someone who had missed his chance or wouldn't have it again."

Throughout his career, most commentators on Israeli politics have dismissed Eban as a possible prime minister because Israelis prefer Eastern Europeans to the Anglo-Saxon Jews from South Africa or England. (Eban was even called Aubrey while he was growing up in England, going back to the Hebrew name he was given at birth when the state of Israel was created.) Israelis are drawn to the hardened kibbutz pioneers who drained the swamps and made the desert bloom rather than to a Cambridge-bred intellectual like Eban. (It is typical of Eban's problem that Yiddish and Russian are not on the list of the six languages in which he is fluent.) Others say that he's just too weak and wordy, too ready to compromise, that he makes complex issues out of simple realities that military men are more competent to judge. They point out that a tougher, open-shirted sabra—a military figure like Yitzhak Rabin—is more attuned to the Israeli character, because he has been in the trenches and speaks, as one journalist put it, "your basic Golda Meir 600-word vocabulary."

Eban argues that events have made him more viable politically than he was before the war. "I believe that there is more consensus in Israel now for a flexible compromise. There is much less euphoria, much less fundamentalism, much less belief that the status quo can go on for twenty years, attitudes which were very prevalent before the Yom Kippur War and which put me in the minority. What was then a minority position has now become the majority position. I even think that those who took a hard line in the past are now changing their attitude under the impact of events—I include Rabin himself, who was a much harder-liner before he had the responsibility than now."

Eban does not deny that the Israeli hawks in the military are an obstacle to compromise (one lesson from the Middle East wars of the last twenty years, military writers point out, is that whoever struck first got an advantage), but he dismisses them as any determinative political force that might push Israel into a preemptive strike against either Syria or Egypt. "The Israeli

military are not a decision-making body," Eban explained
crisply. "They can think what they like. They cannot decide.
You could never get an Israeli cabinet decision for a preemptive war."

What about his reputation as the Adlai Stevenson of Israeli
politics? ("One never remembers what he says, only how well
he says it," someone wrote of both Eban and Stevenson.) "My
feeling," he says with a smile, "is that a discreet measure of
literacy is not a fatal handicap; it can be overcome and lived
down."

He does worry that in Israel "it is a very bad period because
Israelis have not yet recuperated from the melancholy generated by the Yom Kippur War, which shattered very many illusions." One senses that he could benefit from not being in
power during the internal economic crisis in much the same
way that Rabin escaped responsibility for the war by being
ambassador to Washington. "I think it is possible to get Israel
back onto a more stable psychological course—it's a matter of
national leadership—we'll see how the economic measures
work out."

Eban is making the effort to puncture his reputation for
pomposity and bloated oratory, and now that he is out of office
he can even summon up a profanity occasionally to accentuate
a point—though from him it sounds more like a Churchillian
exclamation than the natural expletive of a backslapping good
ole boy. When asked about the fear in the American Jewish
community that Kissinger will have to lean over backward
to placate the Arabs because he is Jewish, Eban shot back,
"That's a lot of damned nonsense because no secretary of state
before him and no likely secretary of state after him has emphasized the common values of America and Israel more than
he. The fact that he has a sense of the Jewish experience is an
added contribution, in my opinion." Having worked with
every secretary of state since World War II, Eban considers
Kissinger to be "exceptional in his originality, first of all, in his
sense of history . . . and a somewhat greater audacity."

Eban brings special intimacy to his denunciation of the United Nations, which he condemns with surprising sharpness: "I don't think the League of Nations was ever at such a low point of prestige and of public respect as the United Nations is today. It is in a moral crisis." He was particularly angry at the "protocolar flattery" of Arafat, and that "nobody got up on the floor and said, 'What the hell kind of precedent is this; who decided to treat Arafat like that?'" And he added, "Paradoxically, if we could get the United Nations out of town, the prospects for peace would increase."

Eban does not accept the argument that Arafat is a moderate who can emerge as a reasonable force for a self-governing West Bank. "That's ridiculous. Anybody who writes of him as a moderate is idiotic. You just have to listen to what he says." He dismisses the recent arrests of PLO hijackers as "a jurisdictional" dispute. "It is not an objection to the principle of it. The PLO says that we must do the killing ourselves—we decide when to murder, whom to murder."

His formula for Israeli policy regarding the West Bank is to wait until the Arabs realize that they have made a mistake with Arafat: "Israel will not give the West Bank to someone who will use it as a springboard for the destruction of Israel. And I hope that when it becomes apparent that Arafat cannot deliver the goods—that is, cannot get a compromise, cannot get territorial change—perhaps more moderate Palestinians on the West Bank, perhaps even together with Jordan, will again begin to articulate a more moderate possibility."

Eban considers himself an optimist who believes that "in spite of all the hot talk, war is not impossible but it's not inevitable." He believes that "if Egypt opens the Suez Canal, it will have a very strong interest in not getting it closed again by renewed warfare" and that détente may convince the Russians "to cool down the arms shipments to Syria to win American sympathy."

He sees a "tremendous anti-Arab backlash" growing out of the oil crisis and feels that they are reassessing their strategy because "if they threaten the collapse of the industrial countries of the advanced world, they'll be destroying their own markets."

Since late summer, the Ebans have been living in the small furnished apartment that the Weizmann Institute maintains on Central Park (he is a former president of the institute) with a beautiful view of the park and a small study for the fifty or so books he brought with him in a couple of suitcases. Eban's wife, Suzy, is studying art at Columbia, and for the first time they have been able to dip into the city's pleasures, seeing plays and movies, museums and galleries.

"The advantage of living in New York for me is improvisation," he explains. "You go out into the streets and go where the spirit takes you, you move with the current in the streets. Even if one doesn't call the city beautiful, it has a pulse, it has a vitality, it has an exhilaration." One would not expect it of a man with the cultural tastes of Eban, but his favorite restaurants run to "rather simple places. We used to like places like Reuben's where you could get very solid food. There's now a place called Wolf's on Sixth Avenue. I don't like elaborate, sophisticated things in general." (Contrary to his silver-spoon image, Eban grew up without social position or money.) All the same, he and his wife occasionally drop by the Plaza, where the United Nations mission had a suite that he stayed in during sessions, and where they are still treated with "great obsequiousness." He smokes long Cuban cigars but is smoking less than when he was in office.

Abba Eban insists that he has not retired but is just pausing, pointing out that Golda Meir and David Ben-Gurion served Israel until they were in their late seventies. Eban's major political strength in Israel lies in his standing with the American Jewish community, which has an emotional attachment to the sound of his voice. Unlike the speeches of many ambassadors to the United Nations, his were undiluted by the dry tones of translators, so that most American Jews experienced the trauma of the past three Middle Eastern wars through his words and personality. To them, his clipped accent and British demeanor dramatized a civilized Israel fighting for a chance to live, but more important, he was an intelligent representative for the non-Jewish American audience as well. Eban was good for the Jews.

His route to power in the past, however, was always by appointment through his standing with Chaim Weizmann, David Ben-Gurion, and Golda Meir. But he has never had any real voter support among the mass of Israelis, and his foreign-affairs portfolios have kept him out of the country much of the time. His popularity in the United States is still his trump card, for "Israel is caught up in a great drama in its dialogue with the world," he says, leaving no doubt about who he feels can conduct that dialogue effectively. So no matter that his immediate plans are to return to Israel; chances are that the American Jewish community will be seeing a great deal of him. Already, in February, he has scheduled a number of speeches, and he admits that he might like another semester at Columbia next fall.

Perhaps if the top post is beyond his grasp now that a new generation of Israeli leaders is emerging, Eban is letting the Labor party know that he will not go to pasture quietly. Some observers have suggested that he would add visibility and reso-nance to the largely honorary position of president of Israel, a post previously reserved for distinguished scholars. Whatever his future, he warmed to the analogy of the restless war-horse pawing the ground in eagerness to get back into the battle.

"After six months, that's a reasonable diagnosis," he says. "There's ambivalence—an appreciation of the tranquility and lack of strain—but also a desire to bring that happy conclusion to an end. If there was really something big to do, then I would give up the tranquility and the privacy to do it."

The "something big to do" turned out not to be elective or appointive office in Israel, but a far-reaching public television idea that evolved into "Heritage: Civilization and the Jews," the nine-hour, award-winning 1984 series that has since been broadcast in fourteen countries, including Russia in the summer of 1992 (where it had a potential audience of 150 million people).

The idea for a BBC-style series on Jewish history had first occurred to me in the 1970s, when my work took me to England to spend time with the staffs of the Kenneth Clark series "Civilisation" and the Jacob Bronowski series "The Ascent of Man." When Abba Eban and I first talked about it in 1978, he was captivated with the idea that a television experience could be created that would not portray Jews as "victims" or Israel as a "problem" but would reach back in time and seek to understand the strands in the tapestry of history and then reweave them into what he called "the long, continuous, somber, sometimes tragic, yet noble story" of the Jewish contribution and interaction with Western civilization.

The "Heritage" series, which was launched by the Revson Foundation and supported by over one hundred contributors, was the product of six years of planning and production. It became one of the most ambitious documentaries in the history of American public television. It was filmed in eighteen countries on four continents and has been seen by hundreds of millions of viewers around the world. In addition, more than two hundred colleges and universities have offered courses based on the series.

Eban is working on a successor to the "Heritage" series, another collaboration entitled "Israel: A Nation Is Born," a five-hour series already broadcast in England that will be offered to public television stations in December 1992.

In a far more intimate role as a witness and participant, Eban as storyteller and narrator will deal with the modern period of Israel since 1948 when, to quote him, "the Jews became a subject of recent history, statecraft and diplomacy and, of course, of tense struggle, illuminated by hope." Because the story of Israel as a modern nation has also spanned the history of television, Americans have been personal witness to the drama of Israel's struggle and have watched Eban play out his public career in the role of chief defender as United Nations and American ambassador. Once, in the late 1950s, my grandfather and I were watching a UN debate, when he turned to me and said in his slight East European accent, "You must learn to speak like Abba Eban." In an unusual way, Abba Eban is part of the collective memory of the American Jewish community, which embraced him like family.

I once asked Eban what he would have done had he not gone into public life. When he answered that he would have been a teacher, I had the presence of mind to respond, "Mr. Ambassador, I think at last we have found a classroom big enough for you."

Now 75, Eban has had a great life of statesmanship and extraordinary eloquence in behalf of justice, freedom, and homeland.

While he wishes to be known as a teacher, future generations who will continue to experience him through "Heritage: Civilization and the Jews" and "Israel: A Nation Is Born," will also surely see him as one of the shapers of Jewish destiny and as the modern voice of the Jewish people.

21

The Electronic Village

Over a number of years, I have written several versions of "The Electronic Village" to make the case for a greater involvement with and commitment to new technology as a vital resource of renewal for Jewish cultural and educational life. It has seemed self-evident to me that an enormous opportunity was being missed to counteract the discouraging trends developing in America and undermining the ancient cornerstone of Judaism throughout history: the Jewish family. These unmistakable patterns have been noted with alarm by a number of analysts of Jewish social history—declining birth rates, increasing intermarriage, and an escalating divorce rate, as well as a population of the young, characterized by their flight from identification with and a lack of interest in Jewish tradition or participation in Jewish life. Moreover, as surveys have confirmed, more than 40 percent and perhaps as many as 60 percent of the Jewish families in America are unaffiliated—that is, not touched by synagogue or temple membership or any organizational tie. The obvious question for the organized Jewish community in America is how to reach out to these families, to involve them in Jewish educational and cultural experiences.

New technology is the overlooked partner in bringing the rich potential of Jewish culture into the home. There is a television set in over 97 percent of American homes; cable television will be present in nearly 100 percent of all homes by the year 2000, as will video cassette recorders (VCRs). Home computer sales continue to move forward, and the compact audio disc, based on laser technology, makes the resurgence of the videodisc just a matter of time and inventiveness.

The proliferation of technology presents a whole new set of opportunities for touching those often considered "lost" to Judaism. I am talking about that large group of individuals who identify themselves as Jewish, who may be interested in aspects of Jewish culture, but who for one reason or another do not participate in the formal institutions of the Jewish community. Telecommunications certainly is not a substitute for such participation, but is a way to reach into the intimacy of the home and supplement it, enrich it, and—this is the great hope and possibility—stimulate those who have lost contact altogether with organized Judaism. Developing technology, though incapable of replacing the small, tightly knit communities that immersed many of our parents and grandparents in Jewish life, does constitute a kind of electronic village, where every family can tap into the richness and diversity of Jewish culture. This vital means of reaching out will increase in importance as the current telecommunications revolution touches virtually the whole population, changing the way we live, work, and learn. And while the primary audience for most of the programming I am going to talk about is Jewish, modern telecommunications—especially television—enables us to reach both Jews and non-Jews with materials designed for a broad audience.

In many ways, cable television offers the most promising prospect. Specifically, though the problems are daunting, plans should be made to create a special cable network for Jewish audiences, because of cable's advance in major metropolitan areas where 90 percent of all American Jews live. It is possible to envision a place on the cable dial for music, dance, and drama presentations; children's shows; interviews with writers, artists, and political figures; live news from Israel on a daily basis; satellite conversations joining intellectuals from several countries with thinkers in Israel; feature films and documentaries. Jewish cable initiatives have made promising starts in Los Angeles, Chicago, Boston, and Miami, and it is possible to foresee a time when enough channels would be available in New York, Philadelphia, Dallas, and Atlanta for a nationwide specialized Jewish Cable Network to be created. Since 1975 more than two dozen such new "networks" have been started, ranging from the Black Entertainment Television Network to the Spanish International Network to Nickelodeon, a children's programming service. I have thought about the prospect of it often over the years—when Natan Scharansky and later the first planeload of Russians arrived in Israel, and there were only snatches of coverage on the U.S. network news programs; when a pivotal Israeli election such as the 1992 election of Yitzhak Rabin demanded more intensive analysis; when a new book was published, such as Martin Gilbert's *The Holocaust*, and I wanted to hear in depth from the author; when Israeli cultural events, such as the opening of the Dayan archaeological exhibit at the Israel Museum, were taking place and received little mention in America. I also imagined the impact of such an outlet when "Rechov Sumsum," the Israeli "Sesame Street," completed the production of 190 programs, and eleven hours of the American version of the show, "Shalom Sesame," were shown on American public television. (That will be discussed later in this chapter.)

Unfortunately, however, cable has been slow to develop in America and has had disappointing results. At present, the limited number of channels would make a nationwide Jewish Cable Network difficult to establish; however, if planning and financing could be organized over the next few years, such a thing could be accomplished as the next generation of cable systems comes into operation with more than 50 to 150 channels in each city. (This is no longer a pipe dream: digital compression could create 500 channels for New York City by the late 1990s if the interminable delays could be overcome, and over one hundred channels are already being planned in Denver.)

But, even so, cable and the other new technologies are just systems for delivering programming, and ultimately these strategies will succeed or fail only if the content and quality meet a high standard. Cable, for example, depends on attracting and keeping an audience, which means delivering high quality material not available more conveniently elsewhere. The technology itself is only a means; it is what we do with it that gives it value. Once the novelty has worn off, the content of the material must be such that people will continue to want it.

While cable's growth potential has been disappointing, what has been promising is how receptive public broadcasting has been to well-produced Jewish material of interest to broader audiences. According to the Neilsen ratings, "Heritage: Civilization and the Jews" reached over 51 million viewers in its first broadcast in the United States, and more than two hundred colleges taught courses using the series. There have also been numerous films shown on individual public stations over the last few years, including *Shoah*, Claude Lanzmann's nine-hour film classic (called by many critics and admiring filmmakers one of the greatest documentary films in history), which drew surprisingly good ratings, even across the American heartland where many found it to be a spiritual experience. And by 1992, all eleven half hours of "Shalom Sesame" had been shown on public broadcasting, with ratings equal to "Sesame Street," which means it reached millions of American homes.

It is also interesting that well-produced Jewish material for children has been accepted on commercial television. *"Lights,"* a delightful and inventive animated film, has been shown for several consecutive Chanukah seasons on commercial stations, and *"The Animated Haggadah"* has had extensive audiences on independent stations and network affiliates during the Passover holiday.

Perhaps the most important and promising development is the speed with which VCRs have made their way into American homes. Video cassette recorders have proliferated so quickly that before long a VCR will be present in almost every American home. The implications of the presence of dozens of video cassettes on bookshelves in the Jewish home video library of the future are far-reaching, and a number of strategies are being devised to take advantage of this new distribution system for quality programs.

The problems today are both leadership and money. Good television cannot be wished into existence; the material produced must be of the highest quality in order to attract, sustain, and build an audience. Every program does not have to cost the millions of dollars required to make "Heritage: Civilization and the Jews," but the quality must be what audiences have come to expect in television. All of us have seen low-budget television on public access channels—amateurish production and television-on-the-cheap—but that would only drive away the very audiences a new initiative needs to attract.

The Jewish Cultural and Educational Service

I believe that, in order to produce material of high quality that reflects the richness and diversity of Jewish tradition and experience, a new entity should come into being that will foster the creation and distribution of such programming. For purposes of discussion I will call this entity the Jewish Cultural and Educational Service. Such a service should be founded with great vision and long-range purpose; it should be independent, national in scope, and open to all. It should draw leaders from all areas of Jewish life and should ultimately be endowed as an independent national service, similar to the Corporation for

Public Broadcasting's Annenberg Fund, the $10 million-a-year fund created by the founder of *TV Guide* to support the development of educational programs involving new technologies. That much money would not be needed, but there should be substantial funds for a five-to-ten-year period. In fact, it would be appropriate if this new service carried the name of its founder or of a philanthropic family that would see the creation of such Jewish telecommunications systems as a long-range way to change the tone, quality, and scope of Jewish life.

The role of the service would be to provide leadership—to stimulate, support, and disseminate superior materials not only for Jewish cable systems, but for commercial television, computers in the classroom and home, video cassettes and video discs, and other technologies as they emerge. It would provide funding and assistance for the production of programs as well as for the training of young talent.

One goal would be the development of a community of artists—the linking of creative film and television talent in Israel and America and the sponsoring of interchanges between talent in both countries; it would thus help to create programs in Israel for distribution and broadcast in America and vice versa. The degree to which the young in both countries are enamored of the media is remarkable: Israel has the largest per capita film-going audience in the world and far greater per capita VCR ownership than the U.S. As an example of American student interest in this idea, within two weeks after "Heritage: Civilization and the Jews," was announced, WNET-Channel 13 in New York City received 2,500 résumés, mostly from young people wanting to work on the series.

The service would act, in some ways, like a foundation, making grants to develop new ideas and giving guidance to local and national organizations, many of which have begun to develop materials for new technologies and will continue to do so. Its staff would be experienced in communications matters and would be available to consult with other funders—foundations, individual givers, and the national endowments.

It would bring together creative talent in broadcasting and the arts for conferences, seminars, and specific projects. It would provide a national umbrella so that local cable services could cooperate with each other and perhaps seed large projects of its own. In a pattern similar to public broadcasting's, strong local entities would produce many of their own programs on both local and general topics, and a national entity would provide funds and develop major ideas in joint initiatives. It would promote charismatic local figures who, as has been the case with National Public Radio and public broadcasting, would provide continuity and a central focus for perspectives from their geographic areas or special points of view. Many local programs could be expected eventually to have national distribution, and the Jewish Cultural and Educational Service could help facilitate that.

The service would link up with, and build on, the best programs of Jewish culture already happening. The 92nd Street Y in New York City, with its diversity of offerings in music, dance, lectures, and discussions, perhaps could be one source of programming. Others might include the Jewish Television Network in Los Angeles, which has begun to produce some programs drawing from the talents of the entertainment industry and has developed a capacity for linking cities by satellite nationwide; the National Jewish Television Service, which has developed a weekly show from Jerusalem and has satellite time reserved and available for other projects; the National Jewish Archives of Broadcasting at the Jewish Museum in New York and the profit-making film distributors like Ergo, which distribute Jewish films; the Institute for Computers in Jewish Life in Chicago, which is developing software for home computers; the Center for Jewish Film at Brandeis University, which acquires and distributes feature films; and the interview programs of the Union of American Hebrew Congregations Television and Film Institute.

Let me describe several of the projects funded by the Revson Foundation over the past ten years which suggest some uses of telecommunications to preserve, record, and share the Jewish cultural experience. The projects use conventional broadcast television, videotape, and videodisc technologies in partnership with books, teaching materials, and home computers to reach individuals of all faiths in homes, schools, and universities as well as in community centers, churches, synagogues, and temples.

"Heritage: Civilization and the Jews"

One of the first grants made by the Revson Foundation launched in 1978 a major documentary series entitled "Heritage: Civilization and the Jews," which was, at the time, the most ambitious project ever undertaken by American public television. The series, narrated by Abba Eban, traced Jewish history from early biblical times to the present, describing and interpreting Jewish experience on four continents and its impact on other traditions. It was conceived, from the beginning, as a project for all Americans and therefore carried with it a special mission of exposition and interfaith understanding.

"Heritage" was filmed in eighteen countries, the major sites of Jewish settlement over the past three thousand years, at a cost of over $10 million from more than one hundred contributors. Eban's book on the series has sold more than two hundred thousand copies in the United States and was also a bestseller in England while the series was being shown. The series has also been seen in Australia, Belgium, Denmark, Holland, Israel, Italy, Norway, Spain, Sweden, Switzerland, West Germany, and, in the summer of 1992, to a potential audience of 150 million in Russia.

The series was special in many ways. It was visually beautiful, being a labor of love for the creative team involved, and featured great variety, because it was filmed all over the world.

The research done for it involved examination of thousands of still photographs, film footage, museum collections, and archaeological locations.

It was also unusual in that the written and teaching materials surrounding the series were not an afterthought but an integral part of the planning and a fundamental core of the project itself. This interaction between the visual and the printed material was unique in the history of television.

Thus, the series was not just a television experience, though millions enjoyed it on that level, but could also be, for those who wanted to participate, a total intellectual and emotional learning experience.

To ensure a lasting educational value for the series, materials for college, high school, adult education, and the general home audience were developed: in addition to the book by Eban with three hundred photographs and text, there are also a second set of two books for colleges to use as a study guide and as a sourcebook of readings from Jewish history, a family viewing guide, and teaching guides for schools, colleges, and adult discussion groups. The series was a noteworthy success in the South and the Midwest, where it had unusually high ratings. Of the two hundred colleges teaching courses around the series, about a third were denominational schools in the Bible Belt. The series was broadcast in the fall of 1984, repeated in early 1986, and will be available on cassette for future use in high school and college classrooms. Jacob Bronowski's "Ascent of Man" and Kenneth Clark's "Civilisation" have been shown in five thousand college classrooms since they were broadcast in the 1970s. "Heritage: Civilization and the Jews" will have the same lasting impact.

"Rechov Sumsum" and "Shalom Sesame"

After three years, the Israeli version of "Sesame Street" has completed 190 programs on Israeli television. It has been an enormous success in Israel, captivating not only the pre-schoolers for whom it is intended but also their older siblings and parents.

The Hebrew-language series is a joint production of Children's Television Workshop, which originated "Sesame Street" in 1969, and the Instructional Television Center of Israel, the educational broadcasting entity of Israel. The series, called "Rechov Sumsum," was funded initially by the Israeli Educational Ministry and the Revson Foundation but has since received funds from over forty contributors.

The programs feature as regular characters children on an imaginary Israeli street, "Rechov Sumsum," animation introducing the Hebrew alphabet, and original film shot in Israel. The film segments highlight the many cultures that exist side by side in Israel, from desert tents to Jerusalem streets. The voices of such Muppet characters as Bert and Ernie, Cookie Monster, Grover, and, of course, Kermit, have been dubbed in Hebrew in a way that captures the personalities of each one of the Muppets without losing anything in translation.

"Rechov Sumsum" is designed to prepare Israeli youngsters for school and to improve relations among the different segments of Israeli society, sowing positive relationships between Sephardim and Ashkenazim, religious and nonreligious people, Arabs and Jews. The Ministry of Education has been training teachers and parents to use the series, which is being seen in the public kindergartens that are attended by almost all three-, four-, and five-year-olds in Israel.

A fascinating aspect of this project has been the adaptation of the series for American audiences as a home video project where it can be an exciting aid to foreign-language learning. CTW believes that "Rechov Sumsum" has the potential to reach millions of American children and adults, providing a window to the culture, traditions, and people of Israel. It can also motivate the learning of Hebrew. Eleven programs, called "Shalom Sesame" and hosted by renowned violinist Itzhak Perlman, have been created and had sold more than one hundred thousand cassettes by 1992, a number unprecedented for Jewish video materials. In addition, all eleven programs have been broadcast on public broadcasting stations, with ratings equal to "Sesame Street" across the country and higher in major cities. That means that "Shalom Sesame" has reached more than twenty million American children.

Yale Video Archive for Survivor Testimonies

A visual and oral history that captures the human dimension of the Holocaust through personal testimony has been established at Yale University as the Video Archive for Survivor Testimonies, with the help of a grant from the Revson Foundation. The project's principal goal is to preserve for posterity the living memories of all survivors who wish to tell their stories, a task that has special urgency because of the survivors' advancing ages. Nearly 2,600 interviews have been collected in the archive, and teaching materials including them have been created for use in the public schools.

The establishment of the archive at a leading American university ensures the preservation of this precious material and its availability for scholarly research and educational purposes. The foundation has also helped Yale to create satellite projects in New York City at the new Museum of the Jewish Experience as well as in other countries (England, France, Poland, Hungary, Russia, and Israel), all of which will be a part of the Yale collection. It is hoped that future generations will learn from the experiences recorded in the project and its affiliated efforts all over the world.

The National Jewish Archive of Broadcasting

The opportunity to look again at people and events that have shaped our time, as recorded on the spot and viewed with the perspective of the intervening years, is an extraordinary gift of modern communications. To ensure that the treasure of programming of the Jewish experience recorded in the media is not lost and that it is accessible to the widest possible audience, the Revson Foundation helped establish the National Jewish Archive of Broadcasting at the Jewish Museum in New York City.

The archive was founded because of a belief that the programs created by broadcasters over the last thirty-five years, if preserved and displayed creatively, could have a profound impact on the transmission of Jewish culture and could contribute to intergroup and interfaith understanding. The results of a detailed study uncovered an extraordinary treasure trove of programming that had Jewish content and interest, including hundreds of hours of documentaries, drama, interviews, conversations, and films. The archive has collected, catalogued, and displayed these materials and now consists of some 2,800 programs.

These programs will be invaluable to scholars and students, especially as the years go by and the people who participated in the events are no longer alive. Visitors to the archive will be able to come face to face with famous figures in modern Jewish history, to experience again the television history of Israel, to hear a story read by Isaac Bashevis Singer or a recital played by Yitzhak Perlman, to see the dramatization of Passover by Sholom Aleichem. All of it is on film and on tape, able to move a new generation of students and adults.

YIVO Institute for Jewish Research, New York

In an innovative experiment joining the old with the new, the latest videodisc technology is being applied by the YIVO Institute for Jewish Research to its unique film and photograph collections. (YIVO is the Yiddish acronym for the Yiddish Scientific Institute, founded in Poland in the nineteenth century and re-created in New York after the war.)

With videodisc technology, more than one hundred thousand images can be stored on a single disc, and an audio track—music, sound effects, or voice commentary—can be added to the visual material. When programmed and linked to a computer, videodisc images and sound track can be retrieved in any sequence desired.

Among YIVO's holdings is an enormous body of audiovisual material on Jewish life in prewar Eastern Europe, including more than one hundred thousand photographs, four thousand slides, twelve hundred records of Jewish music, six hundred hours of field recordings on tape, and eight hours of silent film.

The project has produced a fully programmed disc containing twenty thousand photographs—a kind of visual encyclopedia of prewar East European Jewish life. One side will store the photographs, catalogued geographically, while the other will contain presentations on such topics as synagogues, the labor movement, and the role of women, each using a small selection of stills together with the appropriate audio material. This "smart" or programmed disc will be an invaluable teaching aid in both religious and secular schools at elementary, secondary, and college levels. It will also allow individuals all over the world access to YIVO's collection, which up to now has been available only at its headquarters in New York. The success of the YIVO project may open the way for many other exciting educational and archival activities that would not be possible without the new technology, which is the most efficient means known of storing large numbers of images.

Two New Projects

What these projects have all had in common is that they have been instrumental in making available to broad audiences, as well as to specialized groups and to individuals, material that had previously been accessible primarily to scholars, travelers, and those already deeply involved in Jewish education.

I believe that over the next few years the goal should be to create a new video educational curriculum in Jewish education through the consolidation of existing resources and additions to them. Two new projects would provide the institutional setting for testing, using, and broadly disseminating this curriculum. The proposed new Jewish Museum in New York City should become an institutional innovator in Jewish life, serving not only as the home for the creation, display, and use of the educational materials but also as its primary showcase. To ensure that the materials are used well beyond the walls of the museum, the curriculum could also be packaged and distributed as the Jewish Heritage Video Collection, along with the best feature films made in Hollywood with Jewish themes in the last fifty years. This collection, which would be disseminated as broadly as possible, would ensure that the materials were easily available for use in settings around the world—in schools, in religious institutions of all faiths, in libraries, in community centers, and in homes.

The Redesigned Jewish Museum   After many years of planning, the Jewish Museum in New York has orchestrated a major expansion that will transform it into an institution with national and international impact. At the center of this expansion will be a permanent multimedia exhibition in one or more new buildings that would trace four thousand years of Jewish history. The inspiration for the idea is the Museum of the Diaspora in Tel Aviv, a twenty-first-century museum, which is now (after the Wall in Jerusalem) the second most popular tourist attraction in Israel. Almost $50 million has already been pledged for the project, which will open in 1993.

The plan for the new museum involves the creation of evocative situations for visitors; they would, for example, be able to walk into the middle of sound stages, video displays, and models re-creating places and moments in history. One such situation might depict Jerusalem during the time of the Second Temple; another might depict Toledo, Spain, during its golden era. Throughout, the new museum will employ state-of-the-art video and audio technologies to put people in touch with events, art, culture, and personalities; there will be sophisticated computer use for access to information about families, genealogy, and Jewish history; art and artifacts will be displayed against a backdrop of photographs showing where each piece came from and its meaning.

Planning is also already under way to ensure that the design of the new museum is attractive and accessible to families, from grandparents to young children, and is of interest to people of all faiths. Those involved in its planning are calling one major exhibition of the new Jewish museum "A Walk Through Jewish History," one which will put people in touch with and allow them to experience Jewish history. It is hoped that this museum will be not only a popular New York City–based attraction but also a center for and creator of educational materials for use internationally in schools, universities, and homes.

After the "Heritage: Civilization and the Jews" series was completed, the more than 250 hours of unused film material and research was transferred from WNET-Channel 13 to the Jewish Museum. The Revson Foundation supported an analysis of these outtakes by a group of experienced consultants. They came up with a number of ideas for future steps which involve reusing the existing material creatively both inside a new museum and outside in schools and homes. Here is a brief description of three ideas:

A children's version of the "Heritage" series would recast it with a new host and a special narration for children. The series would be repackaged in twenty-minute units for classroom or possible television instruction and perhaps incorporate animation and other creative techniques that would interest children. A special version would be created for home use, aimed at ten- to thirteen-year-olds.

A videodisc of all the art objects filmed for the series would be created. Some five thousand art objects from museums including the Louvre, the British Museum, the Metropolitan Museum in New York, and the Luxor in Egypt were "animated" for use in the series—that is, beautifully filmed and prepared for on-screen use. Only about one thousand were ultimately used as the series was refined. With this material, it would be possible to create a videodisc that would, in effect, be a visual encyclopedia of a worldwide collection of art of Jewish interest from the great museums of the world. For example, the material includes some sixty images of Moses and of David made over a two-thousand-year period, to which historians, artists, and scholars would, for the first time, have ready access. They, as well as students and others interested in art, would be able to compare and contrast Michelangelo with Donatello, Rembrandt with Rodin.

A more ambitious undertaking that has been proposed would be the creation of a more sophisticated "interactive" disc, which could contain not only the artwork but also two-minute explanations or commentaries for museum visitors. Once created, it could also be made available to other museums and to the more than nine hundred Jewish-studies courses all over the world. A major publisher has expressed interest in a book, which might be called *Art Treasures of the Jewish People*, that would accompany the disc. What is perhaps most attractive about this project is that one of the most expensive parts of creating a videodisc has already occurred: crews went all over the world to film the objects and then prepared the material for television use. Some gaps would have to be filled, but a large part of the task is already accomplished.

A third idea is that the "Heritage" material might be used in the creation of special museum modules—that is, short films for specific use in the redesigned Jewish Museum. As with the art objects, these films would also be made available to visitors on videodisc, with easy access to the material through computer terminals. Some suggested subjects for the modules include: Jewish synagogues through the ages; Jews of the world—from England, America, and Israel to North Africa, China, and India; the vanished world of Eastern Europe; the desert and the giving of the law; and profiles of great figures in history—from biblical figures to Maimonides, Spinoza, Disraeli, Einstein, and Weizmann.

The Jewish Heritage Video Collection   The Jewish Heritage Video Collection was begun in order to make the rich resources of film and television accessible to those interested in Jewish life, culture, and history. One of its purposes is to clear new material, especially broadcast programming, that has not previously been distributed.

The JHVC will be a video library of film and television programs with significant Jewish content, designed for educational use in Jewish and secular institutions and in the home. Its videotape collection will present some of the best films and broadcast programs on Jewish themes produced since the advent of motion pictures and television. Its specially developed curricula will incorporate and interpret these film and television programs for many diverse audiences of all ages, Jewish and non-Jewish, secular and religious.

The project addresses a critical need in Jewish education today: how to make the Jewish experience a part of the patterns and concerns of contemporary life and relevant to the large number of Jews who are currently unaffiliated with Jewish institutions, as well as those who are. There is a hunger for knowledge about Jewish history and culture in America today, as well as for new ways to relate to the Jewish community. Many educators, lay leaders, and institutions, both Jewish and secular, are hoping to respond to this interest with creative programming.

As currently planned, the JHVC will have two components:

One is a series of packages on key topics in Jewish life and culture, each presenting film and television programs along with specially developed study guides. These packages will provide the source material for courses that can be offered by community centers, Y's, libraries, synagogues, schools, and other institutions. And there will be specially developed new packages, such as the first series by Elie Wiesel, entitled "Portraits in Greatness," six beautifully filmed stories on the lives and lessons of biblical heroes from his book *Messengers of God*—Moses, David, Job, Adam and Eve, Cain and Abel, Abraham and Isaac.

A second component is a core collection of fifty to one hundred films and television programs with significant Jewish content recommended as a basic video library by a panel of Jewish, media, and education experts. The collection will be placed at local institutions, where members can borrow these tapes for home viewing just as they now visit their local video stores to rent popular movies.

Viewing tapes, and visiting the local video store to borrow them, have become part of the American routine. But, as anyone who has looked for something besides the most popular feature films knows, video stores generally have very little but recent Hollywood movies in stock. Old films released as "classics" might be found, but not less famous ones. Foreign films, independent films, and television programming are scarce or nonexistent.

Through the National Jewish Archive of Broadcasting at the Jewish Museum in New York, a wealth of broadcast material has been acquired—more than 2,800 television programs dealing with Jewish subjects. The JHVC will make selections from the archive collection available to viewers in communities around the country for the first time.

This project seeks to reinvigorate Jewish culture and education in the Jewish home. I am a historian, and when I was a boy, I would long to hear the voice of Abraham Lincoln and other historic figures. That, of course, is not possible, but young people can be stirred by the personalities of Abraham Joshua Heschel, Martin Buber, Gershon Scholem; the wisdom of Albert Einstein, Elie Wiesel, Isaac Bashevis Singer, Primo Levi; the artistry and personalities of Marc Chagall, Isaac Stern, and Leonard Bernstein; and the charismatic power of the great leaders—Chaim Wiezmann, David Ben-Gurion,

Golda Meir. Those too young to remember can relive events such as the liberation of Europe; Israel statehood in 1948; the Six-Day War; Sadat's trip to Jerusalem; the flight of the Ethiopian Jews and the waves of Russian immigration. The best feature films from Hollywood can be summoned: from *The Jazz Singer* to *Gentlemen's Agreement*; from *Exodus* to *Judgment at Nuremberg*; from *Fiddler on the Roof* to *Hester Street* and *The Chosen*; from *The Diary of Anne Frank* to *The Garden of the Finzi-Continis*. And the simple voices of survivors are a cumulative cry to history to remember.

The task is ahead of us: the challenge to weave real connections—with Israel, Russia, in America—to reawaken millions of people to a rich heritage and to explore this new world. The computer, the telephone, and the television set are all merging. Interactive videodiscs empower the learner. The opportunities to use technology creatively are all about us, waiting to be harnessed to the great tasks of Jewish memory, creativity, and inspiration.

Future Directions

These ideas represent just the beginning of the kind of communications-led renaissance that can be achieved in the Jewish home and with the leadership of new and creative Jewish institutions. If the future communications era is to live up to its promise, however, educators, community leaders, writers, filmmakers, and a responsive philanthropic community will have to seize the opportunities presented by new technology and create exciting materials and ideas for the many new outlets for programming. If they do, this can all be the basis for a reawakening of millions of people to a rich heritage and a means for reaching out to non-Jews.

Not all the programming needs to be large-scale or high-budget; there is room for a full range of creative activities by small foundations and individuals. Much needs doing: training teachers; providing opportunities for young filmmakers to train and work; financing preliminary research of ideas, treatments, and pilot programs; developing oral and video histories of current leaders and thinkers in Jewish life; helping with hardware costs in community and national institutions; sponsoring international and national seminars; evaluation and assessment; setting up awards and prizes to encourage excellence.

Potential grantees might include videodisc creators; independent filmmakers; public television entities; organizations like YIVO and others with film ideas; Israeli-based cultural institutions such as museums, universities, and the Israeli Instructional Television Center and the Israel Broadcasting Authority; and broadcast entities in England and elsewhere. Partners would be needed from other foundations, individuals, and government organizations such as the Corporation for Public Broadcasting and the national endowments.

Creating a significant quantity of superior programming will require new mechanisms of production and distribution, along with, of course, a substantial investment of resources. The question is no longer whether the technology exists that can disseminate ideas; the question is whether the will and the funds can be assembled for such an investment. It takes a long lead time to plan and develop programs; the seeds planted by our own foundation five years ago are beginning to bear fruit. Meanwhile, the technological advances are proceeding rapidly. The time to think about how to organize and finance such mechanisms is now. The dimensions of Jewish programming in the future will be limited only by our imaginations and the resources we are willing to devote to the enterprise. But the opportunities to use technology creatively are all about us, waiting to be seized.

22

A Question of Remembering: Three Reviews

An Assimilated Woman

A few years ago, the *New York Times* printed an article called "Christmas Comes to a Jewish Home" in which Anne Roiphe, the novelist and author of *Up the Sandbox*, celebrated the joys of Christmas trees, Dickens, singing carols, and Santa Claus. She infused the article with a passion for her subject, telling how, on one Passover, when she heard the story of the plagues on the Egyptians and their fate in the Red Sea, out of sympathy for the victims she left the table. "And through eighteen years of combined marriages," she wrote then, "there has always been in my house a Christmas, no longer any seders, no more High Holy Days at the temple, no masses, no born again conversions, just Christmas, a sacred event in our family life." The article brought an avalanche of letters of protest to the *Times*, which printed almost a page of them, charging her with "tooth-fairy theology," and suggesting she study "Jewish texts rather than Frosty the Snowman."

In *Generation Without Memory*, which continues this saga, Roiphe tells of taking her children to their first seder, of spending six months in the Judaica room at the New York Public Library, of interviewing rabbis and their children, psychiatrists, and relatives. The book is part autobiography, part journalism, and part essay. She writes from the vantage of her weekend perch in Washington, Connecticut, in between carpools to Manhattan, trips to the pediatrician, PTA meetings, and children's birthday parties. Against this backdrop of privilege, she spins out the story of her childhood and makes a "desperate effort to browse through the centuries" of Jewish learning.

Her background is the story of an affluent family of Polish and Austrian Jews, who belong to the Park Avenue Synagogue and exclusive country clubs and send their daughter to summer camps in Maine where she can meet German Jews from Atlanta, Scarsdale, Nashville, and Great Neck. "Jews imitated Christians," she writes, "and began to dislike themselves on a sliding scale of how Jewish they appeared." She attended Smith College and Sarah Lawrence and went to graduate school at Columbia in the 1950s. "As my black leotards and sandals demonstrated," she writes, "I was a citizen in good standing of bohemia, of beatnik turf. I thought of myself as tribeless, stateless, countryless, classless, religionless." A few months after her mother's death, she divorced her first husband, who was not Jewish, and married a psychoanalyst, who was. At the age of forty-four, with two young daughters and a stepdaughter, she turned to religious inquiry after years of psychoanalysis that left her unsatisfied ("As the religious Jew daily reaffirms his faith so I now check about my unconscious, rummaging like a bag lady").

Anne Roiphe probably should have waited a while to write this book. *Generation Without Memory* is a self-conscious effort that observes the process of its own writing. With dates sprinkled throughout to give it the feel of a diary, it bounces back and forth from the present to the past. Ideas are presented in no particular sequence, and the result is a disorganized patchwork tumbling out in conversations, anecdotes, and memories. Sandwiched between bits of her personal story are quotations from Einstein, Freud, Isaac Bashevis Singer, and other sages. There is a naïveté behind the selections, as though they were discovered by chance and scattered throughout the text. Such an inquiry takes work—time, reflection, questioning, depth. It is as if one picked up a shell from a beach and presumed a knowledge of the sea from it. After six months of research one does not aspire to be a feminist Rashi.

Yet Roiphe must be commended for the effort. She is an experienced writer, searching for the first time in her life for the meaning of Jewish history. And, because there are thousands like her, her search deserves attention.

At that heralded seder, Roiphe is relieved that her daughters are called upon equally with the boys at the table. She believes the worst aspect of Judaism is what it does to women, and she recalls her own feelings of jealousy at her brother's bar mitzvah, her rage at the expectations for him "to meet intellectual challenges," and for her "to behave in a docile, loving way."

She describes "the gilded ghetto of my childhood with its country clubs, its dancing schools . . . its repression of female aspiration, its materialism that grew like a monster until it finally ate up all the time and energy of its women who were eternally in the stores, worn out from the shopping." She refers to the "assimilation parade" of the Sephardic and German waves of immigrants: "With just a blink of an eye, a subtle shift of the mind, and the parade of assimilating Jews becomes the line on the railroad stations of Treblinka and Auschwitz. For many of us, the Holocaust marks the end of religion, but paradoxically enough, the Holocaust also marks the point of reconnection of this modern assimilated Jewess to Jewishness, to history, to bloodlines . . . a bonding, a coupling, a connection to the victims that is as deep as my genes."

Summarizing her exploration with breezy metaphors, she concludes: "If one modernizes Judaism too far it becomes like a TV game show as compared to a fine Shakespearean performance . . . indifferently, the next generation will be tempted to drift away, to turn it off."

Roiphe's solution does not lie in a return to tradition, for she cannot bring herself to pray for the Messiah, to keep laws that she doubts. "Can there be a truly nonpatriarchal Judaism?" she asks. "Can the new attitudes toward women be infused into the centuries of prejudice? . . . I will start looking for this kind of Judaism." The issues she writes about are alive on college campuses today, in the explosion of Jewish studies courses and Holocaust seminars.

There are, however, a number of curious omissions. Though the state of Israel is talked about as a news event, Mrs. Roiphe has never visited Israel; she does not even discuss what must have been the controversies among her relatives and friends over its creation in the late 1940s. The Christianity she observes in her Connecticut retreat is Congregationalist, reasonable, inviting, warm, and unintrospective. She writes about the church fair, with bake sales and well-dressed polite parishioners under colorful tents with pennants flying. She has not experienced other varieties of Christianity; she does not mention the fundamentalists, or those in the Bible Belt who do not tolerate differences.

This book might have rough sledding in certain circles, but as the faltering first steps made by an assimilated woman back to Judaism it has a topical resonance. Perhaps it will be of use to others who start with a blank tablet in midlife.

New Lives in America

How do human beings recover from the Holocaust experience? How does the physical and psychological turbulence change one's later life—goals, values, attitudes toward family, children, love, and death?

These are primal questions, and in answering them in *New Lives: Survivors of the Holocaust Living in America*, Dorothy Rabinowitz never flinches from the burning eye of history. She has approached her topic not as a philosopher but as a journalist probing the gray spaces beyond clichés for real truths.

Only four hundred thousand to five hundred thousand European Jews survived the German occupation from 1939 to 1945. Most did so by going into hiding or by becoming guerrillas, but about seventy-five thousand somehow managed to live through the death camps. Rabinowitz concentrates on those survivors who came to America (most went to Israel after the war); she has interviewed 108 of them in eleven cities. Her subjects are not spokespersons or intellectuals but common people who speak for themselves, and that is the strength of the book, which, like the people interviewed, is straightforward, unvarnished, spare in its prose yet poetic in its frankness.

In writing about these new lives, Rabinowitz has rescued the Holocaust itself from mass-think. She strives in her book to give individuality back to the millions who suffered death as nameless as the mounds of graves near the camps. The book restores their humanity and distinctiveness, for by exploring the lives of those who survived, Rabinowitz underscores the tragedy of those who perished without record.

The survivors tell a variety of stories about what happened after the liberation and in the years that followed. How they survived depended on their ages, what happened to them in the camps, what they were before the war, whether or not other members of their families survived as well.

Ponder a man who is the only remnant of his earlier life—gone are his brothers, sisters, aunts, uncles, friends, even the village where he grew up; he is totally alone. ("I was newborn," said one woman. Her origin was obliterated, her former life totally erased. "It was as though I had not come from anywhere.") The man finds himself in Memphis, Tennessee, among polite southern society: an indifferent group, preoccupied with possessions, involved in a country-club life and car pools. They avoid him in order to avoid the subject; he overhears them saying his story is an exaggeration. Even distant relatives shrink from him. He is running three tapes in his mind simultaneously—what his life was like before the war, then among the living dead of the camps, and now in America. "The concentration camp experience," he says, "is nothing that endears you to people."

Many survived because they did the opposite of what every-one else did—they ran alone into a forest, hid in a cellar, jumped from a train. The spoiled youngest child of a doting family confessed that it was her independence that saved her, "or as she was sometimes inclined to view it, a capacity not to care too much about anything or anyone." During the Nazi roundup in the ghetto, her brother called to her, but she did not answer from her hiding place. So her family went to their fate together, and she remained alone, the only survivor.

The terrifying lesson an accountant learned from the camps was that he was saved by "improvisation and impulse," his ability to make no friends, establish no ties, to be absolutely alone without feelings for anyone else so that he could seize the split second and dart through the barbed wire.

"Those that were separated from their mothers at Auschwitz were better off," another woman confesses, "for an older person was a burden. The truth is a terrible thing to say, isn't it?"

The book describes a reunion in which three women remember the years of near-starvation, the preoccupation with food; there had been constant chatter in the camps about compli-cated recipes, a fantasy to relieve hunger. When one of the women at the reunion recalls a delicious soup the Germans once served, they all try to re-create it in the kitchen. A nostalgia creeps into their voices. They remember the songs they sang and the jokes they told to keep their spirits up, and "when they talked about the time in the camps, it was not entirely horror that drew them back, but also the memory of their youth."

After the liberation, some survivors got married in the displaced-persons camps to people in similar circumstances; others refused to marry until later, vowing not to marry another survivor. Some were eager to have children and rebuild their lives; others, unable to face the memories of their lost families, refused to have children. "I felt I had no love for the new children in me," a man states.

The survivors deny having any special quality, claiming that it was not destiny but "caprice, chaos, and random chance" that saved them. Still, some emerged with an increased regard for themselves because they were alive, and because they had the will to take risks. "One day in the camp, my father took me aside and told me he had witnessed my brother's death, and that now I must stay alive. He meant it. Then he gave me his bread and I took it . . . because he showed me he would throw it away and not eat it himself if I didn't take it from him."

The book, which is divided into parts such as "1945," "Arriving," and "Settling," is partially organized around the witnesses in a deportation hearing against a former vice-commandant of one of the camps, a woman in Queens living under her married name. Rabinowitz describes the mixed mood in the courtroom, the torment felt by the witnesses who do not want to face the lawyers' badgering or their own unearthed memories, yet who are infused with a duty to bear witness.

None of them was prepared for the feelings of suspicion directed toward them after the war. The question "Why did you survive and not the others?" carried with it the suggestion that they had had "to steal from the starving or cooperate or do other unspeakable deeds to survive." Some even believed that "the best died; the worst of us lived." But most of the survivors deny any guilt about being alive. They describe the American soldiers who liberated the camps as divine messengers carrying out an act of grace. "What else could you want of the Almighty Himself if He had come? He carried her in his arms, he gave her bread, he brought the war to an end."

In a chapter entitled "Honor," Rabinowitz explores the ideology that developed in intellectual circles after the war: "The world had come to believe that the Jews themselves had been accomplices to their murder . . . did not grab guns when the end was in sight . . . had gone like sheep to the slaughter." She calls such questions "absurd," since the "Final Solution had been the fate of ordinary men and women, not, in the main, heroes, poets, or dancers . . . the truth, as they knew it, themselves, was that they had behaved in the way the armed might of the Nazis had dictated that an unarmed and helpless people behave; that there had indeed been bitter resistance and uprising; that most of those that had risen up had, in the end, been killed as had the unarmed and the helpless . . . that all the Jews who died had died with honor."

What is it but "resistance," the author asks, when a man who is about to be gassed gives his shoes to a stranger, knowing that with a better pair of shoes, the stranger has a better chance of surviving?

In a fascinating aside, Rabinowitz writes of the impact of the Eichmann trial on the survivors, who, although they learned no new facts, found the trial to be "a profoundly liberating event." Almost overnight, the trial put an end to the postwar public silence. Many of the survivors witnessed public reaction to the facts of the Holocaust for the first time. Said one, "I thought, 'Nobody knows; that's why I have to live—to tell the world.' Of course, I found out later I didn't have to live just for that; the world knew."

No longer were their stories considered exaggerations; somehow, the "trial lightened the twin burden of silence and cynicism that some of the survivors had carried since the war's end." And, of immeasurable importance to them was the fact that "Jews, acting in the name of a Jewish state, had caught, tried, and punished Eichmann, an event which underscored how far they had come from their former condition of helplessness."

New Lives is not a masterpiece like Bruno Bettelheim's *The Informed Heart*, Lucy Dawidowicz's *The War Against the Jews*, or Elie Wiesel's *Night*, but it is important work, part of the struggle to find the meaning of the Holocaust in human terms. It honors its subjects with a testament to the tenaciousness of the human spirit.

One, by One, by One

Judith Miller, the deputy media editor of the *New York Times*, has written a timely, provocative, and in many respects deeply disturbing book about the ways in which five European coun-

tries and the United States are forgetting, distorting, and politically manipulating the memory of the Holocaust. Traveling as
a journalist in West Germany, Austria, France, the Netherlands, and the Soviet Union, she explores the guilt, the fear,
and the cynicism that cloud this subject in countries that had a
substantial Jewish population before World War II. In *One, by
One, by One*, she also assesses how the United States, separated geographically and morally from the war, is meeting its
social responsibility to history.

The book revolves around the uncomfortable truth that,
while every European country Miller visited seeks to blame the
Nazis for the evil of those years, in each place local citizens
collaborated in the destruction of the Jews.

In France, where the author attended the Klaus Barbie trial
in 1987, she asks unsettling questions about the role, not only
of the Vichy government, but also of the French people as
cooperative instruments of Nazi terror. She observes that the
forty-four Jewish orphans in the little town of Izieu were be-
trayed by a French neighbor and that the Resistance "never
attempted to stop a single deportation train." In Austria,
watching the people defiantly vote for President Kurt Waldheim, the former secretary general of the United Nations, in
the face of documented revelations about his Nazi past, she
points out that "little Austria" supplied nearly 75 percent of
the staffs of the concentration camps and about 80 percent of
the entourage of Adolf Eichmann. During a visit to Kiev in the
Soviet Union, she notes that twenty-two thousand Ukrainians
were fighting alongside the Nazis as late as 1944. Even in the
Netherlands, according to Miller, the celebration of Anne
Frank masks a terrible truth: the well-disciplined Dutch civil
service was so cooperative that the Germans had to commit
only a small number of troops to the job of rounding up the
Jews. As a result, the Jewish death rate in the Netherlands was
the highest in Western Europe—of the 140,000 Jews who lived
there at the outbreak of the war, only 35,000, or 25 percent,
survived.

The burden of such a complex legacy on the next generation in each of these countries requires a willingness to stare into the caldron of this history without flinching.

But Germans, Miller reports, seem to have "mastered the past" by using a number of techniques to relieve the burden of history. For example, by comparing the Holocaust to the bombing of Hiroshima or the Cambodian nightmare, they treat it as "just another manifestation of man's inhumanity to man." By pointing to the loss of life by German civilians during the Dresden bombing, they suggest that the world forgets that Germans suffered too. By emphasizing the normal life of their families during the war, they imply that Nazism was something terrible done by a few brutes who seized power. And finally, Miller points to what the Germans call *Schlusstrich*—that is, "drawing a line at the bottom of an account" to consign the Third Reich to history and make way for the new, democratic, reunified, prosperous "Fourth Reich."

The author is particularly effective in examining the treatment of these issues in television and film. For instance, she notes how the international image of Austria was immensely aided by the 1965 film *The Sound of Music*. It portrayed Baron von Trapp as an ardent nationalist who defies the Nazis by daring to sing "Edelweiss" at the songfest competition. The audience joins in on the line "Bless my homeland forever," and the Nazis in the film are furious. But, the author suggests, "history, as opposed to Hollywood, tells us that the overwhelming majority of Austrians preferred the German national anthem to their own," and the film, until the Waldheim affair awoke Austria from its amnesia, covered over "Austria's love affair with Nazi Germany [and] its vicious persecution of the Jews."

In the Soviet Union, Miller visits a classroom in Minsk where an old woman is describing Russia's suffering during World War II. This was "the Great Patriotic War" that unified the country at a cost of twenty million Soviet lives, more than forty times the losses of Britain and seventy times the losses of

the United States. No one in the class mentions, nor do the
history books note, the Holocaust, the Hitler-Stalin pact of
1939, or the more than seven hundred thousand Russian Jews
who were killed. "Why divide the dead?" asks one Soviet
official. "What's six million when you have lost twenty million?"

Yet, finally, Mikhail S. Gorbachev allowed a slight ray of
light onto this subject through an agreement granting Western
scholars access for the first time to the Soviet archives on the
Nazi occupation and through the easing of restrictions on Jewish culture and emigration. "Despite the obstacles," Miller
writes, "the Soviet Union has been doing what many European
nations have been reluctant to do: it has been confronting its
wartime experiences squarely and facing unpleasant truths
about itself."

In her chapter on this country, the author examines the
difficult and acrimonious history of the United States Holocaust Memorial Museum in Washington and the struggle over
what form the memorial should take. She quotes the concern of
many critics about "vulgarization" and the "considerable
threat to dignified remembrance." A museum setting must
inevitably begin the "gentrification" of the Holocaust in an
"unwitting effort to remove the component of horror and mystery from the event," Miller writes. Yet the risk in the other
direction is that of turning the event into "chambers of horror"
in a series of sound-and-light exhibits that will inevitably be
"an American version of kitsch." Her own preference is for the
quieter work of the scholarly community and for video archives. She calls these oral history projects "among the most
powerful ways of transmitting the memory of the Holocaust to
those who did not experience it. The survivors' own voices and
faces and stories remind us that "the Holocaust was not six
million. It was one, plus one, plus one."

In light of the revolutionary events that have opened up the
countries of Eastern Europe, one hopes that Miller will follow
her quest to other countries with large prewar Jewish popula-

tions, including Poland, Hungary, and Lithuania. The powerful questions she raises about West Germany should be met with a similar study of East Germany, with visits to its abandoned ghettos and schools and graveyards and interviews with its people and officials. The conscience of history suggests that a fuller, more honest understanding of the Nazi period needs to be reached by all of the countries involved, especially the two Germanies.

There are many issues of interpretation in *One, by One, by One* that will attract scholarly criticism. The journalist's trade—interviewing extensively, searching for the telling anecdote, and talking to historians, sociologists, and psychologists who often speak more superficially than they write—has shortcomings. Yet Judith Miller, as a *New York Times* reporter, has had access that few freelance writers could equal. She has taken her mission seriously and has written a troubling and thought-provoking exploration into a dark world of memory and redemption.

23

American Jewish History for Children

Love of history attaches children to their roots, gives them a sense of belonging, and builds bridges of pride and understanding between generations. But the writers of literature for Jewish children are missing a real opportunity by concentrating on just stories from the Bible—staples such as Noah's ark, Moses and the Exodus, Jonah and the whale, and the Maccabees—and about the holidays, and then jumping, almost directly, to the Holocaust and Israel.

There is also a rich history of Jews in America. The landing of twenty-three Jews in New Amsterdam in 1654—the first Jews to settle permanently on the North American continent—stands as one of the signal events in American and Jewish history. It is a pleasure to report that it has been dramatized nicely in two new books.

In her novel for young adults, *Out of Many Waters*, Jacqueline Dembar Greene captures the desperate and lonely world of a twelve-year-old Jewish girl named Isobel Ben Laza, who was kidnapped from her parents and forced to work as a Jewish slave in a monastery in Brazil (such cruel events did happen). Determined to find her parents, the girl stows away aboard a Dutch ship and, hungry and afraid, is befriended by the historic band of Jewish men, women, and children headed for New Amsterdam.

The book moves along with pirates and storms, first love, and Isobel's dreams of being reunited with her family. We meet Asser Levy, leader of the group on this Jewish *Mayflower*, who became the first Jewish citizen of North America; we learn of the failed effort of the peg-legged governor, Peter Stuyvesant, to expel these penniless Jews, whose cause was defended by the Jewish stockholders of the Dutch West India Company. Greene has made a relatively seamless weaving of history, drama, and narrative into an arresting story and avoids the failing of many children's historical novels in which the history shows up from time to time like lumps in oatmeal.

In her non-fiction book *The Jews of New Amsterdam*, Eva Deutsch Costabel uses a more straightforward approach for a younger audience. As a writer-illustrator (she was also educated as an art historian in Europe), she combines a factual narrative with colorful drawings done in the flat, folk-art style of paintings of the seventeenth century.

The book is honest and, in keeping with the trend to treat children seriously, does not paper over difficult issues, pointing out, for example, that Queen Isabella and King Ferdinand of Spain used some of the money seized from the Jews during the Inquisition to help finance Columbus's voyage to America. The glaring errors brought about by oversimplification found in so many children's books do not occur here. The author acknowledges her debt to Rabbi Malcolm Stern, the generous president of the Jewish Historical Society of New York, who has advised scores of history writers, adding integrity and accuracy to their work.

The problem, as with so much writing of this genre, is the obvious tension the reader senses in the author's struggle to combine education with entertainment. Costabel clearly chooses the educational side of that balance wheel, and my guess is that as a "read alone," children may find it a little dry.

But for schools, the inventive Sunday School teacher, or the involved parent, Costabel has made a sound contribution that educators can trust.

Personally, I favor the more fanciful techniques for dealing with Jewish history as well as with other subjects: time machines and magic carpets, rocket ships and rabbit holes, talking animals and adventure dreams. Growing up, I loved *K'tonton*, about a Jewish Tom Thumb who would spin on a runaway Chanukah top or ride the back of a bird to an island where the animals would celebrate holidays with him. It is the "Twilight Zone" approach, such as taking a fantasy subway and getting off in the middle of the Battle of Jericho, that involves a child in great events.

The history of Jews in America is filled with accomplished lives and dramatic tales that would lend themselves to children's literature. I can imagine a series of children's books concocted from the legends my grandparents told me when I was young and stories about the heroes my parents admired. My grandfather was a peddler in the South who progressed from a pack on his back to a horse and wagon to a family store (there are dramatic stories also about the pioneer Jews who settled the West, such as Levi Strauss, who used the blue denim in his tent for his first jeans). My grandmother left a diary telling of her arrival from Eastern Europe at Ellis Island and her memories of Emma Lazarus's poem on the Statue of Liberty. In Baltimore she met Henrietta Szold, who founded Hadassah in the early 1900s and later, at the age of seventy, began Youth Aliyah to save thousands of Jewish children from the inferno of Eastern Europe. My parents admired Louis Brandeis, lawyer and champion of social justice, and the other Jewish Supreme Court justices, Benjamin Cardozo and Felix Frankfurter; they shared in the triumphs of Herbert Lehman, the Jewish governor of New York, of Judge Sam Rosenman, who served on Franklin Roosevelt's brain trust, and of Bernard Baruch of South Carolina, the financial seer who advised presidents from a park bench. My parents embraced Albert Einstein as an American immigrant like their parents, rumpled and beloved, pondering the secrets of the universe, and ardent believer in the state of Israel, and they took pride in Jonas Salk, who conquered polio. And my aunt, who studied music, loved the violinists Jascha Heifetz and Yehudi Menuhin, who were playing concerts at the age of five, and the pianists Artur Rubinstein and Vladimir Horowitz.

As a boy, I grew up with uncles and cousins and friends who were passionate fans of Hank Greenberg, who hit fifty-eight home runs in a season and almost overtook Babe Ruth; Sid Luckman, quarterback of the Chicago Bears; the boxers Max Baer and Benny Leonard; and Sandy Koufax, who, legend had it, would not pitch for the Brooklyn Dodgers on Yom Kippur. And of course there were Al Jolson, Eddie Cantor, the Marx Brothers, Fanny Brice, George Gershwin, Irving Berlin, Rodgers and Hammerstein, Jack Benny, and Leonard Bernstein.

I later discovered many lesser-known Jews, such as Commodore Uriah Phillips Levy, who abolished flogging in the navy and went to Virginia to save Monticello from ruin, and Penina Moise of Charleston, whose poems were published in the first book written by a Jewish woman in America.

The stories are all about and everywhere, waiting for the inventive eye, to build links in the chain of American Jewish history and stir the imaginations of children.

Part V

Southern Images
and Culture

24

The Changing Image of the South in Movies (1979–1992)

At one point in my life, I was considering writing a book on the history of the South in the movies. I went to see films about the South at a feverish pace; I read film literature and went to lectures. It seemed to me that so much of what America thought about the South was shaped by movies and television, and I was beginning to sense subtle changes. Politically, it fascinated me. From Jimmy Carter to Bill Clinton, southern candidates for national office have been defined by the mass media images of the South and have suffered from the way the South resonates in the mind of America. In that sense, the distance from *Gone With the Wind* to *The Prince of Tides* is not so great. But some changes began to occur at the end of the Carter administration, and by 1981 films were beginning to catch up with the new interest that the Carters of Georgia had stimulated in southern matters.

Films of the 1980s

Between 1979 and 1981 actress Sally Field and director Martin Ritt almost single-handedly broke the South out of its well-worn clichés in two films about the southern soul.

Back Roads, their first collaboration since *Norma Rae* in 1979, is the story of two endearing hustlers in Mobile, Alabama, who stumble toward California in search of the good life. Field's co-star is Tommy Lee Jones, who played Loretta Lynn's husband in *Coal Miner's Daughter* and once again grabs his woman by the scruff of her neck to get her out of the South. Their thumbs-out escapades, "traveling on wit and grit," as he puts it, involve them in constant cheap schemes for small change—rolling drunks or staging fights in roadside diners to avoid paying the check but always ending up falling on their faces or buried neck deep in a mud hole, flat broke but chin up, looking west for salvation.

Martin Ritt, the blacklisted director of the fifties, loves underdogs and the South they live in, as is evident in a number of other movies he has made, such as *Sounder*, *Hud*, *Conrack*, *The Sound and the Fury*, and *The Long Hot Summer*. He obviously feels affection for working-class women, such as the characters played by Sally Field, whether they work all day in a textile mill or walk the streets all night on the honky-tonk side of Mobile.

These characters—Norma Rae and Amy Post in *Back Roads*—share a great deal. Both are rebellious and dynamic personalities, in the tradition of southern women from Scarlett O'Hara to Blanche DuBois, hopeless romantics living in a fantasy world where the harsh realities close in from time to time to tear their dreams apart. Both radiate an eternal optimism, a small-town innocence coupled with a spunky street sense and anchored by love for their illegitimate children who give them emotional roots in a cruel world. And both fall under the spell of strong men, who channel their zeal for a better life from daydreams into action.

Norma Rae and *Back Roads* bookend significant changes in the image of the South in the movies. Three other films of note made in 1980 and 1981—*Coal Miner's Daughter*, *Wise Blood*, and *The Great Santini*—present a composite portrait of the soul of the South that provides mass audiences with new insights into the people who inhabit that most mysterious of America's regions. Each of the movies is about ambition—the characters' desires to rise above the stifling traditions and servitude of the South, to change conditions, to survive, or to get out. Together, they comment on the subconscious fantasies of poor southern whites and on the primary institutions of escape—the Grand Ole Opry, the church, the military, the unions, the open road.

Like *Back Roads* and *Norma Rae*, these films are about true believers. In *Coal Miner's Daughter*, Sissy Spacek plays Loretta Lynn, the southern waif from Butcher Holler, who marries at fourteen, hears the siren song of Nashville on her radio, and sings her way out of a dead-end life to the pinnacle of country music stardom. Brad Dourif, who plays the returning military veteran, Hazel Motes, in the film adaptation of Flannery O'Connor's first novel, *Wise Blood*, seeks his own salvation by founding the Church Without Christ, "where the blind don't see, the lame don't walk, and what's dead stays that way." Robert Duvall's "Bull" Meacham in *The Great Santini* is the head of a family caught up in the "hack it or pack it" rootlessness of military families moving from base to base, settled finally for a time near Parris Island in Beaufort, South Carolina.

These films trace the lives of charismatic figures who act out a southern dream, attracting intense loyalties and facing bitter destinies as a result of their absolutism and their willingness to break with illusion, to challenge the dictates of the gods. But the South does not tolerate challenges to the way things are. Loretta Lynn crumbles into a nervous breakdown under the pressures of stardom; the factory owners try to destroy Norma Rae's future by revealing her past; the Mexican madam and her pimps drive Amy Post back out to the Greyhound buses and the freight trains; Hazel Motes must turn to self-destruction to prove to the street-corner preachers and himself that his soul is purified and he will be saved; "Bull" Meacham finds the martyrdom that eluded him "between wars," in the peacetime military of the early 1960s.

The women in these films are not fluttery southern belles but strong-willed, courageous heroines. In that sense, the films probe the fiber and the grit of southern womanhood more deeply than any films in a long time. Although Blythe Danner's character in *The Great Santini* is the suffering southern-sweet wife of a dawn-to-dark marine, she strives to pass on to her son the gentleness of nature that is at war with his father's hardened expectations. Robert Duvall, fresh from his portrayal of the war lover in *Apocalypse Now*, energizes "Bull" Meacham, with his swagger stick, as the military version of Big Daddy, as authentic as Burl Ives in *Cat on a Hot Tin Roof* and as bellicose as Orson Welles in *The Long Hot Summer*.

The major stars of these films all had previous southern films to cut their teeth on—Sissy Spacek as the innocent Texas runaway in Terrence Malick's *Badlands*; Sally Field in *Stay Hungry* as the down-home girl from the wrong side of the town in the country-club world of Birmingham, Alabama; and Robert Duvall as the deaf mute in *To Kill a Mockingbird* and the dirt farmer in *Tomorrow*.

A friend of Flannery O'Connor's family wrote the screenplay for *Wise Blood*, lovingly translating its prose and persuading John Huston to direct it as a small project to be shot in eight weeks. It is a rare movie because it has no known star to carry it and because the entire film, from script to photography, is so uncompromising. Every character in it is what southerners call a little "off." (One is reminded of O'Connor's famous insight that "the South is Christ-haunted.") Hazel tries to convert the South away from its Bible Belt obsessions, but in the end his own religiosity rises to smite him. Brad Dourif's character has eyes intense enough to attract other crazies, but he is no phony, no Elmer Gantry or Marjoe. From the hood of his beat-up jalopy, he preaches that "a man has redemption if he has a car," but he refuses to milk the locals. He throws back the money, for he is a prophet. And if the world merely rejects its prophets, the South crucifies them.

Coal Miner's Daughter combines the luminous presence of

an authentic Texas-born actress, Sissy Spacek, with the talents of a British director, Michael Apted. Apted had never worked in America before, but in the first half of the film he captures the essence of mountain family life in the coal country of Kentucky. "I had great interest in Appalachia," he told an interviewer, "because it was first settled by Englishmen. I wanted to explore the culture, and this was my chance."

He was one of a long line of English artists fascinated by the South. Vivien Leigh mastered the southern accent to such an extent in *Gone With the Wind* that she could virtually drop it in the scenes with Clark Gable, who refused to even try one, then dip her language in honeysuckle when she was with Hattie McDaniel and Butterfly McQueen. Charles Laughton, who portrayed the Sam Ervin character in *Advise and Consent*, told an interviewer that the southern accent was the easiest American accent for him to use because when the English had settled in Virginia, plantation life just slowed down their cadences.

It took the South decades to escape from the long shadow of D. W. Griffith's *Birth of a Nation* and from *Gone With the Wind.* The plantation genre has been a haunting presence, from Walt Disney's *Song of the South*, which was picketed by the NAACP in the late 1940s, to *Mandingo*, Dino De Laurentiis's "spaghetti southern" made in the mid-1970s.

In a book entitled *Media-Made Dixie*, author Jack Temple Kirby links the changing image of the South in the movies to historical trends. First came the romantic era of the early classics; then the films of the 1950s, which he identifies with the "visceral South" of Erskine Caldwell, Tennessee Williams, and William Faulkner; in the films of the 1960s and 1970s the "devilish South" was represented in *Easy Rider* and *Deliverance*, where redneck savages stalked the terrain. In all three decades, he notes, a few films were made reflecting the "mellow South," Southern movies containing somewhat liberal messages of reconciliation such as *To Kill a Mockingbird, The Defiant Ones, The Heart is a Lonely Hunter*, and *The Member of the Wedding.*

But no matter which South is being portrayed, the region has been trapped in clichés throughout its movie history. Images of rednecks, moonshine, and hillbillies have played in the minds of moviegoers for over forty years, from John Ford's 1941 version of *Tobacco Road* to *The Last American Hero*, with Jeff Bridges as the Junior Johnson character who rises from moonshiner to stock-car king. Southern chain gangs have been used as metaphors for sadism and escape in *The Defiant Ones* with Tony Curtis and Sidney Poitier and *Cool Hand Luke* with Paul Newman. Corrupt southern politics have featured in such classics as *All The King's Men*, with Broderick Crawford as the Huey Long figure, and Elia Kazan's *A Face in the Crowd*, with Andy Griffith as the guitar-picking country slicker who uses television to achieve power. Some films set in the South have centered around country music: *Urban Cowboy*, Robert Altman's *Nashville*, and a number of early Elvis Presley films such as *Love Me Tender* and *Kissin' Cousins*.

The South is one of America's enduring myths, and the best of America's Yankee-born acting talents have tried a turn as southern characters: Jack Nicholson as the southern lawyer in *Easy Rider*; Robert De Niro as the ill-fated ballplayer in *Bang the Drum Slowly*; Elizabeth Taylor as Maggie in *Cat on a Hot Tin Roof*; Marlon Brando as the southern air force lieutenant in *Sayonara*; Gregory Peck as Atticus Finch in *To Kill a Mockingbird*.

The more recent films have not only shown a more authentic world but have been truer to their sources than most previous films. Most of Faulkner's books suffered terribly from their Hollywood treatment in the fifties. But *Coal Miner's Daughter*, *Wise Blood*, and *The Great Santini* were faithfully adapted from interesting books, and *Back Roads* and *Norma Rae* were created from original screenplays, the latter drawn from the real-life story of Crystal Lee Sutton, a J. P. Stevens worker in Roanoke Rapids, North Carolina, who stood up on a table and slowly rotated a sign reading "UNION" until the police took her away. None of these were big-budget films but succeeded as small movies exploring characters and the inner terrain of the region.

One big void in these films is the interior world of black southerners, which has been consistently ignored by Hollywood. There are rare exceptions: Ethel Waters lent her dignity to the extraordinary film *The Member of the Wedding* and to a number of lesser films such as *Pinky*, *Hurry Sundown*, and *The Long Hot Summer*; Cicely Tyson in *Sounder* and in the television movie *The Autobiography of Miss Jane Pittman* showed the heights to which a black actress could rise when the scripts were available. But traditionally, movies about the South have depicted the archetypal mammy, the slave, and a parade of other black stereotypes, along with a good bit of gratuitous violence.

Films of the 1990s

In the 1990s, the South's image has continued to change, even as its political life has included periodic spasms of racism in the midst of an overall trend toward moderation. Nothing could illustrate the two Souths more vividly than Louisiana's flirtation with David Duke, the ex-Klansman, in a gubernatorial campaign in 1991, and the rise of Bill Clinton of Arkansas and Al Gore of Tennessee in 1992, both men from states that are more typical of the moderate South.

David Duke's rise paralleled the public excitement over movies that explore the themes of fear and violence lying just below the surface in the poor white South. *JFK*, set in New Orleans where Duke's roots were nourished in the swampwaters of racism and the masked conspiracies of the French quarter; *Cape Fear*, the hair-raising remake that stars Robert De Niro as the pentecostal devil of vengeance; and *The Prince of Tides*, with Nick Nolte's career performance as the son of a South Carolina shrimper who comes north to exorcise the dark secrets of his family's past, all reflect the public's fascination with the Yoknapatawpha stereotype and the enduring mythology about the white South. All have origins in literature—in the earthy novels of Erskine Caldwell, the soul-searching fiction of

William Faulkner, and the plays of Tennessee Williams. And all explore the dysfunctional lives of white rural southerners raised on fire and brimstone in the revival tents of the post-war era.

Ramblin' Rose and *Fried Green Tomatoes* are films that are warmer in tone; they deal with memory, love, and friendship among powerless women in a South populated by eccentric families and oddball female characters (echoing the success of *Driving Miss Daisy* and *The Color Purple*).

All five of these films have been heralded by critics and nominated for Academy Award performances; but what is remarkable, given the times we live in, is that only one of them—*Fried Green Tomatoes*—deals at all with race. In the others, blacks are almost invisible or are minor characters of little importance. The one film in 1991 that explored racial themes directly—*The Long Walk Home*—was a story revolving around the 1956 Montgomery bus boycott, and it was a box-office flop in spite of the producers' earnest efforts to give it a chance by releasing it several times. The film starred Sissy Spacek as the white-establishment wife (a role she reprised in *JFK*) who befriends her maid, portrayed by an understated Whoopi Goldberg. Her character is a symbol of all the blacks in Montgomery, who, led by the young Martin Luther King, Jr., showed quiet courage as they walked miles to and from work each day.

Of course, Oliver Stone, Martin Scorcese, and Barbra Streisand are pursuing much larger purposes in their films. In *JFK*, Stone turned Jim Garrison's 1969 wild and flamboyant trial concerning the Kennedy assassination into an American legend of grand conspiracies involving the FBI, the CIA, the military-industrial complex, the Secret Service, big-oil magnates, and Lyndon Johnson. Whether or not one finds the premise reasonable, the film does capture the peculiar flavor of the New Orleans netherworld—its underlife of strip joints, cross-dressing, homosexual masquerades, and general wildness that has characterized it since its early days as a raucous port

city. The movie shares the same fondness for the neon vulgarity
of the French quarter that was the backdrop for *Blaze*, Paul
Newman's story of Governor Earl Long, and *The Big Easy*,
which revolved around Cajun culture and the Louisiana Mafia.

Martin Scorcese's remake of *Cape Fear* features an ensemble
of southern types as a backdrop to Robert De Niro's virtuoso
performance as the tattooed pentecostal prisoner who returns
to a small town just up the Cape Fear River from Wilmington.
De Niro becomes the menacing, insanely sadistic Max Cady,
whose whole being has been turned into a sinister instrument
of revenge against the lawyer, played by Nick Nolte, who did
not defend him honestly of rape and aggravated battery fourteen years earlier, ignoring evidence that could have kept his
client out of prison. Joe Don Baker, a squinty-eyed graduate of
the Buford Pusser films, and Fred Thompson, who was Senate
counsel to the Watergate committee, lend southern authenticity to the film, and Jessica Lange and Juliette Lewis are
appealing as the female quarry. "The South has a fine tradition
of savoring fear," De Niro says to the captured family, and he
molds a performance of single-minded evil that combines the
feeling of southern doom he displayed in *Bang the Drum Slowly* with the frenzy of his assassin in *Taxi Driver*. Gregory Peck
and Robert Mitchum, who played the lawyer and the killer in
the original film made in 1960, make cameo appearances.

The Prince of Tides, filmed in Beaufort, South Carolina,
and in New York City, is Barbra Streisand's beautiful and
affecting transformation of Pat Conroy's novel; she even enlisted Conroy as one of the screenwriters. Here Streisand at
last directs a movie that doesn't focus just on her; she uses her
directorial and acting talents in the service of the story. And
Nick Nolte inhabits the role of Tom Wingo, the angry football
coach raised on the South Carolina out-islands, who joins a
Jewish psychiatrist (Streisand) in the search for the family
secrets that have driven his sister to attempt suicide. As his
marriage falls apart, his wife, Sally, played by Blythe Danner,
reaches out to him as an understanding southern wife similar to

the one in *The Great Santini*, the 1979 film also made from a book by Conroy about his boyhood with a stern professional marine of a father. Some critics believe that Pat Conroy, Willie Morris, William Styron, Thomas Wolfe, and other southern writers secretly want to experience Jewishness through their characters and are drawn to write about Jewish themes and Jewish women because of the fundamentalist atmosphere of their boyhoods and the mixture of anti- and philo-Semitism they were raised with. Tom Wingo's love affair with Susan Lowenstein gives Conroy the opportunity to explore the Jewish connection, just as Thomas Wolfe did in his two urban novels, *Of Time and the River* and *The Web and the Rock*, which described his real-life affair with Aline Bernstein. "Lowenstein, Lowenstein" becomes Wingo's mantra, his door to the past and to an understanding of life and family. For her part, Barbra Streisand, who has played opposite a variety of Wasp superstars such as Robert Redford and Ryan O'Neal, portrays a character who exclaims at the end of the movie, "I've got to find me a nice Jewish boy; you guys are killing me."

Southern Women

Ramblin' Rose is a small movie that also makes use of flashbacks. Robert Duvall is brilliant as the head of a household into which Laura Dern, as Rose, moves, just as she is reaching the age of full flower, that moment when southern girls are beginning to sense their power as they hover on the cusp of full-blown sensual womanhood. She is cast opposite her real-life mother, Diane Ladd, who contributes her own memorable performance as Rose's protector and a truth-teller.

Ramblin' Rose is a mood film reminiscent of *A Trip to Bountiful*, the 1985 adaptation of the Horton Foote story starring Geraldine Page (who won an Academy Award), about a final visit to an ancestral home overgrown with vines and strangled in memory.

Fried Green Tomatoes, adapted by Fannie Flagg from her own novel, is a vehicle for two previous Academy Award winners—Jessica Tandy and Kathy Bates—who sink their acting teeth into the characters of southern misfits. Mary Stuart Masterson and Mary Louise Parker give glowing performances as the childhood friends whose implied lesbian love for each other transcends marriage, wife-beating, the Klan, and even murder. Flagg, with her peculiar brand of low-class southern feminism, creates a send-up of eccentric southern women in group encounter sessions who are trying to overcome powerlessness by unleashing the power of "Towanda, the avenger." The Whistlestop Cafe is the center of a town where trains mean both freedom and tragedy, and where the whites eat inside and the black folks out back. Jessica Tandy, as the all-wise occupant of an Alabama nursing home, makes use of a southern accent and mannerisms as she did in *Driving Miss Daisy*.

The stories of *Fried Green Tomatoes* and *Ramblin' Rose* take place in the dreams of the off-screen narrators who take the audience back to the long ago South. They are films that see the South and its changing world through the eyes of women. They resemble *Steel Magnolias* and *Crimes of the Heart*, in that they deal with southern women as complex beings. The women in these films are not the southern belles of plantations and cotillions, but strong, small-town, up-front women, dominating the lives of their men and their communities with toughness and straight talk. These are not women capable of losing themselves in dreamy illusion, but women seeking emotional roots in a cruel world. Such women have always existed—and still exist today, as documented in *Sherman's March*, Ross McElwee's docu-comedy tribute to the southern women in his life.

In addition to grappling with new images of women in the South, in the late 1980s and early 1990s, a cluster of films sought to probe beneath the surface of the stereotypes of whites and blacks in the South and to penetrate the clichéd image of the historic South in the movies. What better time to examine this phenomenon than more than fifty years after *Gone With the*

Wind, when both the original novel and its sequel, *Scarlett*, are both on the bestseller list?

Alfred Uhry's *Driving Miss Daisy* explores the strong and enduring links between blacks and whites that are created through complex relationships in southern homes and families and that often last for many years. Less noticed by reviewers was Miss Daisy's German-Jewish origin, which adds a fascinating dimension to the interaction. Uhry stayed close to his Pulitzer Prize–winning play in the film adaptation, but there were some differences. In the play, when Miss Daisy hears of the bombing of her Reform temple in Atlanta, she says in her shock, "I could have understood if they had bombed the synagogue, but *our* temple . . . " It was an unfortunate omission in the film. Like the Jews of Germany in the 1930s, the Jews of Atlanta discovered in 1958 that to the Klan, there were no distinctions based on origin or class. Miss Daisy and Hoke are at that moment united as victims of a common hatred. It is a powerful moment, written with a complexity indicating that this drama about a black chauffeur and his white employer is beyond the ordinary.

It is somehow fitting that Morgan Freeman should have starred in both *Glory* and *Driving Miss Daisy*, released at about the same time. He could be his own ancestor, and the two films, if seen together, have an eerie connection. The black 54th Massachusetts Regiment in *Glory* is made up of ex-slaves, and the range of black characters portrayed in the movie is impressive. The distinguished historian Shelby Foote served as adviser, so there is a brutal authenticity to the battles not seen in a Civil War film since *The Red Badge of Courage*. *Glory* and the equally shocking and violent 1990 *Mississippi Burning* are films that give a new reality to the tortured history of the black experience in America.

Two films that preceded *Fried Green Tomatoes*, *Steel Magnolias* and *Crimes of the Heart*, also examine the modern varieties of the white experience in the South. Filmed in Natchitoches, Louisiana, *Steel Magnolias* provides a look at life in a small southern town where the local beauty parlor is the crossroads of gossip. In both that film and in *Crimes of the Heart*, the 1986 movie made from Beth Henley's Pulitzer Prize–winning play, the cloistered, smothering lives of the women in town are revealed through episodes of joy, scandal, and heartbreak. As did Mary Stuart Masterson and Mary Louise Parker in *Fried Green Tomatoes*, Sally Fields, as the mother of a dying daughter, has to play tragic scenes in an otherwise comic film. In previous films, particularly *Norma Rae* and *Places in the Heart*, she had honed her accent, and she did so with the special combination of vulnerability and strength that has been the hallmark of her southern heroines. While Olympia Dukakis's Greek-southern accent seems out of place, Shirley Mac-Laine, as the madcap neighbor with overalls and crazy hats who drops one-liners with manic bluntness, plays her role with the assurance of a native Virginian who knows the territory well.

Louisiana Politics

Earlier films about the politics in New Orleans and the city's nighttime stirrings influenced the moody atmosphere of *JFK*. In *Blaze*, Paul Newman brings Uncle Earl K. Long to life as the vulgar, boozing, woman-chasing governor of the great state of Louisiana. Earl Long was a cartoon character of a southern politician, a buffoon whose cronyism was a lifelong habit and whose hubris brought him down. Newman may seem to be overacting in the film, but anyone who had ever seen Earl Long recognized him in the Newman characterization: the sodden figure of a swaggering public man, who prowled the back streets, did his stump-speaking from a flatbed truck, and flaunted his open indiscretion with the queen of burlesque he once introduced in a public gathering as a "performing artiste on the cultural scene."

"In a certain way," says Blaze Starr, "we're both in show

business." And Earl Long replies, "You're catching on to the wheels of government real fast." This movie itself has several film antecedents. *All the King's Men*, the 1949 film about Earl's older brother, Huey Long, starred Broderick Crawford as Willie Stark, the fictional creation of Robert Penn Warren. Both films convey the corruption and the ruthlessness of Louisiana politics under the Long dynasty as well as the outsized personalities that strode the great stage of southern politics before television. "I never bought a senator or a congressman," said Earl. "I rent 'em. It's cheaper." (One is also reminded of the 1988 film *Bull Durham*, which *Blaze* writer and director Ron Shelton created about minor league baseball in the small-town South. I grew up in Durham with those languorous summer nights of lightnin' bugs and baseball and can testify that Shelton got it right. He is a filmmaker who cares about the mood and tone of his film.) The "feel" of *Blaze* is as sure-handed as a chef mixing jambalaya and as lazy as the meandering Mississippi River: the earthy glitter of the strip joints and bars in the French Quarter; the sweat-soaked shirts of the men in the campaign motorcade in the humid swamplands of rural Louisiana; the Mussolini-style public buildings "my brother built"; the "pea patch" shack where Blaze strips just for Old Earl, who dives into bed with his boots on "to get better traction." There is a visual sensibility at work in *Blaze* (and *Bull Durham*, as well), a cultivated eye for the way in which the South haunts the soul, inhabits the psyche, and entwines like kudzu around the memory. Haskell Wexler, the director of photography, gives every scene the look of a southern watercolor.

Paul Newman cut his teeth on movies about the South. Thirty years ago, he starred in *Cat on a Hot Tin Roof*, *The Long Hot Summer*, and *Sweet Bird of Youth*, and throughout his career, he continued to explore the archetypes, in *Hud* and in *Cool Hand Luke*. He has thought a lot about the South, as one would expect of a man married to actress Joanne Woodward, who is from Thomasville, Georgia. And as a well-known liberal Democrat, he must have been attracted to the political ambiguities in the Long story. They were populist demagogues who attacked the banks and the establishment, but they also fought the white supremacists by opposing the poll tax and favoring voting rights for blacks. It was pragmatic, as the film points out, because the poor of both races voted for them. "It's not Blaze Starr; it's my progressive ideas," says Earl. "The best friends the poor folks ever had was Jesus Christ, Sears Roebuck, and Earl K. Long."

The Southern Actor and Actress

It has been an interesting decade for the depiction of southerners in films. Holly Hunter in *Broadcast News* was allowed to portray the rarest of women—a brilliant television producer with a rural Georgia accent, miserable because she was smarter than everyone around her. In *sex, lies, and videotape* (filmed in the suburbs of Baton Rouge, Louisiana), Andie MacDowell of South Carolina, whose glowing beauty masks an affecting talent, gives a sensitive portrayal of the neglected wife of a lawyer she discovers is having an affair with her sister. And she is emerging as a major star in *Green Card* and other films that allow her beauty and intelligence and southernness to shine through. Throwback films do show up, such as *My Cousin Vinny*, but it is as much a hilarious spoof of Italians from New York as it is of rural southern boobs. Its depiction of stereotypical Yankees in the backwoods is reminiscent of the old Ma and Pa Kettle films.

A growing number of southern-born actors and actresses can take us beyond the world of rednecks, hillbillies, and moonshiners into the subtle varieties of the southern experience. Dennis Quaid's character in *The Big Easy* gets caught up in the corruptions, both petty and large, of the New Orleans police department; the film captures, through accents and music, the fascinating Cajun subculture. In a little-noticed and underrated performance in *Everybody's All-American*, Quaid portrayed a football hero from his college years to old age, the all-American halfback from LSU who marries his beauty queen sweetheart and matures into a paunchy dreamer who will never recover from his glory days. His co-star is Jessica Lange, who proclaims with regal sexuality that her mother taught her the secret of keeping a man—not batting her eyes but "owning a deep fryer." Lange added to her own southern credentials with *Sweet Dreams*, the story of Patsy Cline, the ill-fated country music singer who was killed in an airplane crash when she was at the peak of her career.

Writers and actresses have used regional accents to radiate a down-home toughness and courage in characters such as those played by Jodie Foster in *Silence of the Lambs* and Emily Lloyd in *Going Home*. One longs to see new southern stories written for the experienced group of older stars: Ned Beatty (of *Deliverance*, *Nashville*, and *The Big Easy*); Esther Rolle (who recreated the Ethel Waters role in the television version of *The Member of the Wedding*); Sissy Spacek (of *Coal Miner's Daughter*, *JFK*, and *The Long Walk Home*); Joanne Woodward (who, with Geraldine Page, is surely the best southern actress of her generation); Elizabeth Ashley (the first southern woman to play Maggie on Broadway in *Cat on a Hot Tin Roof*); Tommy Lee Jones (of *Coal Miner's Daughter*, *Back Roads*, and *JFK*); and Robert Duvall (who may have delivered one of his most memorable performances in *Ramblin' Rose* but whose favorite role, he has told friends, was in a small film made from a Faulkner story entitled *Tomorrow*). Filmmakers can also call on the talents of the emerging group of younger southern actresses such as Holly Hunter and Andie MacDowell, Tess Harper (*Tender Mercies*), Mary Steenburgen (*Cross Creek*), Lisa Jane Persky (*The Big Easy* and *The Great Santini*), and actors Danny Glover (*Places in the Heart*), Stan Shaw (*Fried Green Tomatoes*), Dennis and Randy Quaid (*The Last Detail*), and David Keith (*An Officer and a Gentleman*).

The Burden of Southern History

The recent emergence of a cluster of black and ethnic directors and the success of a number of their films gives one some hope. Films about the South continue to indicate that white Hollywood is not going to deal with the world of race and the black experience. But some new filmmakers are beginning to grapple with racial themes. In *Daughters of the Dust*, director Julie Dash has made a lyrical film set in 1902 on the South Carolina Sea Islands about a Gullah family struggling with the decision to move to the mainland. (Interestingly, *The Prince of Tides* probed the whites on the islands.) *Mississippi Masala* is an idiosyncratic film set in 1972, written and directed by a team of women filmmakers from Bombay, about an Indian family running a motel in Greenwood, Mississippi, and their spirited daughter's love affair with a local black, portrayed by Denzel Washington. "Masala" is the name of an Indian mixture of spices, and the film is a black-white-brown cross-cultural stew of an exotic community in the South.

The shadow of *Gone With the Wind* has lingered for over fifty years. Perhaps now, with its sequel published and its images giving way to new insights, writers, directors, and producers can be freed up to look at the varieties of southern experience in all its quilted diversity and patchwork richness. Doing so would enable Americans to come to grips with the burden of southern history and the ways in which people have endured in that struggling, mysterious, and complicated region that has given America so much of its literature, its tragedies, and its soul.

25

Revisiting the Saturday Westerns: Back in the Saddle with Hoppy, Gene, and Roy, Oh Boy!

"I was raised on matinees on Saturday afternoons,
Looking up at Hoppy, Gene, and Roy, oh boy.
I grew up a-thinkin'
The best a man could do,
Was be a rootin', tootin', straight-shootin'
Cowboy Buckaroo."

Mason Williams,
songwriter and singer

"Saturday meant all day in the movies. I'd watch the feature twice and the cartoons and serials three times, all for nine cents admission—and five cents for popcorn popping fresh right there so you could smell it all over the Rialto Theater. . . Late in the afternoon, I'd wander bleary-eyed out of the movie to start my weekly ritual . . . Walking down Main Street I would always drop in on a few of the Jewish merchants who would give me a big hello and let me roam around their stores."

from *The Provincials*

Gene Autry, Roy Rogers, and Tex Ritter used to meet for an occasional marathon game of cards that climaxed with scrambled eggs at 5:00 A.M.; Bill Boyd, dressed as Hopalong Cassidy, would often ride as Grand Marshall in small town parades waving and smiling at the crowds while muttering under his breath, "Hello, you little bastards"; Tom Mix once said, "If God was good enough to give me a full head of hair, the least I can do is keep it dyed"; "Lash" Larue has been married nine times, and after a life that has included very hard times, is now working with an evangelist, bringing people into the church by doing whip tricks outside.

And that's just the beginning. Clayton Moore, who played the Lone Ranger in the 1950s, was once standing in a hotel lobby with another western star. When the star pointed Moore out to a youngster seeking autographs, Moore ran from the room with his face in his hands. Later, he said to his colleague, "Don't you ever identify me without my mask again."

These were just some of the stories making the rounds at the Fourth Annual Western Movie Festival—a four-day affair in 1974 in the new Nashville Hyatt-Regency, where six screening rooms were open seventeen hours every day to show over 200 old western films and serials. More than 900 people showed up from all over the country and paid $20 a person for this cowboy orgy—western film buffs; dealers who buy, sell, and trade films; entrepreneurs who collect western movie stills, comic books, and lobby cards, to mingle with returning stars to relive those thrilling days of yesteryear. Buster Crabbe was there (the Flash Gordon and Buck Rogers who also starred in forty-two B-Westerns as Billy the Kid) and Eddie Dean (a late forties singing cowboy who accidentally referred to himself as "Roy Autry"); Ray "Crash" Corrigan (one of the original "Three Musketeers" who claimed he taught Leonard Slye of Cincinnati, later known as Roy Rogers, how to mount a horse). There were also assorted other supporting stars like Ray Whitley (a backup musician who claimed he designed the first fancy guitar and wrote "Back in the Saddle, Again" for Gene Autry after a 4:00 A.M. phone call saying they needed it for shooting that day); Reb Russell (now in his late seventies, who knew Tom Mix and Gene Autry and who asserted "Gene was a clumsy musician, not a cowboy"); and Russ Hayden (who played "Lucky" in the Hopalong Cassidy series). Past years' guests had included a number of villains and comic sidekicks.

The festival was conceived by three men in their thirties who discovered accidentally their mutual love for the genre. "Packy" Smith, who sells baby chicks out of Nashville, would visit the small Bristol Theater in Memphis on Tuesday nights when B-Westerns were running. A postal employee, Michell Schaperkotter, ran the theater as a hobby, and he knew Wayne Lackey, a printer from Trenton, Tennessee, who had hundreds of stills and had been collecting films since he was seventeen. They all began collecting films of their own and became linked into the national network of collectors and dealers through the various publications and mailing lists like *The Nostalgia Journal*, *Film Collector's Review*, and *The Big Reel*. The idea for the western film festival came from the success of the comic book and super-hero conventions; at first, they just wanted to meet the people from whom they were buying films. Then they decided to invite the stars to draw crowds. The first year, 160 people came, and the convention has grown steadily ever since, mostly by word of mouth.

One of the most striking aspects of the festival was that the stars were all thirty years older than the audience—because the fans were all kids watching them once, and one could sense that same adulation all over again at the two-hour "Panel of the Stars" that took place every afternoon of the festival, in which the movie buffs asked questions and the stars told earthy stories about each other and their friends.

The festival added some 1950s films of Audie Murphy, Joel McCrea, and Randolph Scott, in order to bring in younger fans and broaden the appeal to families.

"Basically, though," said "Packy" Smith, "it's a man's area. There are many women interested but there are few women

collectors. It's economics. Most women prefer to put their money in clothes and other things."

Smith owned about 200 films and described the economics
of collecting. A film, he said, usually costs from $85 to $100
and a serial anywhere from $350 to $500. A 16-mm sound
projector can be bought for anywhere from $200 secondhand to
$900 new, though more exotic equipment is available. Thus,
he has about $15,000 to $20,000 sunk in his hobby, "but it's
an investment. There are more people collecting everyday."

I'm certain that the western movie holds one of the keys to
the American male personality, that its values shaped part of
the fast-draw character of the men who sent the marines to
Lebanon and thought up the Green Berets, that the American
fascination with violence, over-simplification of conflict, and
search for hero-presidents is partially derived from western
films. But those are all the heavy side of the western—the
nostalgia boom is less about western films and more about
validating and making valuable any and all artifacts from earlier times. And if the growth of the festival is any indication,
the B-Western and the serial are on the edge of a rebirth.

The audience for the festival was mostly small-town, white,
and southern, from places like Marbleton, Georgia; Church
Hill, Tennessee; Hopkinsville, Kentucky. Some of them wore
Stetsons and cowboy clothes, and were what the sponsors of the
festival called "squirrels," with a consuming obsession for
western films. One, who wore a pearl-handled Colt pistol in a
silver-studded black holster, told me he had bought old theater
seats and a popcorn booth to recreate his boyhood in his basement. Another was a forty-eight-year-old bachelor, who had
seen Tex Ritter nineteen times in person, had collected all his
records, books, and photos and spent most of his spare time
with the Tex Ritter Fan Club, keeping the legend alive. ("Did
you spend your childhood in a theater?" I asked. "No, my
mother wouldn't let me, but she can't stop me now," he replied.)

I saw only four blacks in the three days. One of them, in a
big western hat and shirt, was a security man for Sears and

Roebuck, who grew up in rural Mississippi where "Saturday westerns and Sunday church were the only things we had to look forward to." He said the western was "part of my heritage" and that he was there because he couldn't afford to collect films, but he could come down to see them. "Hell, one out of three cowboys on the trail were black or Mexican, but you don't hear much about that."

For the most part, the participants in the festival were collectors with ten or so films, who came to the festival to trade off the films they were tired of for ones they wanted to see.

Buster Crabbe was the biggest star in attendance, and because his career roamed beyond the western, so did the questions from his middle-aged fans. Though Crabbe had gotten into movies as a swimmer, he admitted that he had not been able to beat Johnny Weismuller in the three times they had raced. Later, Crabbe said, they met in the same film when he played a villain in one of Weismuller's *Jungle Jim* series. The finale consisted of a water fight in which Crabbe held Weismuller under water for several minutes to get the bubble effect the director wanted. "You S.O.B., are you trying to drown me?" Weismuller spluttered. Crabbe looked mournfully at the audience at the film festival—"Now, I ask you, can you imagine anyone drowning Johnny Weismuller?"

Crabbe seemed some kind of figure out of a family album— there he was on the screen as Flash Gordon in the thirties, as Billy the Kid in the late forties, and today as a well-preserved, but sixty-seven-year-old man. It was unsettling and not what anyone there had wanted. Films freeze the stars in memory, as dancing images of our boyhood—to meet them as old men is to be reminded of one's own mortality.

Roy Acuff, the country-western singer, made a "surprise" appearance at the festival, as attracted to a Nashville crowd as anything else. Someone next to me muttered, "He ain't no cowboy," but he had once been in a western movie called *Night Train to Memphis* and he contributed his print to the festival. The papers had been full of a brewing controversy over the film *Nashville* (Producer Robert Altman had said, "You people are

trying to do the same thing to this movie as the Army did to
M.A.S.H."), and Acuff was said to be one of the inspirations
for Henry Gibson's portrayal of Haven Hamilton in the film.
Acuff, who once ran for governor of Tennessee, denied any
resemblance but observed that "Everything in films can't be as
fine and as Christian-like as it should be." Haven Hamilton
would have said the same thing.

While Nashville's natural ability to attract celebrities drew
larger numbers of fans each day, the crowd also included a
smattering of doctors and lawyers, as well as a number of
professors who were drawn to examining the values of the
B-Western in an effort to understand the subconscious roots of
American values.

Michael Nevins and Ed Mitchell were young professors who
taught film courses on the western at St. Louis and Ohio universities and met every year at the festival. They came because
"this is about the only place left to see these films" and because "understanding the western film is vital to understanding
American culture."

Nevins said that "for the intellectual here, the attraction is
the ideology in the films. Nobody cared what the plot lines
were, nobody cared what the writers and directors were doing.
It was the freest medium, so the ideology is a true reflection of
the times." Nevins pointed out that in the thirties, the villain
behind the outlaw was invariably a "Mister Big," usually in
eastern clothes. "He was most often a banker trying to seize
land for the railroad, the old abandoned mine, the water. He
was trying to manipulate the little people. Since the B-Western
enjoyed its greatest popularity in the South and Midwest, the
plot played on the small-town mistrust of the establishment and
reflected the populism of the Depression."

Another theme, according to Mitchell, was the ineptness of
the local official. "The U.S. Marshall or the Texas Ranger is
the hero. The Sheriff is too old or corrupt or needs help. The
federal government is acting to clean up a local mess." He
pointed out that "Vengeance was a popular theme," and that
"death was always painless, bloodless and acrobatic."

The movies were all fifty-five minutes long so they could fit on a double bill with a serial. Watching parts of dozens of films over a three-day period, you realized that the plot lines were so similar that you could walk into any film at any point and pick up the story in less than thirty seconds. The B-Westerns were very cheap films, shot in less than a week, with lavish use of stock footage of stage coach chases and cattle herds; they used classical music because it was in the public domain and cost nothing (the explanation for the Lone Ranger's famous William Tell overture). For the most part, good guys really did wear white hats and rode better horses, which animated the chase scenes and made the heroes easily identifiable in group brawls in saloons (the festival allowed the viewer to overdose on the great horses who could nibble a rope loose or be summoned to a jail cell with a high whistle—not just Trigger and Champion, but Ken Maynard's Tarzan, Buster Crabbe's White Flash, and Bill Boyd's Topper). Even with identical plots and settings (many of the westerns were shot at "Crash" Corrigan's ranch, Corriganville, so that stock footage could be more easily blended into the film), the mood of the films varied with the personality of the stars and can be distinguished from each other by the originality of the comic antics of the sidekicks like "Smiley" Burnette, Gabby Hayes, and "Fuzzy" Knight. Buster Crabbe said flatly that "Al 'Fuzzy' St. John carried our entire series," because his humor was improvised right on the set.

Peggy Stewart played the leading lady in much of the Red Ryder series that starred "Wild" Bill Elliot and Allan "Rocky" Lane. She was married for awhile to another Red Ryder star named Don "Red" Barry, a feisty, 5'6" Irishman whom she referred to as the "Cagney of the Plains." She always played the local school marm, or the daughter of an aging rancher whose land was more valuable than he realized. (Because of budgets, I was told, there were rarely any mothers in B-Westerns.) At the end of the picture, she would ask the hero to stay; he'd blush and talk about settling down, but then would ride off into the sunset as she waved to him wistfully. It was the perfect scene to appeal to adolescents struggling with sexuality.

"I wanted to ride fast and shoot straight in a couple of pictures," she said, "but mostly, it was the same simpering roles because the system featured the men and we just had to accept it." For her, like most actresses, the B's were not an end but a vehicle to other jobs in the movies. However, because of ironclad contracts, few made it out—it was so rare that the festival took pains to feature a film with Marguerita Casino (later Rita Hayworth) and a very young Jennifer Jones.

"For the men, it was different," she said. "Don Barry still acts and Bobby Blake (who played Little Beaver in a string of Red Ryder movies) is now Robert Blake of the *Baretta* series on TV." Not that acting was a necessary requirement to be in western films. Reb Russell confesses that he had "two expressions necessary for success—constipation and relief."

Peggy Stewart was filled with tidbits—that well-known villain Roy Barcroft off-screen was a "pussycat" who played the clarinet; that Lash Larue bragged that he could recite more than 800 poems and would launch into Shakespeare for hours.

The festival attracted its share of serial freaks, who stayed up till 4:00 A.M. watching all fifteen chapters (that's five hours) of a favorite cliffhanger. *Flash Gordon* was far and away the most popular serial ever, mainly, as Crabbe pointed out, because it was the only one with a large enough production budget to experiment with special effects. But Flash was for the masses—this crowd couldn't wait to see *Dick Tracy vs. Crime, Inc.*; *Captain Marvel*; *Tiger Woman*; and a World War II thriller called *Spy Smasher*.

For the afficionados, the heroes of these serials were not the stars, but the stunt men who did the daring 50-foot leaps from burning buildings and the spectacular fight scenes in the lumber mill in front of the proverbial conveyor belt to the spinning buzz saw. The reason that so many of the serials were built around comic-strip heroes who wore masks—Zorro, Captain America, The Phantom, Batman—was because they were written for a stunt man named Tom Steele whose name never appeared on the screen. Since they weren't supposed to exist, the stunt men never received billing but remained to all but trivia fans as anonymous as the masked heroes they played.

The festival showed 21 different serials including a dozen of the most action-packed from Republic studios. I clocked several segments of *Spy Smasher* ("The *Citizen Kane* of serials," one fan said), and there was a fight, a chase, or a gun battle every three minutes. In one 20-minute chapter, the only line of dialogue was "Hold it. Drop that gun." A stunt man named David Sharpe was so catlike, I was told, that directors at Republic kept a line on the wall of their offices at his height and picked their stars accordingly. To preserve the illusion, stunt men wore flesh-colored straps on their cowboy hats to make sure the hats wouldn't come off during fight scenes; and since Sharpe was small in stature (though perfectly proportioned), he created his own demand for small villains. His size also allowed him to don a wig and a dress to do stunts for women in serials. William Whitney, the director of the most popular Republic serials, claimed that staging fights for Sharpe was like watching a great dancer at work. When asked recently where he got the inspiration for these fight scenes, Whitney replied, "Busby Berkeley."

The most famous western stunt man in movie history was Yakima Canutt, who doubled Tom Mix and most everyone else in the silent era and often played a villain after sound arrived. It was not unusual, I was told, to see a chase scene with Canutt doubling the hero chasing himself as the villain. Much of what we remember about the star was really his double—for instance, Canutt did the famous scene in John Ford's *Stagecoach* when the driver was shot and John Wayne leapt into the horses running at full gallop, suddenly fell beneath them, and grabbed the rear of the stagecoach as it ran over him and climbed back over the top to try again. Canutt galloped off high cliffs into water, jumped over canyons on horseback, and fell off hundreds of horses when shot. "The greatest tribute to Yak," said one of the stars, "is that he's still alive."

The not-so-quiet talk in the halls was of the copyright problems and the recent visits by the FBI to dealers or collectors
buying from a West Coast firm suspected of selling illegal
prints of popular new films. The case arose from pirated versions of big-budget films like *The Sting*, *The Exorcist*, and *The
Godfather*, that showed up in South Africa and Rhodesia without any studio contracts or royalty agreements.

A collector of ten films complained to me of having his
collection confiscated by the FBI. To get some answers, more
than 150 people showed up at 9 A.M. on the last day of the
festival to hear a lawyer discuss copyright problems.

Jack Irvin, a Nashville copyright lawyer, said that because
"studios kept no records of 16-mm prints prior to 1970, the
true pedigree of a print is impossible to trace." Thus, he said,
"no one can tell whether a given print is legal or illegal."

However, he warned the group against selling prints they
knew to be illegal, and against charging admission for the
"exhibition" of a film if they bought it for "private use." He
emphatically said that "You are not liable for possession of a
film you bought in good faith."

Irvin predicted that the videotape recorder would stimulate
new studio interest in the titles to old films, and that studios
would someday offer videotapes of favorite films the way record
companies issue phonograph records. At the present time,
Irvin said about 100,000 people owned at least one old film.

The audience unanimously agreed, when asked, that they
would prefer to buy films directly from a studio (thus assuring
the quality of a mail-order purchase; now, I was told, a mail-
order print can arrive so scratched you can't even run it).

"Packy" Smith resented the FBI harassment because he felt
that "these films wouldn't exist today had not a lot of people
who cared wanted to preserve them." He said there were only
500 active western film collectors in the country; another
dealer complained, "We are being punished because of a few
rotten apples on the big new films."

The rarest films were the most valuable: *The Trailblazers*
with Hoot Gibson, Ken Maynard, and Bob Steele; any sound

version of Tom Mix (he only made nine); early movies of John Wayne or Gary Cooper before they left B-Westerns for the big time; a couple of movies in which Robert Mitchum played a villain. According to the dealers at the festival, the most popular hero this year was probably Buck Jones, a square-jawed straight arrow who died in the Coconut Grove nightclub fire in 1942 "trying to save a little child."

There were cult favorites, too. Lash Larue, a moody, brooding tough guy whom some called the "Bogart of the Badlands," had a strong following, and his *King of the Bull Whip* was especially popular. So was a kinky Linda Sterling serial called *Zorro's Black Whip* in which a sweet Linda in a long dress decides to adopt the Zorro black mask, black horse, and black hat to avenge her dead brother, and takes on the villains as a woman everyone thinks is a man, but the audience knows is a woman dressed as a man. (It was really a stunt man dressed as a woman dressed as a man!) I was also told that one could buy a solid hour of excerpts from jungle girl serials of women fighting each other.

Many of the people I interviewed also collected guns, comic books, still photos, and posters. A number were looking for other kinds of films—particularly gangster and horror films, and Bogart classics like *The African Queen*. One looked forward every year to the mystery writers, the comic book, and *The Star Trek* conventions. Most were rather eccentric, introverted men, who collect western films the way religious pilgrims must have bought icons. There was a strange patriotism to it—articulated by the stars—that the nation was coming apart, entertainment was too decadent, and that if everyone watched B-Westerns, this would be a better country.

Four days of 35-year-old movies caused me to fantasize about the nature of a similar event in the year 2010. Crowds of fifty-year-olds will gather in their jeans and T-shirts at the Rock Music Nostalgia Festival where they will be showing *Help*, *A Hard Day's Night*, and *Gimme Shelter*; old Beatle record albums will be selling for $50 apiece; the FBI will be investigating the sale of unauthorized tapes and cassettes. A pair of wizened and wrinkled seventy-year-olds named Mick Jagger and Paul McCartney will reminisce at the "Panel of the Stars" about drug busts and the groupies in the good old days in Liverpool. A few professors will be musing about the cultural applications of adolescent sexual fantasies in the rock era, and someone will try to remember a Southeast Asian country that begins with a "V."

But still, the western film is something special. It is an enduring myth, reborn again to new generations on television. It has its modern reincarnation in the vengeance movies like *Dirty Harry*, *Death Wish*, and the *Kung Fu* series. It is suggested in the broad-brimmed hats and white Cadillacs of the Broadway pimps. It creeps into politics ("The American people admire the lone cowboy riding unarmed into town on his horse," said Henry Kissinger to Oriana Fallaci in explaining his popularity. "We're eyeball-to-eyeball and somebody just blinked," said Dean Rusk during the Cuban missile showdown). It is a recurring theme of folk and rock music, from Bob Dylan and James Taylor to Elton John:

The great sequin cowboy who sings of the plains,
Of roundups and rustlers and home on the range,
Turn on the T.V., shut out the lights;
Roy Rogers is riding tonight.
                    Elton John from *Yellow Brick Road*

26

All the Candidates' Clothes

Fashion represents an odd way to look at presidential campaigns, but the way a candidate dresses, especially in this
television age, often is an extension of his campaign themes, or
unconsciously can give the discerning voter clues about the
candidate's politics.

Jimmy Carter was not the first candidate in history to wear
jeans as a political tactic; Calvin Coolidge tried it in 1924, but
photographs of him in the fields in starched, creased overalls
and a pair of well-shined black shoes made him an object of
national ridicule. Jeans were an authentic part of Carter's
wardrobe, however, and the well-worn fit of them proved that
he felt at home in the Plains, Georgia, uniform of the day. It
was not lost on political advisers during his presidential campaign that jeans mean one thing to the young people around
Harvard Square and another to the farmers in Iowa—thereby
cleverly attracting voters of opposite political views.

Because media and politics have merged in the modern
political campaign, running for office has become a kind of
extended theater—taking a song-and-dance show on the road
for public affirmation. Looking at a campaign the way candi-

dates must—as a series of nightly two-minute television news spots—one can see that clothing becomes costume, as important in conveying an image as the other crucial indicia of modern leadership—the smile, the haircut, contact lenses instead of glasses.

During the 1976 primaries Jimmy Carter starred in an almost weekly television series Tuesday night until June, and though he could have worn bib overalls he invariably chose a blue pin-striped suit or a dark blue blazer. (Media specialists have been telling candidates for twenty years that blue is "sincere" and "presidential.")

The country-slicker image fit in with Carter's overall political plan. For fifteen years, George Wallace had worn the double knit, mail-order look as part of his act in the North. Wallace didn't want to look "big time"; he was the little man's little man, the bantam-weight counterpuncher, lashing out at the "pointy-headed briefcase-totin' bureaucrats," and he took pains not to look like them.

Part of the genius of the Carter primary campaign was to recognize that southerners, with their inferiority complex, really yearned for a better representative to the North. The elections of New South governors showed that southerners were tired of the yahoo image. With attitudes of racial moderation gaining favor, the South was ready to send the smiling son of light, not the angry son of darkness, off to do battle with the Yankees; because Watergate made sin an issue, they wanted him to look like a choirboy. Carter could have taken instruction years ago when the Planters advertising people used a top hat, cane, and monocle to elevate the humble goober. The Democratic nominee didn't go that far, but if Wendell Willkie was the "barefoot boy from Wall Street," then Jimmy Carter was the pin-striped peanut farmer from Plains.

My father, who was elected mayor of Durham six times from 1951 to 1963, and I recently talked about clothes and politics.

"The important thing when you run," he said, "is to wear what you've always worn. If you try to dress up, people will say you're puttin' on the dog; if you dress down, they'll say you're pretending to be humble."

Indecision was Gerald Ford's problem with clothes after he became president. In the first year of his term, he dressed the way midwestern congressmen dress, in plaids and double-vent jackets with brightly striped shirts and colorful ties—a man of the people. Every man who has ever rented a tuxedo can identify with a president who met Emperor Hirohito of Japan wearing striped pants hiked up above his ankles with his socks showing—no airs for good ole Jerry. When Ford asked Harvey Rosenthal, the White House tailor whose father had made clothes for Dwight Eisenhower, to give him a more "presidential look," Ford's reelection game plan began to fall apart. He should have followed the example of our only haberdasher-president, Harry Truman; the loud shirts he wore in Key West gave him the "everyman" look that raked in votes across the farm belt and didn't hurt with working people either.

Perhaps Ford's own transformation during the presidency (to the point where he wore a vest to the mid-August Republican convention) dictated his choice of Senator Robert Dole of Kansas as his running mate. He now needed a man in midwestern congressional garb to remind the voters of where he came from. Besides, by picking someone who mirrored his own fashion tastes, geographical appeal, and philosophy, he shattered conventional wisdom and confounded the Democrats; they had predicted he would pick someone who would broaden his appeal.

Politicians cannot dress too fashionably. You never see them wearing Saint Laurent suits, Gucci belt buckles, or loafers made of old Rolls Royce seat covers. My father pointed out the reason: "Men don't like dandies. Women notice clothes more and respond to them. So you have to dress more carefully when appearing before women's groups but not go too far, or you'll offend men." That's the reason that candidates who especially appeal to women, such as Ronald Reagan or Ted Kennedy, seem to dress against type. If they wore untraditional clothes that suggested a rakish quality, they would risk turning off the male vote.

Liberals have a special problem in dress. While appealing to liberal voters with their ideas, they must also reach conservatives with a solid image, which means clothes that are respectable, stable, and without flair or a hint of originality. Walter Mondale personified the liberal candidate; dressing like everyone else allowed him to think differently. They should be contrasted with Ronald Reagan's cowboy clothes, as the conservative movie hero saddles up in the west to gallop into the White House.

A president's leisure-time dress reveals a great deal about the man and his roots. John Kennedy's tastes ran to Cape Cod slickers and the sailing clothes he grew up in; Eisenhower loved golf outfits, which obviously came from years of visiting officers' clubs and golf courses on military bases; Lyndon Johnson relished Stetsons and ranch clothes, which emphasized that he was a westerner (being a southerner was not a political plus in the sixties); Franklin Roosevelt's cape was a necessity, the most convenient garment for a president in a wheelchair.

Richard Nixon's clothes, however, hid his character behind a facade of propriety. There has been nothing distinctive about his dress in the last twenty-five years; even his leisure clothes murmured simply, "I am the president." He once tried to have a Kennedy-esque picture taken on the beach at Key Biscayne but spoiled it by wearing dressy blue trousers (shades of Calvin Coolidge). Nixon, however, mastered the full-dress confession speech: He always wore dark-blue or neutral gray suits for moments of national contrition—in the 1952 Checkers speech and in his 1974 "But it would be wrong" resignation.

In the 1992 presidential campaign, the political differences between George Bush and Bill Clinton were reflected in their physical appearances. Bush, relaxing in Kennebunkport, Maine, radiated the self-confident Ivy League look of the pure preppy, from polo shirts to topsiders. Even at a press conference, the blue blazer and open shirt gave a certain duplicitous subtext to his claim of Texas citizenship. When he does "go western," as happens from time to time at the quadrennial quail hunt or ranch-sized barbecue, he is still the patrician on a dude ranch who dons a cowboy hat and looks like an embarrassed Yale extra in a John Wayne movie.

Bill Clinton introduced the dark glasses and saxophone look to late-night talk shows; Bush, forgetting his own effort once to play blues guitar with Lee Atwater, tried to turn it into a blunder, comparing it to Michael Dukakis's miscast tank helmet. While Clinton occasionally moved to plaid shirts and Levi jeans for press conferences in the farm belt, he obviously worried about not appearing too regional or too young in his campaign stops outside the South. Tending to wear double-breasted suits in the dark and reassuring colors of a more mature world statesman with a weight problem, he also revealed in his choices of striped club ties and white shirts a past influenced by Oxford University and Yale Law School. His advisers had an instinct for the messages of costume: he changed caps and sweatshirts when he huffed and puffed on morning jogs, and the day after Ronald Reagan addressed the 1992 Republican convention in what looked like a tailor-made shirt with tiny red dots and a white collar (as befits a man who once made $100,000 for a single speech in Japan), the Clinton and Gore families joined former President Jimmy Carter in work clothes to hammer in a few nails and raise the walls of a Habitat for Humanity house in Atlanta for a poor family.

Thus did the 1992 campaign echo the ones of 1976, with Hope, Arkansas, playing the role of Plains, Georgia, while the Republican country-club aspirations remained constant.

27

The Emperor's Fall Clothes

And it came to pass that a man who sold shirts was
smitten by hard times. Neither did any of his
merchandise move nor did he prosper. And he
prayed and said, "Lord, why hast thou left me to
suffer thus? All mine enemies sell their goods
except I. And it's the height of the season . . . "
And the Lord heard the man and said, "About thy
shirts . . . "
"Yes, Lord," the man said falling to his knees.
"Put an alligator over the pocket."
"Pardon me, Lord?"
"Just do what I'm telling you. You won't be sorry."
And the man sewed on to all his shirts a small
alligator symbol and lo and behold, suddenly his
merchandise moved like gangbusters . . .

Woody Allen
Without Feathers

In the spring of 1975, the editor of the *New York Times Fashion
Magazine*, which comes out twice a year, asked me to attend
all the fashion shows that spring and write a piece for them.
When I protested with the timeworn phrase that I was "just a
country boy" and knew absolutely nothing about fashion, she
answered, "That's just what we are looking for." I figured that

looking at beautiful models parading down runways could not be too burdensome for a young man in New York, so I dropped into the fashion world, going to hotels, designer showrooms, lofts, and suites to write something about fall and winter clothes in the rising temperatures of late spring.

I had never been to a fashion show. I do not read *Women's Wear Daily*, *Vogue*, *Mademoiselle*, or *Glamour*. I cannot identify designers and rarely do more than glance in the windows of the boutiques on Madison Avenue. But I did have parents who were once in the retail business, and the impression had filtered down even to North Carolina, where we lived, that Saks Fifth Avenue, Bergdorf's, and Lord & Taylor were important symbols to American women, their labels quietly conveying the same message of class as the more public alligator on a French shirt.

I was expecting the shows to be a glamorous New York experience and pictured myself climbing the pinnacle of chic where I would be the envy of my friends. It was a short climb. The buyers storming Seventh Avenue watch the proceedings with expressions I haven't seen since the livestock bidding at the North Carolina State Fair.

First of all, in May, when everyone else is naturally dreaming of summer, an entire world is caught up in tweed overcoats, wool sweaters, and high boots. They have to think cold and live warm, see green and draw gray. The fashion business is always out of sync, I realized, which may explain why the atmosphere on Seventh Avenue is so nutty.

I kept telling myself that, basically, it's just cloth. The Seventh Avenue magic show can wrap it, dye it, drape it, sling it, and pin it tight, but after the seven hundred outfits I saw in ten days, the whole thing became as confusing as three teenage couples in the back of a Dodge pickup. I was told that the "if-it's-Tuesday-it-must-be-Halston" syndrome inflicts itself on every fashion writer, who must see several thousand outfits each season in approximately fifty shows and seventy-five showrooms.

With so many identical designs being shown, everything can't be as "fabulous" as the women's magazines report. *Women's Wear Daily* and the fashion magazines seem to exist not to provide criticism, but to tell their readers what's "in," to applaud whatever's flashy with lavish adjectives and action verbs, to surround the millions of dollars in advertising space with radiant copy.

Thus, when I would write down "orange," the woman next to me wrote down "apricot"; I scribbled "dark brown," she wrote "chocolate." The big trick in fashion writing is to describe colors with tasty adjectives: "cinnamon," "plum," "oatmeal" and "paprika." *Women's Wear Daily* even went so far as to call a table full of raw vegetables at the Calvin Klein show "a still life of beige, green, and white" (meaning mushrooms, asparagus, and cauliflower).

The designers seemed to be following my mother's advice to me years ago when I helped out in the family store before Easter: "Sell her the dress she wears into the store." The women's magazine press, the buyers, and the fashion groupies flocked into the shows wearing the same daytime clothes that were showing on the runway, as the economy forced the designers to keep their ideas just slightly ahead of what was selling last year.

It was my first exposure to the so-called "layered look" from Paris—a turtleneck with a blouse, with a sweater, with a vest, with a raincoat, with a cape. Frankly, it looked hotter than a simmering pot of grits, but perhaps it was the ultimate fashion for the time of an energy crisis. (Maybe Seventh Avenue knew something Henry Kissinger didn't about the Middle East.) The shows recalled the untaped moments of the Nixon years with a tentative gesture to the Chinese influence, still more silky Madame Chiang Kai-shek than Mao, though the quilted coolie jacket might have scored with fashion-conscious American women who were looking over their shoulders and worrying about being out of step with 700 million Chinese.

The fascination of the upper classes with working-class clothes led Seventh Avenue some years ago to develop the skin-tight silk bib overall—a nostalgia item for small-town southerners like me who recall, whenever we see them, our friends slopping hogs at feeding time. Another such trend was the jumpsuit, probably inspired by long lines at the gas pumps, an impression confirmed in a Lower East Side thrift shop featuring a real auto mechanic's jumpsuit in its original smudged white.

In some ways, the conjunction of politics and culture with clothes is the most intriguing part of the fashion world. The theory is that fashion ideas seep into the public mind from the images we see on television and in newspapers. It's a less depressing way to respond to the news, letting the pictures wash over you and wondering how this or that event will influence women's clothes. After all, from the Vietnam War era came the gunbelt-and-brass-button look.

The black models stole the shows. At the shows of the major black designers—Scott Barrie, Stephen Burrows, and Willi Smith—the models were unrestrained enough to skip down the runways and occasionally toss off an all-out, high-stepping, syncopated wipe-out step, turning an ordinary jersey dress into two hound dogs in a burlap bag.

Since the industry has adjusted to using black models, one wonders why it can't make other concessions to the real world and design clothes for, say, plump women or anyone un-young or un-thin.

In spite of all the change that American women claim to be going through, the ideal as celebrated in the fashion magazines still persists—the tall, slender woman with long legs, a lanky demon that causes deep depression around the mirrors of any department store. In some ways, high fashion is a cartoon, but to the degree that it represents arch-commercial judgments aimed at women's deep-seated insecurities, it's oppressive, because its major impact is to make women thoroughly dissatisfied with their looks. But one can't blame the industry; it exists to sell, not to struggle, to create the tide and ride it, not to fight the seasons and the sea.

Personally, I like materials I can touch as well as look at. In the fifties, we felt each other's sweaters to prove they were not cashmere, and my most vivid prom memories involve dresses that invited me to brush up against them. I suppose that's the reason I liked some of Oscar de la Renta's pale chiffon concoctions, Holly Harp's flowing pants-skirts, and Calvin Klein's mixing of dark velvet with silk in blouses of unusual color.

The trouble was that there was no place in New York to wear those clothes—jeans had invaded ballet, theater, and gallery openings so assertively that everyone else felt overdressed. The only designer to solve that problem was Halston; his Ultrasuede was the perfect outfit to wear when shopping for another Halston.

Ultrasuede was a triumph of ecology—the synthetic that cost more than the original skins, created for the woman who never goes near the washing machine, who can tell everyone how serviceable her laundress says the dress is. The international spy and detective look were featured, either because the CIA was so much in the news or because Halston felt guilty about the prices he was charging.

Ralph Lauren and Oscar de la Renta presented polar views of how women could dress. Lauren's blazers and pants suits were practical daytime clothes that one could run around in; de la Renta's chiffon visions were for nighttime wear, an alternative for opera-going when the jeans are in the laundry.

Not one show ran counter to the Paris trends, which is disturbing for a country that asserted during the disastrous mini-to-midi switch years ago that American women could wear clothes any length they liked. Sometimes the slavish adherence to Paris trends reveals how thoroughly manipulated American women can be. The emperor's new clothes tale that year was played out afresh in the guise of the "big look"—the

tent dress that surely ranked as the most democratic garment
out of Paris in decades: it looked universally terrible on everyone. While its popularity mystified me, one explanation might
be that a woman's attitude toward clothes is probably influenced by how she feels about her body—what she believes
needs accentuating and especially what "deficiencies" need
covering up. Since the tent dress enveloped everything, it
emerged as the biggest "no-risk" look since the sack.

I do enjoy shopping with women, especially when they are
doing the buying. To find out whether a woman dresses for men
or for other women, you must develop strong opinions—women
who are on the edge of deciding whether to blend in or stand
out don't appreciate wishy-washiness. I was once the only male
around on the designer floor at Bonwit's, where I was watching
a girl friend celebrate a new promotion. Near us, a woman with
an off-season tan had winnowed her way through a morning of
indecision; it came down to a long brown knit dress or a white
flowing number. She turned to me, a stranger, for advice.

"Can I ask you for a frank opinion?" she said, while looking
in the mirror at the white one she was wearing and holding over
one arm the brown one I had noticed her in a few minutes
earlier. "As a man, which one do you like best?"

"Well," I answered, compelled to be decisive, "frankly, I
thought you looked better in the brown one."

"Good," she beamed, turning toward the cash register. "I'll
take them both."

28

Jericho: **Shout of Silence**

After traveling through the South together, the painter Hubert Shuptrine and James Dickey, the Georgia-born poet, combined their talents to produce *Jericho*, an unusual book with over one hundred watercolors and drawings and an accompanying text.

It was a good idea, harking back to Dickey's hero, James Agee, whose travels with photographer Walker Evans in the thirties resulted in *Let Us Now Praise Famous Men*. ("James Agee," Dickey once said, "for me, word by word and sentence by sentence, is the writer I care more for than for anybody else I've ever read in any language.") But whereas the Agee-Evans book was published quietly (fewer than six hundred copies sold at the time) and was an underground classic until rediscovered more than twenty years later, *Jericho* came out with all the yahoos of a rebel yell as *the* gift book of the Christmas season in the suburbs from Baton Rouge to Richmond.

The sheer bulk of the book has made it an easy target for ridicule: 12½ by 16 inches, weighing seven pounds, it could be used as a coffee table itself. The first printing of 150,000 numbered copies (mine was No. 76,362) showed that the good old boys who conceived the book at Oxmoor House in Birmingham have learned well from publishing the successful *Southern Living* magazine how to manipulate the southern need for status. (Dickey, the former ad man, knew no New York publisher had that kind of whole-hog faith in the South as a market.) The press release accompanying the book sets a new standard for southern chic, pointing out to sensitive art lovers that the book required "28 carloads (one million pounds) of paper and 31 miles of cloth." It's as if the poet decided to give himself over to the Alabama Chamber of Commerce for a few months.

But statistics and salesmanship are not the issue.

The book succeeds in capturing that haunting character of the white southern spirit which echoes with the hollow sound of defeat and battered pride. It is astonishing, however, that a book about the South could be written in the seventies that does not mention the black struggle for freedom, that does not even make reference in word or painting to the civil rights movement. The tapestry also fails to acknowledge the emerging South that has registered more than two-and-a-half million black voters since the Voting Rights Act of 1965 and has elected more than 1,300 blacks to office including mayors, city councilmen, school board members, sheriffs, and state legislators. The story ignores the New South governors and the strong image of racial reconciliation that major white political leaders must project to win election. (Even George Wallace appointed a black to his cabinet.)

Instead of showing a young black lawyer arguing his case before an integrated jury, the paintings depict the sad face of a black woman fishing or a group of black folks in the fields chopping cotton. It's as if the book had been written in 1953, or even before that, before any of the southern present caught up with its tormented past. In some ways, however, no book has better captured the South that white southerners like to *think* they live in.

If the book has value, it is in the creation of a nostalgic mood that confirms the white southerner's view of himself as the citizen of Jericho, the destroyed but resurrected city. Dickey took his title from the book of Joshua: "And the captain of the Lord's host said unto Joshua, Loose thy shoe off thy foot; for the place whereon thou standest is holy."

Says Dickey: "Hubert and I are Southerners. This is one of the reasons we have chosen the title *Jericho*. That the South has been traditionally a Bible-oriented culture is only part of the reason. We wished to behold our land, each in his own way, with something as near to Biblical intensity as we, personally, could get." What is ironic about this choice of title is that "Joshua Fit de Battle of Jericho" was one of the anthems of the civil rights marches, its line "and the walls came-a-tumbling down" a reference to the barriers against freedom and opportunity that the white folks inside the city erected to keep the blacks out.

As a southerner myself, I know that southern history shrouds the psyche, smothering the present in gauzelike memories as thick as the mist hanging over the Georgia marshes. That's the South that Shuptrine paints, Wyeth-like—coonskins and old men whittling, hound dogs and Confederate gravestones, broken-down barns and buggies and rocking chairs and moonshine. Dickey seems blinded by the sights and tastes of the South, intoxicated with the smell of corn bread baking and the sounds of fried okra sizzling (recipes are included in the book). This aspect of the southern character thrives not only on the abandoned plantations, but in the hearts of the common men that Dickey recalls—the wild, hoop-and-a-holler possum eaters, skinning rabbits and marrying kin until their genes were as played out as the land.

Dickey, as far as I know, has not directly addressed the civil rights issue since 1961, when he wrote a short essay before he left the advertising business called "Notes on the Decline of Outrage." Dickey knew the score then, for he described the unfolding drama of the blacks' struggle as "pointing up, as nothing else in this country has ever done before, the fearful consequences of systematic and heedless oppression for both the oppressed and the oppressor, who cannot continue to bear such a burden without becoming himself diminished, and in the end debased, by such secret and cruel ways. . . . It is not too much to say that in the 'Negro problem' lies the problem of the South itself."

Then how to explain the void in *Jericho*? For *"Self Interviews"* in 1968, Dickey talked into a tape recorder over a period of several weeks. He had been criticized for his silence on Vietnam and on racial issues; while Robert Kennedy's funeral was being broadcast on a television set in the next room, Dickey laced the more fashionable poets who wrote according to the political mood and the critics who "call you 'out of it' if you don't write about the Watts and Washington riots and the march on Selma . . . but the universe exists as well. Why should we slight that? . . . one must not be coerced. . . ."

While writing *Deliverance* (which also avoided racial themes), Dickey elaborated on this defense of his creative choice by saying, "It excites me more to write about a river than to write about violence in the streets. And if that's what excites me, by God, that's what I'm going to write about."

As a poet and novelist, Dickey was on defensible ground, I think, because a writer of his sensibilities must write from the emotional edge, calling on the fragments of experience that move him. But *Jericho* is an interpretive history, announcing its theme as "the South beheld." An omission as immense, as egregious as the changes the civil rights movement brought about in black and white attitudes—not to mention the longing and anger that punctuate all of southern black history, so tellingly revealed to us in *All God's Dangers: The Life of Nate Shaw* (in fact, the two books should be read together)—raises a fundamental political and psychological question about the intentions of the authors. Perhaps the question is the sales strategy of their sponsors. With *Jericho*, Dickey cannot any longer retreat onto the platform of poetry or the prerogative of creative preference by professing a lack of interest in southern racial struggles. No southern writer can write about southern history without addressing this tiger directly. *Jericho*, then, shouts with Dickey's silence.

Had Dickey begun to explore the impact on blacks of the image of Jericho, he might have come upon fascinating possibilities. Despite the efforts of white planters to immerse the slaves in Christian fundamentalism, blacks turned to the Old Testament for solace and inspiration. They were attracted to the Israelites and their great journey out of the land of slavery into the land of freedom. "Go Down, Moses . . . Let my people go" was a Negro spiritual, not a Baptist hymn; the river Jordan with its chariots, Daniel's den of lions and Joshua's walls were all real places to the newly freed slaves. The stories in the Old Testament were alive for black people. It was no accident, then, that civil rights leadership emerged from the pulpit and expressed itself in the idiom of the Old Testament; to the masses of black people, Bull Connor was a modern Pharaoh, Martin Luther King was their Moses, and the marchers were the children of Israel headed for the Promised Land.

Dickey and Shuptrine might have done great things with the biblical themes had they tried to see the South through the eyes of the millions of black people who live there and to whom history means burned-out churches and the fear of night riders, the Dexter Avenue Baptist Church in Montgomery where King preached in the shadow of the state capitol a block away, sit-ins at Woolworth's in Greensboro, the successfully integrated schools of the seventies, and the black mayors in Atlanta and dozens of other cities whom whites helped vote into office.

There's another omission, serious because it was conscious and the authors had to work so hard to achieve it. Southern writers, including Pat Watters (*The South and the Nation*) and John Egerton (*The Americanization of Dixie*), have pointed to the crumbling values of southern life as every little town begins to look alike, every main street an identical patchwork of chain stores and fast-food diners. This is how Dickey coped with intrusions as he traveled and wrote: "He sent his pictures. I put them on the floors, on the walls, on the ceilings of innumerable cinder-block Southern motel rooms, where, cramped between a Home of the Whopper and a tire-iron-wangling Shell station, I went to sleep looking at a Negro sliding placidly across the ceiling . . . in the blue of Hubert's water-color sky . . . the quality of a Southern motel will never be quite the same for me again, because I carry my Shuptrines with me and by the magic of Scotch tape can cover my living spaces with the images of my land, with the fixed and limitless mysteries of place."

And so it is that this book papers over the real South, shielding its blemishes and changes from the reader; it is commercially successful because its subliminal message is what book-buying southerners want to hear—that the last twenty years didn't happen, that they are still living in a white paradise without any recognition that the paradise—if it was paradise—has been lost.

For Dickey, one of the most publicized American poets since Frost and Sandburg, the gap between his new book and reality is profoundly disappointing. He sells his South short. In so many ways, the South is now the most optimistic section of America, embarked on its long process of healing while northern cities are exploding with white violence.

Perhaps the South *is* Jericho, destroyed by the war, tempered by protest, and now rebuilt to new strength and vigor on the shoulders of a committed leadership of both races that see cooperation between blacks and whites as a key to regional vitality and national reconciliation. That's the Jericho that could have unfolded in this volume; that's the political and emotional reality of the South in the seventies that Shuptrine and Dickey could have captured for the next generation. The sad thing is that the opportunity to do it in such a dramatic format will probably not come again.

Part VI

Home

29

Sports: The Bond between Fathers and Sons

Love of University of North Carolina football and basketball has been in my blood since I was a small boy, when my father took my brother and me to games at Kenan Stadium in Chapel Hill on Saturday afternoons in the autumn and to Woolen Gym during the winter months. Like millions of other southerners, I was raised in the fire and brimstone of athletics, and it was only later that I discovered that the delirious ecstasy I experienced during a primeval battle between the Duke Blue Devils and the North Carolina Tar Heels was just as intense for others in the hordes of worshippers who flocked to the cathedral-like stadiums throughout the South. They came for the soul-saving frenzy of the Ole Miss–LSU annual Armageddon, the Georgia–Georgia Tech battle of the "dawgs" of hell, or the Alabama–Auburn blood feud. These annual passion plays were more like holy wars than ball games, and the atmosphere was heavy with that old-time religion, including a congregation of true believers speaking in tongues, and a scripture that recounted past miracles and fabled heroes.

Sports has become the most fundamental of American metaphors, stirring enduring myths, lasting loyalties, and the deepest of emotions. There are special local variations in every corner of the country, in small towns and big cities alike. Especially in this century, with the emergence of film, radio, and television as major cultural forces, the sports experience seems to have become the national touchstone of communications between the generations.

Recently, in the Atlanta airport, I found myself standing next to Alex Webster. New York Giants football fans remember Webster as the star fullback in the championship years of the 1950s and later as one of its coaches; but to me, Alex Webster was the punishing runner of the postwar North Carolina State Wolfpack, the John Riggins of his time, all the more awesome then in the impressionable years of my boyhood.

"Mr. Webster," I said, my heart jumping, to this hulk of an aging icon, "I remember you from your college years in North Carolina where I grew up. You were one of the greatest runners I ever saw."

A smile came over his face as he looked down at me, savoring, I knew, a rare eyewitness compliment from a pre-television age when football heroes were not in your living room holding up deodorant but were down on the stadium grass every Saturday pounding out legends.

"How's it going, son," he said, the squeeze of his hand on my shoulder sending me back to 1949. Old feelings began to wash over me. The truth was that I had hated Alex Webster.

My father had gone to the university in Chapel Hill, just eight miles from Durham where I grew up. All through my boyhood, my heart belonged to the Tar Heels; my soul was blue and white. UNC was the graduate center, Thomas Wolfe's alma mater, where students learned of Chaucer and Beethoven and went on to graduate schools in law, medicine, and business (learning to drink beer and chase coeds along the way). NC State was "cow college," the agricultural school where the farm boys went for courses in animal husbandry and horticulture. So when Alex Webster came to Kenan Stadium in Chapel Hill, he was searching not just for first downs but for self-respect. The pine-tree-framed setting turned into an autumn stage for his team to unleash a good ole country boy head-knocking between the sons of the soil and the princes of book learning.

My true hero was Charlie "Choo Choo" Justice of Asheville, UNC's triple-threat tailback from 1946 to 1950 in the old single wing, whose number 22 my mother sewed on a sweat-shirt I lived in during the days before they sold such things. "Choo Choo," who weighed just 165 pounds, not only could run "like a runaway train" but could pass and kick and was a master of improvisation who could return punts and kickoffs, too. The whole stadium rose to its feet every time he caught a punt and faded back twenty or thirty yards for running room, weaving through the opposing team, picking up blockers, swivel-hipping by a sprawling "would-be tackler," fancy high-stepping all over the field and back again, for touchdowns— TD's, "pay dirt," the end zone. "Choo Choo" was our All-American Heisman candidate (runner-up to SMU's Doak Walker in 1948) who took the Heels to three bowl games.

So why didn't I kick Alex Webster in the shins? He was the archenemy, the bruiser who brought his dreaded bull-dozing, blast 'em, ball-control, three-yards-and-a-cloud-of-dust of-fense to Chapel Hill. Invariably, it was a battle of brothers that only sibling rivals in the same state could wage. They were white boys playing before all-white crowds in the days when even professional ball had not been integrated. I remember the black kids sitting on the limbs of the trees around the stadium to get a glimpse of the action.

But meeting Webster turned me for a moment into a stam-mering kid in dirty jeans and brought back a flood of old feelings—the excitement in downtown Durham on Saturday mornings in front of the Washington Duke Hotel where visiting teams such as Tennessee boarded the bus early to go play at Duke and Carolina, and where my friends who were button and pennant hawkers sang out, "Give 'em hell, Tennessee," in order to sell their wares to the raucous visiting fans; running with my older brother to my father's downtown store to ride home with him in the ritual of departure for the game; bundling up in warm clothes, finding the blankets and the lost field glasses; my mother insisting we have a healthy lunch when all I wanted was to stuff peanuts into a Pepsi bottle and slurp them out one by one. My brother, my father, and I were enveloped in a warm bond of comradeship as we bounded into the car for the trip to Chapel Hill, joining the stream of traffic from every part of the state flowing into the town of 8,000 with a stadium that held 42,500. We hugged each other after scores, watched bandleader Kay Kyser take a turn as a returning alumnus cheerleader, and win or lose, sang the solemn alma mater "Hark the Sound" at the end of every game. My mother rarely went to these games, for she sensed a rite of passage going on.

I've tried to understand the origins of these loyalties, these passions. My father was a track star at Carolina in the late 1920s, inspired, he said, partly by Harold Abrahams, the English Olympic runner portrayed in *Chariots of Fire*. We were Jews in the South, and perhaps the intensity of my zeal was a form of assimilation crafted by my subconscious to forge a closer bond to the South itself, making me a Jewish southerner with a Talmudic mastery of statistics and local lore. The son aching to belong was not the athlete his father was, but at least he could be a superfan, the archetypal southern boy like his friends.

Dad passed on the stories of Carolina's sports legends: basketball heroes such as George Glamack, who, in 1941, was playing with eyes so bad he had to find a spot on the floor and shoot by memory; "Hook" Dillon in 1942, whose sweeping hook shot I imitated in my backyard; "Bones" McKinney, who took Carolina to the national finals in 1946. He told of the time after Pearl Harbor when Duke lost to Oregon State in the Rose Bowl, which was played in Durham because of the fear of another Japanese sneak attack on a helpless crowd in Pasadena.

My own college years at Chapel Hill added to the continuity of memories that to this day are crucial bonds between my father, my brother, and me, as if we are reciting oral histories in some aboriginal tribe.

When Everett Case brought big-time basketball to North Carolina State by recruiting Indiana ballplayers, UNC countered with Frank McGuire's New York City "subway southerners." Finally, in 1957, after a titanic struggle lasting years, in my junior year Carolina's basketball team went 32 and 0 and beat Wilt Chamberlain's Kansas team in a triple overtime for the national championship. It was almost the last all-white national championship college team. Twenty-five years later almost to the day, in 1982, when Carolina won again, on Michael Jordan's big shot, with four blacks in the starting five, my first instinct was to call my father and my brother to celebrate.

There was lots of grand history dancing in our dreams. My family's Jackie Robinson was Charlie Scott, the first black superstar in southern basketball, who carried North Carolina in the late 1960s over the barriers of redneck abuse all the way to the Final Four. NC State made the transition with David Thompson, the 6'5" "skywalker" who, the story went, could get a fifty-cent piece off the top of a blackboard and leave the change, leading State in 1974 to a national title over UCLA. And when NC State won another NCAA basketball championship in 1983 with an all-black starting five, and the country boys poured out of their dorms into the streets of Raleigh to celebrate, just as the Tar Heels had in Chapel Hill the year before, only the color of the uniforms mattered. The change was complete. Perhaps Dean Smith's greatest achievement in over twenty years of coaching is what he and Carolina basketball were able to do for race relations in North Carolina and the South since the 1960s as the drama of the nation was played out in the hearts of sports fans.

"There's no way on earth you could possibly understand this family passion," I once tried to explain to my wife. These were not mere games but life itself, stirring memories of fathers and sons in the South, passages to manhood across time, of changes in race in America's soul, of the yearning for youth in middle age. Sports gives that to men—the capacity to feel again, to care again, to soar again, to belong to a brotherhood, to rekindle the fires and feel the magic return in these exquisite moments of madness.

Sports talk is the universal language of adult men, and I am always grateful to my father for giving me the legacy. He passed on to me the vocabulary, the images, the attachment to history that enabled me to feel a surge of security that first day on shipboard in the navy when an enlisted man said to me, a nervous, fuzzy-cheeked ensign, "So who do you root for, sir?"

To this day, when my father and I call each other or walk together in our old North Carolina neighborhood as we have done all my life, we can invariably start a conversation with "Tell me, how do you think they'll do this year?"

30

The Call from Home

"The Drama" awaits every New Yorker who comes to the city from somewhere else—the call from home with the dreaded news of a parent's fatal illness or death.

"It is very serious," the doctor from Duke University Hospital said of my mother's cerebral hemorrhage when he reached me late at my office, "and I suggest you come home as soon as possible." I had been in New York for almost twenty years, but when he used the word "home," it sounded very natural to me. Durham was home, my mother was dying at the age of eighty, and I had to return to my roots, to that place where all the memories and connections and lifeline entwine. The phone call transported me almost mystically back into childhood, drawing me back to the relationships and the soul-forces that have shaped me.

"Your father is with her now," he replied to my questions, "but she is in a coma and will not come out of it. I'm telling you this because your father has not accepted it. She is on life-support systems, but we do not know how long she will last." He had tried to reach my older brother, Bob, but was told he was on a plane to the West Coast.

Was there hope? The doctor left none, but he had implied that she was alive, on "life support systems." I desperately wanted to be at her bedside, to talk, to hold her hand, to tell her of my feelings. Perhaps she could hear or maybe just know. But deep down, I knew the truth. And as I put the receiver back, I burst into tears and put my head on my desk and sobbed.

In a few minutes, I sat up and my mind began to race along a thousand tracks at once—reservations, arrangements, my schedule for the coming week, notifying relatives. Almost involuntarily, memories of scenes of my childhood surfaced among the thoughts of practical matters. I called my wife, Judith, who was at home with our one-year-old son, Joshua. Her mother had died six months before, and this news brought back her own mourning. She and my mother had had a very special relationship, and, beyond that, she and I both understood what these twin losses would mean to our little son. He would have no grandmothers. At least both of them had seen him and held him, had gloried in his arrival. Last Chanukah, his first, my mother had sent gifts that were inappropriate for a baby—toys and games, trucks and trains meant for an older child. I had complained to her that it was excessive. "Put them away," she advised. "You never know."

Mom had laughed at my antics and my excitement when Joshua was born. On a trip to Chapel Hill, I had scooped up some North Carolina soil from the UNC campus and brought it with me back to New York. I put it in a vial and took it into the New York University hospital delivery room where my son was being born; and with one hand, I held Judith's hand and with the other, I clutched the southern soil. I would later tell people that I simply did not want him to be born altogether as a Yankee, but the truth was that I wanted him to know his roots and I believe that one had to begin to create family legends early. So whenever I reported to my mother that Joshua wanted his shoes off or was diving into some grits, Judith would say on the other line, "The dirt's working." Later I told that story to the national convention of the United Daughters of the Confederacy and they gave me a standing ovation.

Soon after his birth, we flew down to Durham and I presented Joshua to Mom. She hurried out of the house to greet the car and it was a primal moment for all of us, mother and grandchild, a lifelong dream come true. My mother's tears were overpowering; the look of fulfillment and profound joy on her face expressed the emotions felt by a grandmother toward her fourth grandchild, her first by the younger son. She had not been able to come to the *bris* (the Jewish circumcision ceremony held eight days after birth) because of my father's illness; now, she eagerly took Joshua into her loving arms and spoke to him. She called him "sugar," with that deep southern accent, lilting and endearing. It was so simple for me to imagine myself being similarly stroked and cuddled. "Let me have a look at you," she said, peering at him on the dining room table where she propped him up to study his features and his coloring and his shape. We had decided to call him Joshua, my father's middle name, since he had arrived during my father's serious illness when we were not sure Dad was going to make it through. Joshua had also had his brush with danger during the pregnancy, and the name in Hebrew meant "saved by God." Dad had been so proud of the choice.

But, sitting in my office after that fateful call, these thoughts were all swift and jumbled. There were necessities of the moment. The last plane to Durham was leaving in two hours and I had to grab a cab home and get out to LaGuardia airport. I hurriedly packed enough clothes for a week; Judith had already checked schedules and was gathering clothes to bring Joshua down the next day. As I said my goodbyes to my family, I lingered a moment to feel the grasp of Joshua's little hand on my finger. He was so innocent and unaware of the tragic meaning of all this; it was reassuring to realize that he was part of the wheel of life, to look at Sara's grandson and feel his breathing and smell his cheeks and touch his neck with my lips.

After the plane took off, I put the seat back and closed my

eyes, and let the stunning news of the last few hours wash over me. The sadness would, from time to time, bubble uncontrollably to the surface, but it felt good, in one sense, to yield to the feelings. Pictures of her danced through my head: with my father under an umbrella at Myrtle Beach, watching us play in the water; in home movies, at family reunions, laughing with her seven sisters and her brother and all of the uncles and the aunts and the twenty-two first cousins; at her typewriter in her office at the family store, where she typed sixty words a minute with two fingers; holding my hand as I climbed the stairs at the Watts Street Elementary School for the first day of school; practicing her Hadassah speeches in the bedroom in front of the mirror, as she prepared for a speaking tour in behalf of Israel, taking the Zionist message in a southern accent to Tennessee or Mississippi; listening intently and approvingly as I showed photographs and talked about my first trip to Israel in 1956; the scene in the rearview mirror of my car, standing beside Dad to bid a brave good-bye to me as I drove off to California to meet my navy ship for eighteen months in Japan, and the young officer saw, for the first time, both his parents dissolve in tears; pride at my graduation from Yale Law School, my work in the White House, my career in philanthropy in New York.

"Hang on, Mom," I said to her as the roar of the engines subsided into the clouds. "I know you are waiting for us all to come. I know that. And I am coming."

I had my private moments with her, sacred and personal, holding her hand, which was still warm. She lasted several days, until my brother could return from Los Angeles and the rest of the family could arrive, from Florida, Texas, West Virginia, and North Carolina. All were able to visit her for final good-byes.

The rallying of a large family at a time of such sadness is an extraordinary comfort. Her sisters and only brother came without being asked, out of their own impulse to hold each other and share the burden of the loss of their oldest sister. For almost all of them, she had been a substitute mother, had raised them and stood firm for the old values. She had become the grand dame of the family.

For infrequent visitors to Durham, like my brother and me, there was comfort and support in other ways as well. The sense of community, for someone used to living in the beehive of New York City, was almost overwhelming. For example, under Jewish law, the body of the dead is not to be left alone. Volunteers and members of the Women's Chevra Kadisha of Beth-El Synagogue, where my parents had been lifelong members, dressed her in the shrouds and stayed with the body around the clock. They were Durham friends, and I knew most of them. It was very moving for us to know that she was never abandoned, that loving friends watched over her and performed these sensitive and blessed tasks with dignity, respect, and caring. The rabbi gave us the list and I thanked each of them; one of those who had volunteered for the midnight to 4:00 A.M. shift had been a girl in my Hebrew class who had married and stayed in Durham.

Large minyans (prayer groups) of twenty-five or so people gathered each day at the house with all of us to say the mourner's kaddish, the prayer of memory. As customary, people sent pies and fruit salads and cakes and even whole turkeys for visitors to nosh on during the week.

I plunged myself into the mundane tasks of planning the funeral, calling relatives, letting friends in the national office of Hadassah know, and preparing a news release for the local paper and for the Jewish press in the South. I took the release down to the editor of the Durham *Morning Herald* along with my father's favorite photograph of her. It appeared on the front page the day of the funeral under the headline "Mrs. Sara Evans, Wife of Ex-Mayor, Dies." I sent copies to wire services for the other state papers, to the Jewish Telegraphic Agency in New York, and to the *Southern Israelite* in Atlanta, which goes out to over twenty-five thousand homes across the South. I was instinctively using my experience in politics, working the press in my mother's behalf. I thought she would have wanted it that way.

The article said:

SARA N. EVANS

July 2, 1905–*March* 23, 1986

Sara Nachamson Evans, long-time civic and lay religious leader in Durham, died on Sunday, March 23rd, at the age of 80 at Duke Hospital.

Mrs. Evans, the wife of Mayor Emanuel J. Evans, served as the "first lady" of Durham from 1951 to 1963. Known affectionately as "Miz Evans" by her friends and family, she was, in her own right, a prominent local, regional and national leader of Hadassah, the women's Zionist organization with a national membership of 300,000 Jewish women, who work for causes in Israel and in Jewish communities around the world. Mrs. Evans served on every level of the organization during her lifetime. She was president of her local chapter in Durham, president of the Seaboard Region of nine states from 1942–1945; National vice-president from 1954–1957 and was a life member of its National Board since 1942. She was a dynamic public speaker who was known as Hadassah's "Southern accent" and she traveled across the South in the late 1930's and 1940's organizing local and state chapters. During World War II the Evanses signed more than fifty affidavits for refugees from Hitler's Europe, personally guaranteeing a job from an American citizen in order for them to receive a visa. Many worked in the Evans store and she counted meeting their children as some of her proudest moments. After the creation of the State of Israel in 1948, with her husband she worked for the political support of Israel among North Carolina Senators and Congressmen as well as among other political leaders in the South.

Mrs. Evans inherited her passion for Israel from her parents, Jennie B. and Eli Nachamson. Mrs. Nachamson, also a long-time Durham resident, founded Hadassah in the South in 1919 and found time to lead it in Eastern North Carolina even as she raised her nine children. Sara, the oldest of eight consecutive daughters and then a son, accompanied her mother on a memorable trip to Palestine in 1933 that, for the rest of her life, fired her passion for a Jewish State in the Holy Land. All eight sisters have served as presidents of local chapters of Hadassah across the South and the family was of such legend in Jewish circles, that when the sisters went to Israel in 1968 for Mrs. Evans's 40th wedding anniversary, *The Jerusalem Post* ran a photograph and a headline which said "Sara and Her Seven Sisters." In the synagogue famous for its Chagall windows in the Hadassah Hospital in Jerusalem, is a plaque commemorating the occasion.

Mrs. Evans came to Durham as a young girl when the Nachamson family moved here from Kinston in 1921 and opened United Dollar Store. She attended Duke University, where she played the flute in the Duke Orchestra, and worked in the family store. When her father became ill, much of the responsibility for running the store fell upon her. She met E. J. "Mutt" Evans of Fayetteville while he was attending the University of North Carolina, and the unusual Duke-Carolina marriage in 1928 at the Washington Duke Hotel in Durham, with the sisters as bridesmaids and her brother as ring-bearer, was a major social and religious event discussed for years.

"Mutt" and Sara Evans built the Durham store into a chain of stores in North Carolina and Virginia called United Department Stores. She was both a talented business executive and a corporate officer of several corporations. She also headed the Women's Division of the United Way campaign in Durham in 1952; was a member

of the N.C. Board of the American Association of United
Nations from 1961–1963; the League of Women Voters
and the United Fund Campaign in 1960.

In the last fifteen years, she and her husband created
and supported the Judaic Studies Program at Duke University and UNC.

Mrs. Evans is survived by her husband; by her two
sons, Robert M. Evans of Atlanta and Eli N. Evans of
New York City; and four grandchildren. She is also survived by her sisters: Grace Taylor of Miami Beach, Florida; Ethel Zeiger of Pompano Beach, Florida; Eva Stewart
of Charlotte, N.C.; Mary Wynn of Miami, Florida; Doris
Frankel of Cape Coral, Florida; and her brother William
Naxon of Dallas, Texas.

The funeral was a rite of passage for the Durham Jewish community, signalling the passing of one of its most powerful personalities. Over five hundred people attended, including leading figures of the non-Jewish community who had served on the city council with Dad when he was mayor or were business friends; many were the faces of people who had loomed large in my years of growing up. Now retired, they had been, during my childhood, the store owners downtown who had operated the pawn shops, jewelry stores, clothing stores, and shoe-repair shops; the local lawyers; doctors out at the Duke medical school and Duke professors; and the wives who had been my mother's colleagues and protégés in Hadassah and in the Beth-El Sisterhood and in the United Jewish Appeal-Federation fund-raising drives. And a number of black business and political leaders came out of respect for my father.

Bob and I had decided that the funeral service would not have a grief-stricken tone but should be a celebration of a life, a great and giving life. And the community did not disappoint us in the response to it. There was an embracing quality in the mood of the service, as if the whole town were enveloping us in its arms. We had asked Dr. Eric Meyers, the director of the Duke-UNC Judaic Studies program, which my mother and father had worked so hard to create, to give the eulogy; he was a family friend who had come to know her very well over the seventeen years he had been at Duke. We had met with him to tell anecdotes and share feelings. During the service, he quoted from my book, pointing out the passages about her business skills, which had been honed in the family store she began working in when she was eighteen, when her father first became ill and she inherited responsibility for the business.

> It forced her to grow up in a hurry, to pretend she knew all about merchandising, to learn to order around men three times her age, even hire and fire managers and muscular stockroom clerks. A crisp business personality masked a painful shyness she had to overcome every day. She maintained a deep intimacy with the older employees, whose children she would buy prom dresses for or send to Duke Hospital for expensive operations. The older women who ran ladies' ready-to-wear and the lingerie departments respected her judgment for the decades they worked with her and loved her for the respect they got back.

I wanted them to understand her warmth, her energy, the way in which she lived life all out, even into old age. Eric told one of my favorite stories about her: "When *The Provincials* was first published, Sara wanted to sell copies through Hadassah and to give copies away to people she hoped would read about her kinfolk in the South. So Eli called his publisher and asked for one thousand copies for his mother. There was astonished silence from the publisher who then replied, 'We've just never had a mother like that before!'"

He ended with a kind of coda to her life: "Today we rejoice in the life that Sara Nachamson Evans lived. She was a pioneer woman in every sense, ploughing the fields of Carolina so that it would be a better place for Jews to live with their Christian

brothers and sisters, and seeding the land of Israel with vine-
yards of hope through Hadassah. Her name has been a
blessing—may it forever remain so. Amen."

And then, just as I had suggested to the rabbi the previous
day, the pallbearers wheeled the coffin slowly out of the synagogue while the gathered congregation sang "Hatikva," the
song of hope of the Jewish people and the national anthem of
the state of Israel. At the cemetery, each of us trickled a
handful of earth into the grave, a Jewish custom that asserts
that a loved one should be buried by family and friends. We
picked up small clods of the North Carolina red clay mixed
with black earth, all moist and rich with the potential of spring,
and broke it up in our hands. The sound of bits of it striking
the coffin resonated with her history and her life. It was something all members of her large family could do together, a
healing act of respect. As a group all the family visited the
weathered tombstones of Jennie and Eli Nachamson's graves;
Mom had picked a site just forty feet away because the day she
had visited there, she was able to see her mother's and father's
stones from the spot where she would be buried. She had
planned it that way, so that the families' memories would be
blended and the generations unified.

After the funeral, the whole family gathered at the house as
friends dropped by to pay their respects. Bob greeted people,
and I stayed near the phone that was jangling off the hook with
calls from people who had read the news stories. They were
shocked because she had always been in good health and had
indefatigable energy, and had gone so quickly (one wise and
elderly friend said to me that if one's time had come, quickly
was the best way). I began to be exhausted from the emotional
interactions with her Hadassah friends from around the country, and old employees from the store, and just plain people for
whom she has done special things over the years. In the living
room, everything was revolving around Joshua, who was on the
floor, crawling over to this aunt or that one, a centerpiece of

joyful innocence to break up the somber clouds of the day. I will never forget the sight of my father holding his grandson on his lap, while visitors came over one after the other to give him their condolences.

In the months before my mother's death, she and I had been planning a family reunion in Durham. As part of the get-together, I had arranged with the new owners for a visit to the house on Minerva Street where the Nachamson family had lived when they first came to Durham in 1922. Their original store had been in a crossroads of a town in eastern North Carolina named Dover, with fewer than a thousand people and a dirt main street on which my grandfather drove the first car in the town. Half the daughters had been born there or in Kinston nearby; my mother and three of the sisters had been born in the Baltimore slums before the family decided to take a chance on the South. For new immigrants to the South the store was the stage in life that followed peddling; it came after the Jewish peddlers had earned enough money to buy a wagon and after the roads had gotten good enough so that the farmers could come to town. My grandmother had left a diary of those times, filled with astonishing stories about the farmers who came into the store to be blessed in the "original Hebrew," or to ask my grandfather, the local expert on the Bible, what he thought the percentage of alcohol was in the wine that was drunk at the Last Supper. Ever on the defensive from the temperance ladies, they were thrilled when he told them "about 18 percent."

However, it was a time of isolation for Jennie and Eli, summed up in a phrase she used to describe their religious lives: "The lonely days were Sundays." She tried to compensate. In Baltimore, Jennie had met Henrietta Szold, the founding mother of Hadassah, and had been fired with such idealism from the association that in 1919 she founded one of the first Hadassah chapters in the South. Consider a mother of nine children, who worked every day running the family store, caring enough about the Jewish people to carve out the time to launch and lead, among the scattered farms and flatlands of eastern North Carolina, an organization devoted to the health and hopes of a future Jewish state in Palestine. One of her proudest moments, she recalled, was introducing the great Rabbi Stephen S. Wise, who spent days on the train coming to eastern North Carolina to speak to nineteen people gathered in Jennie's home, from towns across the state.

Jennie had a keen eye and a strong sense of family values. When I read her diaries years later and then asked the daughters to write their own memories of growing up, I was struck by their descriptions of the way she managed the family, judged disputes among the girls, and always kept an ear tuned to realities. As the daughters got older and more attractive, and as boys started hanging around the house and coming by the store, Jennie decided it was time to open a store in Durham, because Duke University was there and the University of North Carolina nearby and the girls would have Jewish boys to go out with. Besides, Durham had once had a comparatively large Jewish community of several dozen families, some of whom had been recruited as a group off a picket line in New York by Buck Duke himself, because they had been cigarette rollers for the czar and the royalty of Russia; they would be the originating work force of the Bull Durham tobacco company. Eli himself could roll a cigar with one hand, a skill he brought from the old country and used at tobacco market time to draw people into the store.

The rambling three-story brick house, with arches and an ample yard and enough bedrooms for the growing family, suited Jennie's needs just fine. Even sixty-five years later, in the hands of new owners who were restoring it lovingly and were thrilled to greet the large family of the early occupants, it had a stately presence on the street. Just half a block away was Durham High School that almost all the sisters as well as Bob and I had attended. The afternoon after my mother's funeral, the whole family, Dad included, piled into cars and drove across town to the house.

Mom's sisters and her brother had not been in the house in decades and were as excited as schoolchildren to be going back again, all of them together. Sara, they all agreed, would have loved being there with them, too. They stood in the parlor where the family had held open house every weekend, remembering how they had folded back the rug to dance with the Duke and Carolina boys who dropped in. They recalled the rooms that each of them had slept in and showed us the second-floor screened-in porch where Jennie lined up cots dormitory-style in the summer to catch a breeze. Bob showed me the room in which he had first seen me after they brought me home from the hospital. In the attic, a ballet bar and a full-length mirror still existed where Jennie had made sure the girls learned the gracefulness and confidence of ballet and music. On the first floor, I made a wonderful discovery: the wallpaper had been stripped and there on the wall were the height charts of the youngest kids. I summoned everyone from all over the house to see it: "Bill, age three; Dodi, age five; Bobby (my brother) age two," and so on. The many layers of wallpaper had preserved the Nachamson family mark on the house.

In the corner, where the phone used to be, was a phone number and the words "Morris, Johannesburg." Not every member of the large Nachamson family of Linkerva in Lithuania had been able to get a visa to come to America, and Morris Nachamson had been one of the brothers who had gone to South Africa when Eli came to America. He never had children, and in his final years, he traveled to North Carolina to live with the only family he had. Each of the daughters, by this time most of them married with families of their own, took turns hosting him. His greatest fear was that he would die and not be remembered. In the late forties, when he lapsed into a coma, he miraculously lasted eight weeks, finally dying on the same day that Eli had died, fifteen years before. So when members of the family lit a Yahrtzeit candle on the anniversary of the death of their father, they lit one for Uncle Morris, too. It was a family legend so powerful that when the family visited

Jennie's and Eli's graves after my mother's funeral, we all stopped by Uncle Morris's grave, too. He surely must have been smiling somewhere.

Over four hundred letters poured in as the weeks went by. We had the eulogy printed up and sent to everyone who had written, along with a note of appreciation. A neighbor's son moved in with Dad, and he had to begin the terrible adjustment to a life he had thought he would never have to live.

As I returned to New York, the taxi ride from the airport past the crowded cemeteries in Queens formed a depressing punctuation to the trip. It was a metaphor for the city itself—anonymous and busy, too many lives and too little space, people too hurried to form the attachments to ancestors and to soil that is so much a part of the South I had just left. Could I ever sink roots into such a place? Like so many southerners, I vowed that I would not be buried in New York. Home would always be Durham. Even though I was now separated from my boyhood home physically, I felt more deeply attached emotionally to the place where my mother now rested.

I still had the soil from North Carolina that I had brought to New York when Joshua was born. This was Sara's treasured grandchild, and I had one more mission in order to complete the ritual of her death—a task to be performed during a forthcoming trip to Israel that had been planned two months before she died. It was a trip I knew she would have wanted me to make.

"She brought Durham to Jerusalem and Jerusalem to Durham," the rabbi had said at the funeral. I felt the need to attach her to Israel in some symbolic way, especially to the land itself and her beloved Hadassah. And so I left less than a month later with an idea of what specially to do and, to share the experience, I kept a diary and wrote to the family from Jerusalem the last night of my trip:

April 20, 1986
Jerusalem

Dear Family,

I'm writing this from Jerusalem where I just experienced in the last few days the most extraordinary event out at the Hadassah Hospital. I had come to Israel for a trip planned two months ago that I decided to go through with because I felt Mom would have wanted me to do it. She always relished my trips to Israel and wanted to hear every detail to experience it vicariously. And I called Dad several times to tell him of the warm and touching occasion that this letter will describe.

Jerusalem is such a mystical place to visit, but to come and wander its ancient streets and religious sites in a state of heightened emotion gives it a special poignancy. I called the Hadassah Hospital with a personal request—I wanted to come and plant a tree with my own hands in my mother's name in a quiet corner of the hospital grounds. I arrived at the appointed hour on April 17.

I had expected a simple ceremony with one or two people in an obscure spot, but instead, to my surprise, there was a delegation of officials and volunteers awaiting me, including many of the women who knew her and loved her and had learned through my request of her passing.

The women hugged and kissed me, and were so saddened to hear the news. But mostly, the institution as an institution stepped up to the idea of the tree, embraced it as a tribute to one of its important figures and made it more moving and ennobling than I could possibly have imagined.

The site of the tree is central, at the hospital's entrance, across from the Chagall synagogue, beside a beautiful fountain with Agam's sculpture *The Beating Heart*, just in front of the mother and child garden where mothers bring their newborns for their first air, and children are constantly at play. From the entrance to the Medical Center, you look across the fountain to the tree and beyond it out across a wide sloping hillside into the valley below.

The staff handed me a simple typed program for a souvenir, and we strolled into the sunshine of a bright and perfect spring day of blue skies and soft breezes.

The tree is a flowering cherry, the first one of its kind in Israel, chosen by the chief gardener for its elegance, fragrance, and color. It was lying down when we arrived, its roots carefully enclosed in plastic to nurture its life.

Two of the women who knew her spoke warmly and personally of Sara's deep commitments to Hadassah and to Israel, of the times at Hadassah conventions when they stayed up into the night talking of ways to convince American Jews to care about Israel. The mood was informal and conversational, family talk radiating in tone and mood the family feelings of people who loved her and wanted me to know how wide was her influence and her friends. The director of the hospital, Dr. Samuel Penchas, is a young man who replaced her friend and the longtime director, Kalman Mann, and though Penchas did not know Mom personally, he spoke of her as a "legend in the history of Hadassah."

I had brought copies of my book in English and in Hebrew to present, at their suggestion, to the head of the volunteers, a sweet-faced older woman with smile crinkles around her eyes who had worked in the wards of the medical center for over forty-two years. She remembered Mom's many visits and especially the visit of "Sara and her seven sisters." She was most concerned that I know of her recollections, and she listened intently as I spoke.

I was on the edge of tears throughout the presentation because I knew how much this would have meant to Mom, and because I realized that something very remarkable was happening. I had called the hospital with a simple and personal family request to plant a tree. I really expected something spare and personal somewhere on the hospital grounds, alone with my own thoughts and meaning. Instead, because they knew of her, they had transformed the request into an institutional recognition of her role in their history, into a tribute to her years of what they described as "heroic service." By dedicating a tree in a prominent place at the entrance of the hospital, they were recognizing their national strength and honoring all the women from small towns who gave so much of their lives and emotions to the organization.

I have to confess that my voice quaked a little as I tried to hold back the emotion. I spoke quietly of Jennie Nachamson's friendship with the founder of Hadassah, the charismatic Henrietta Szold in Baltimore, and of how Jennie started the first Hadassah chapter in the South in 1919. I told of how in 1933, in the middle of the Depression, our family scraped together the money to send Jennie and Sara to Palestine to see for themselves the dream of a Jewish state, and how Jennie had passed the torch of Zionist commitment first to her oldest daughter and then to the rest of the Nachamson girls. And I spoke of those years in the late thirties and forties, when Sara traveled and spoke and organized across the South and began her service on the National Board. I told of the affidavits she and my father signed during the war to guarantee a job and thereby a visa to more than fifty Jewish families in Europe and the proud moment years later when she met a roomful of their children. The commitment to saving the children of Europe orphaned by the Holocaust extended from her personal actions to embrace the hundreds of thousands of children Hadassah saved during and after the war through Youth Aliyah.

I wanted to lighten things and give a local insight, so I opened *The Provincials* and read a paragraph or two describing how each successive generation of Duke wives went through Miz Evans's training seminars on how to organize the annual Hadassah donor affair. The passage ends with the exchange, "Then a shy, hesitant voice might complain, 'But this is my first year, Miz Evans, and I've never spoken before a crowd that big before.'

"'Don't worry, Ruthie,' she would say, 'we'll write it all out for you and you'll stand up there straight and it'll be terrific.'

"Jewish pygmalions, all of them, and thus did Hadassah in Durham go on and on."

The meaning for me, I told them, was that no matter how high she went in the national structure, she was never too busy for local work in Durham nor too self-satisfied to train the next generation of leadership.

I recalled the visits to Durham of the national leaders—women like Anna Tulin, whom I had accidentally run into the day before in Jerusalem and who hugged me dearly when she heard. Now over seventy-five, I remembered her in the 1950s as a spectacularly beautiful woman with strawberry blonde hair she wore on one side of her face, traveling the South to speak for Hadassah and stopping by Durham to get briefed at the breakfast table about each city on her tour; other women visited, such as Ann Samuels and Mildred Efros of Baltimore and Miriam Kroskin of Norfolk—fabulous women, really, who in the pre-feminist era of postwar America channeled all their love and energy into Hadassah.

And finally, I read from the inscription I had written in the book: "To the officials, friends and patients of Hadassah Hospital at Ein Karem,

In appreciation for a warm and wonderful day of dedication and affection for my mother, Sara Nachamson Evans, who gave so much of her energy and hope and aspiration to this place.

Thank you for planting such a beautiful tree for her—

she loved the trees of Israel and she loved all of you as her Hadassah family.

With best wishes
from the author."

I walked over and presented the Hebrew and English versions of the book to the head of volunteers who hesitated and then kissed me lightly on the cheek.

As the director and I turned to plant the tree, I explained that "it is customary, I know, for Jews to take the earth from Jerusalem back to the diaspora; but I brought with me a little bit of the earth of North Carolina—not just any earth, but a small bit of earth I kept in my pocket in the delivery room when my son Joshua—Sara's grandson—was born a year ago. I had wanted him to know his roots but today I want also to connect him and the South to this occasion. And in a way, it is fitting. For Hadassah's roots extend from here all over the world and especially to America and into the American South."

I sprinkled the bit of earth into the scooped-out place prepared for the tree and then the gardener cut away the plastic from the roots of the tree and stood it upright. It was just over chest-high on me, and I took a hoe and raked all of the moist earth around the roots, patted the gardener's broad shoulder and whispered, "Take good care of it." He nodded warmly.

Then Dr. Penchas presented a plaque for me to attach to a large stone which had been prepared for it. It said, simply:

SARA NACHAMSON EVANS
Hadassah Pioneer in the American South
July 2, 1905 *to March* 23, 1986

Dr. Penchas, at my request, read in Hebrew the Sabbath prayer that is sung after the Torah is returned to the ark: "It is a Tree of Life to them that hold fast to it, and everyone that upholds it is happy. Its ways are ways of pleasantness, and all its paths are peace." I have discussed it with Bob and Dad, and we will inscribe that verse on her tombstone.

I then finished by saying, "You are always thanking Hadassah members for all they have done to help the Hadassah hospitals and Israel; on this occasion, let me thank you for all you have done for us—giving our parents and their families the opportunity to attach themselves to a wider world and participate in Jewish history." I thought to myself how at home and natural I felt shedding tears with people halfway around the world who knew and loved her, too.

We retired to tea and coffee inside the hospital where other staff members and visitors greeted me. I bought a little Hadassah nurse doll for Joshua—she was an academic nurse doll, holding a small diploma, which Dr. Penchas inscribed to him. Only in Israel would they have created an academic nurse doll!

And then, the director of the donations department asked if I had time to look at the other inscriptions in the hospital with my parents' name. I was astonished to see a stack of three-by-five cards in her hand.

We walked into a special room filled with glass cabinets and large leather-bound volumes. The cards referred to the volume and page numbers. It was all there—a microscope given in her name in 1953 by the Durham chapter, other equipment, bricks, this and that. It was deeply impressive because it spanned so many decades.

She then asked me to follow her into the Chagall synagogue, where I have visited many times, but because the sunlight is always different, it is always a fresh experience. The windows, on this clear and special day, glowed with springtime light and had never looked more beautiful.

Nothing gave Mom more pleasure than the many friends and family who came back from Israel and told her they had seen the family plaque in the Chagall synagogue. She felt it attached her friends to Israel to see Durham so prominently mentioned, and that it helped to build bridges.

I said my good-byes and walked out to look at the tree one last time. I thought of how much this honor would have meant to her and how we, her family, must now cherish it for her. I thought, too, of Jennie's early dream of extending the Hadassah movement into the South and how right it was that the plaque proclaimed her oldest daughter's success, here at this hospital, in the land the two of them once visited. While the tree closed the circle, it also deepened a connection. I could imagine myself standing before it with Joshua a decade from now, my son and I also rooted in this holy soil. The growth of Sara's tree and its reblossoming season after season will link the Nachamson and Evans family to this land ever more.

The tree already seemed firm and enduring in its new home. Small children were at play behind it and a Yemenite mother, dressed in a long robe of deep purple and reds with spangles glistening in the sun, walked out of the mother-child clinic clutching a small bundle of life to her. The breeze played lightly on the tender branches of Mom's tree with its single pink blossom and I saw a white butterfly flutter by. It was, in this moment before departure, a scene I would remember forever—of unsurpassed serenity and hope.

Much love,
Eli

Acknowledgments

Because the articles and essays in this book span the last twenty years, there are many people who have helped along the way.

First, as honest and creative critics, I will always be grateful to Avery Russell, my colleague at the Carnegie Corporation and old friend from North Carolina; and to Lisa Goldberg, my associate for ten years at the Charles H. Revson Foundation. Their generosity and insights have shaped individual pieces at each point of completion through the years and both have read this manuscript with empathy and intelligence.

I also owe a debt to Carol Weiland, who has worked with me as an editor both at Carnegie and at Revson; to Jack Nessel, who, as managing editor at *New York* magazine and editor-in-chief at *Psychology Today*, made assignments and talked through issues both as a friend and as a professional; to Willie Morris, whom I first met when he was editor of *Harper's* when he sent me across the South in the 1970s for what ultimately became *The Provincials*; and to Joanne Prichard, executive editor of the University Press of Mississippi, whose enthusiasm for this book and editorial intelligence have helped to organize these articles in a way that gives depth to this book.

At the Carnegie Corporation of New York, where I worked for ten years, I would also like to thank its presidents Alan Pifer, John Gardner, and David Hamburg; at the Charles H. Revson Foundation, I was encouraged to pursue my writing by my board of directors and particularly three board chairs— Judge Simon Rifkind, Adrian DeWind, and Matina Horner.

I also am grateful to Margaret Rose and Terry Sanford; to Mayor Teddy Kollek of Jerusalem; to the late Avraham Harman, president of Hebrew University; and to Abba Eban, for all that knowing them has done to inspire me to dream of a better world.

Almost a fourth of this book appeared in the *New York Times*, and I would like to thank Eden Lipson, an editor of the Sunday *Book Review*, who assigned almost all the reviews; and Howard Goldberg, a senior editor of the Op-Ed page, who encouraged me to submit opinion pieces over the years.

A number of the various articles deserve specific acknowledgment and appreciation.

Bob Spearman traveled through the South for the project on black lawyers; Bill Ferris, director of the Center for Southern Culture at the University of Mississippi, invited a contribution on Harry Golden for the *Encyclopedia of Southern Culture* and asked me to join Alex Haley, Shelby Foote, and William Styron on two trips on the *Delta Queen* down the Great River. The trips stirred me deeply and were an inspiration for this book. I would also like to thank Macy Hart and Marcie Cohen of the Museum of the Southern Jewish Experience in Mississippi, who are so deeply committed to this subject; Joseph Cohen, chairman of the Department of Jewish Studies at Tulane University, who conceived the idea of interviewing me for the *American Jewish History Quarterly*; former presidents of the Southern Jewish Historical Society, Saul Viener of Richmond and Sam Proctor, head of Jewish Studies at the University of Florida; Hodding Carter III, PBS commentator and former publisher of the *Delta Democrat Times*, who hosted me in the early 1970s when I first traveled in Mississippi; and Rabbi Malcolm Stern, my mentor on Southern Jewish history for over twenty years.

In North Carolina, a number of people through the years have been steadfast partners in a mutual concern about the future of the state: Mary Duke Semans, family friend and former mayor pro-tem of Durham; two old friends from my college years in Chapel Hill—Joel Fleishman, vice president of Duke University, and Tom Lambeth, the president of the Z. Smith Reynolds Foundation; the late Jimmy Wallace, mayor of Chapel Hill, and his wife Nina; Walter Dellinger, former dean of the Duke University Law School, and his wife Anne; UNC Chancellor Paul Hardin; novelists Doris Betts; John Ehle and his wife, the actress Rosemary Harris; and Carol and Eric Myers, who founded the Judaic Studies Department at Duke University.

In Israel, a number of people have remained friends through the years and touchstones on every aspect of Israeli life: Walter Eytan, former ambassador to France and brilliant observer of history, politics, and people; Edo Rozenthal, correspondent for Dutch radio and television; Alan Rosenthal, documentary filmmaker and friend for thirty years; Alex Keynan, of the Israel Academy of Sciences and, in many ways, my teacher on matters of science in Israel; the late Mildred Efros, lifelong Hadassah friend to my mother, whose husband was one of the founders of the Tel Aviv University, and her daughter, Gila Scharfstein; Rabbi David Geffen, formerly of Atlanta, whose roots uniquely embrace both Israel and the South; Ora Ahimeir, director of the Jerusalem Institute for Israel Studies; Horace Richter, of the Delson-Richter art gallery, and North Carolina family friend for fifty years; Ruth Chessin, president of the Jerusalem Foundation; Elihu Katz, head of the Communications Department of Hebrew University, and his wife Ruth; Arthur Fried, director of the Rothschild Foundation, and his wife Susan; Rabbi Levi Weiman-Kelman of Congregation Kol

Haneshama and Hebrew Union College; and Bonnie Boxer of Mayor Teddy Kollek's staff.

Rue Canvin has worked as my assistant for more than twenty years and labored over every aspect of this book in its original form and as a collection; and Michele Lyman was patient as she put the manuscript onto a word processor and never let constant changes bother her.

And finally, I would like to thank my family—Gail and Bob Evans of Atlanta for the years of helping to talk it all through; my nephews Jason and Jeffrey and my niece Julie Evans, the next generation of family historians who have already accepted the baton of writing about the family into the next century. I want to pay special tribute to my father, Mayor E. J. "Mutt" Evans, who has inspired my interest in people, politics, and Southern life. I also want to acknowledge the memory of my mother, Sara N. Evans, who raised her family, even in a small town, to believe that Southern Jews have a role in shaping Jewish history, and a responsibility to care.

Finally, it would have been impossible for me to complete this book without the inspiration of my seven-year-old son, Joshua, and the support of my wife, Judith, who shares the loyalties in my life and whose faith in me as a writer helps to get me through the day.

A number of the essays and articles collected here have appeared in a different form in other publications:

The *New York Times*: "Southern Liberals and the Court," Sept. 3, 1974; "Emperor's Fall Clothes," Aug. 24, 1975; "Going Through the Mill," Jan. 27, 1976; "All the Candidates' Clothes," Sept. 19, 1976; "Southern Jews, Baptists, and Jimmy Carter," Oct. 20, 1976; *Natural Superiority of Southern Politicians* by David Leon Chandler and *Ethnic Southerners* by George Brown Tinsdale, Jan. 16, 1977; "In the Shadow of Southern History," July 5, 1977; *Members of the Tribe* by Richard Kluger, Sept. 25, 1977; "The City, the South, and the Caribbean," July 26 & 27, 1978; *Transformation of Southern Politics* by Jack Bass and Walter DeVries, Aug. 15, 1979;

Jericho by James Dickey, Jan. 5, 1981; "Movies Alter the Image of the South," May 24, 1981; *Generation Without Memory* by Anne Roiphe, June 7, 1981; *Crescent City* by Belva Plain, Oct. 7, 1984; *Out of Many Waters* by Jacqueline Dembar Greene and *The Jews of New Amsterdam* by Eva Deutsch Costabel, March 19, 1989; *One, by One, by One* by Judith Miller, April 29, 1990.

New York: "Abba Eban at Columbia," Dec. 16, 1974; *Newsweek*: "A New Generation Takes Over," July 9, 1984; *Village Voice*: "Back in the Saddle with Hoppy, Gene, and Roy, Oh Boy!" Sept. 29, 1975; Chronicle of Higher Education: *New Lives: Survivors of the Holocaust Living in America* by Dorothy Rabinowitz, June 10, 1977; *Washington Star*: "George Wallace Could Turn the Yahoos On," Mar. 26, 1976; University of North Carolina Press, "Harry Golden" in *Encyclopedia of Southern Culture*, June 1989; University Press of Virginia: "Southern Jewish History: Alive and Unfolding" in *Turn to the South*, Nov. 1979; *UNC Alumni Magazine*: "Sports: The Bond Between Fathers and Sons," May 1984; *Durham Morning Herald*: "Miss North Carolina Is Jewish," June 12, 1973; American Jewish History: "Four Books on Jews in the South," Dec. 1985, and "An Interview with Eli N. Evans," Dec. 1988; National Foundation for Jewish Culture: "Electronic Village," May 1987; Carnegie Corporation: "A Step Toward Equal Justice," April 1974; Jewish Publication Society: *Strangers Within the Gate City: The Jews of Atlanta 1865–1915*, June 1978; *Zionism in America*: "Zionism in the Bible Belt," June 1978.

About the Author

Eli N. Evans was born and raised in Durham, North Carolina. He graduated from the University of North Carolina in 1958 and spent two years in the U.S. Navy, stationed in Japan. After graduating from Yale Law School in 1963, he served on the White House staff from 1964 to 1965 as a speech writer for President Lyndon Johnson. From 1965 to 1967, he was staff director at Duke University of a nationwide study of the future of the states that was headed by former North Carolina Governor Terry Sanford. From 1967 to 1977, he traveled extensively in the South as a senior program officer for the Carnegie Corporation of New York, the national education foundation.

He is the author of *The Provincials: A Personal History of Jews in the South* (Atheneum, 1973) and *Judah P. Benjamin: The Jewish Confederate* (Free Press, 1988). Since 1977, he has been president of the Charles H. Revson Foundation, which makes grants for programs in urban affairs, education, and Jewish philanthropy. Mr. Evans currently lives with his wife and son in New York City.